I0754583

TREASURES

FROM

THE PROSE WRITINGS

OF

JOHN MILTON.

"Hath he not always treasures, always friends, —
The good, great man?"

COLERIDGE.

BOSTON:
TICKNOR AND FIELDS.
1866.

Entered according to Act of Congress, in the year 1865, by
TICKNOR AND FIELDS,
in the Clerk's Office of the District Court of the District of Massachusetts.

UNIVERSITY PRESS: WELCH, BIGELOW, & CO.,
CAMBRIDGE.

To

JOHN GREENLEAF WHITTIER,

THIS EDITION OF

TREASURES FROM MILTON'S PROSE WRITINGS

IS DEDICATED

BY THE PUBLISHERS.

PREFACE.

THE Prose Writings of Milton, inspired by the stirring events amid which they were written, form his contribution to the literature of freedom. To them were given the matured powers of a mind enriched by varied studies, and ripened by meditation. They form the labors of his life, grand in thought and expression, as the poetic recreations of his earlier and later years are sublime and beautiful. In them his opinions, character, motives and conduct are portrayed with singular fidelity.

It is the aim of this volume to present a selection from Milton's Prose Writings, comprising some of the author's best thoughts, and setting forth as clearly as possible Milton himself, showing impartially his merits and faults as a writer and as a man. It will not have been prepared in vain, if it shall serve to make more widely known the Treasures of truth and beauty in these Prose Writings, and the true greatness of soul in their much abused author. And may the principles of civil and religious freedom, here so eloquently defended, triumph everywhere.

FAYETTE HURD.

July 12, 1865.

CONTENTS.

FROM THE TREATISE

OF REFORMATION IN ENGLAND.

AMIDST those deep and retired thoughts, which, with every man Christianly instructed, ought to be most frequent of God, and of his miraculous ways and works amongst men, and of our religion and works, to be performed to him; after the story of our Saviour Christ, suffering to the lowest bent of weakness in the flesh, and presently triumphing to the highest pitch of glory in the spirit, which drew up his body also; till we in both be united to him in the revelation of his kingdom, I do not know of anything more worthy to take up the whole passion of pity on the one side, and joy on the other, than to consider first the foul and sudden corruption, and then, after many a tedious age, the long-deferred, but much more wonderful and happy reformation of the Church in these latter days. Sad it is to think how that doctrine of the Gospel, planted by teachers divinely inspired, and by them winnowed and sifted from the chaff of overdated ceremonies, and refined to such a spiritual height and temper of purity, and knowledge of the Creator, that the body, with all the circumstances of time and place, were purified by the affections of the regenerate soul, and nothing left impure but sin; faith needing not the weak and fallible office of the senses, to be either the ushers or interpreters of heavenly mysteries, save where our Lord himself in his sacraments ordained; that such a doctrine should, through the grossness and blindness of her professors, and the fraud of deceivable traditions, drag so downwards, as to backslide one way into the Jewish beggary of old cast rudiments, and stumble forward another way into the new-vomited paganism of sensual idolatry, attributing purity or impurity to things indifferent, that they might bring the inward acts of the spirit to the outward and customary eye-service of the body, as if they could make God earthly and fleshly, because they could not make themselves heavenly and spiritual; they began to draw down all the divine intercourse betwixt God and the soul, yea, the very shape of God himself, into an exterior and bodily form, urgently pretending a necessity and obligement of joining the body in a formal reverence and worship circumscribed; they hallowed it, they fumed up, they sprinkled it, they bedecked it, not in robes of pure innocency, but of pure linen, with other deformed and fantastic dresses, in palls and mitres, gold, and gewgaws fetched from Aaron's old wardrobe, or the flamins vestry: then was the priest set to con his motions and his postures, his liturgies and his lurries, till the soul, by this means of overbodying herself, given up justly to fleshly delights, bated her wing apace downward: and finding the ease she had from her visible and sensuous colleague, the body, in performance of religious duties, her pinions now broken, and flagging, shifted off from herself the labor of high-soaring any more, forgot her heavenly flight, and left the dull and droiling carcass to plod on in the old road, and drudging trade of outward conformity. And here, out of question, from her perverse conceiting of God and holy things, she had fallen to believe no God at all, had not custom and the worm of conscience nipped her incredulity: hence to all the duties of evangelical grace, instead of the adoptive and cheerful boldness which our new alliance with God requires, came servile and thrallike fear: for in very deed, the superstitious man, by his good-will, is an atheist; but being scared from thence by the pangs and gripes of a boiling conscience, all in a pudder shuffles up to himself such a God and such a worship as is most agreeable to remedy his fear; which fear of his, as also is his hope, fixed only upon the flesh, renders likewise the whole faculty of his apprehension carnal; and all the inward acts of worship, issuing from the native strength of the soul, run out lavishly to the upper skin, and there harden into a crust of formality. Hence men came to scan the Scriptures by the letter, and in the covenant of our redemption, magnified the external signs more than the quickening power of the Spirit; and yet, looking on them through their own guiltiness with a servile fear, and finding as little comfort, or rather terror, from them again, they knew not how to hide their slavish approach to God's behests, by them not understood, nor worthily received, but by cloaking their servile crouching to all religious presentments, sometimes lawful, sometimes idolatrous, under the name of humility, and terming the piebald frippery and ostentation of ceremonies decency.

But, to dwell no longer in characterizing the depravities of the Church, and how they sprung, and how they took increase, when I recall to mind at last, after so many dark ages, wherein the huge overshadowing train of error had almost swept all the stars out of the firmament of the Church; how the bright and blissful Reformation (by Divine power) struck through the black and settled night of ignorance and antichristian tyranny, methinks a sovereign and reviving joy must needs rush into the bosom of him that reads or hears; and the sweet odor of the returning gospel imbathe his soul with the fragrancy of heaven. Then was the sacred Bible sought out of the dusty corners where profane falsehood and neglect had thrown it, the schools opened, divine and human learning raked out of the embers of forgotten tongues, the princes and cities trooping apace to the new erected banner of salvation; the martyrs, with the unresistable might of weakness shaking the powers of darkness, and scorning the fiery rage of the old red dragon.

He that, enabled with gifts from God, and the lawful and primitive choice of the Church assembled in convenient number, faithfully from that time forward feeds his parochial flock, has his coequal and compresbyterial power to ordain ministers and deacons by public prayer, and vote of Christ's congregation in like sort as he himself was ordained, and is a true apostolic bishop. But when he steps up into the chair of pontifical pride, and changes a moderate and exemplary house for a misgoverned and haughty palace, spiritual dignity for carnal precedence, and secular high office and employment for the high negotiations of his heavenly embassage, then he degrades, then he unbishops himself; he that makes him bishop, makes him no bishop.

Thus then did the spirit of unity and meekness inspire and animate every joint and sinew of the mystical body: but now the gravest and worthiest minister, a true bishop of his fold, shall be reviled and ruffled by an insulting and only canon-wise prelate, as if he were some slight, paltry companion: and the people of God, redeemed and washed with Christ's blood, and dignified with so many glorious titles of saints and sons in the Gospel, are now no better reputed than impure ethnics and lay dogs; stones, and pillars, and crucifixes have now the honor and the alms due to Christ's living members; the table of communion, now become a table of separation, stands like an exalted platform upon the brow of the quire, fortified with bulwark and barricado, to keep off the profane touch of the laics, whilst the obscene and surfeited priest scruples not to paw and mammoc the sacramental bread, as familiarly as his tavern biscuit. And thus the people, vilified and rejected by them, give over the earnest study of virtue and godliness, as a thing of greater purity than they need, and the search of divine knowledge as a mystery too high for their capacities, and only for churchmen to meddle with; which is what the prelates desire, that when they have brought us back to popish blindness, we might commit to their dispose the whole managing of our salvation; for they think it was never fair world with them since that time.

I AM not of opinion to think the Church a vine in this respect, because, as they take it, she cannot subsist without clasping about the elm of worldly strength and felicity, as if the heavenly city could not support itself without the props and buttresses of secular authority.

How should then the dim taper of this Emperor's * age, that had such need of snuffing, extend any beam to our times, wherewith we might hope to be better lighted, than by those luminaries that God hath set up to shine to us far nearer hand? And what reformation he wrought for his own time, it will not be amiss to consider. He appointed certain times for fasts and feasts, built stately churches, gave large immunities to the clergy, great riches and promotions to bishops, gave and ministered occasion to bring in a deluge of ceremonies, thereby either to draw in the heathen by a resemblance of their rites, or to set a gloss upon the simplicity and plainness of Christianity; which, to the gorgeous solemnities of paganism, and the sense of the world's children, seemed but a homely and yeomanly religion; for the beauty of inward sanctity was not within their prospect.

But it will be replied, The Scriptures are difficult to be understood, and therefore require the explanation of the fathers. It is true, there be

* Constantine's.

some books, and especially some places in these books, that remain clouded; yet ever that which is most necessary to be known is most easy; and that which is most difficult, so far expounds itself ever, as to tell us how little it imports our saving knowledge. Hence, to infer a general obscurity over all the text, is a mere suggestion of the devil to dissuade men from reading it, and casts an aspersion of dishonor both upon the mercy, truth, and wisdom of God. We count it no gentleness or fair dealing in a man of power amongst us, to require strict and punctual obedience, and yet give out all his commands ambiguous and obscure: we should think he had a plot upon us; certainly such commands were no commands, but snares. The very essence of truth is plainness and brightness; the darkness and crookedness is our own. The wisdom of God created understanding, fit and proportionable to truth, the object and end of it, as the eye to the thing visible. If our understanding have a film of ignorance over it, or be blear with gazing on other false glisterings, what is that to truth? If we will but purge with sovereign eye-salve that intellectual ray which God hath planted in us, then we would believe the Scriptures protesting their own plainness and perspicuity, calling to them to be instructed, not only the wise and learned, but the simple, the poor, the babes, foretelling an extraordinary effusion of God's Spirit upon every age and sex, attributing to all men, and requiring from them the ability of searching, trying, examining all things, and by the Spirit discerning that which is good; and as the Scriptures themselves pronounce their own plainness, so do the fathers testify of them. . . . .

But let the Scriptures be hard; are they more hard, more crabbed, more abstruse, than the fathers? He that cannot understand the sober, plain, and unaffected style of the Scriptures, will be ten times more puzzled with the knotty Africanisms, the pampered metaphors, the intricate and involved sentences of the fathers, besides the fantastic and declamatory flashes, the gross-jingling periods, which cannot but disturb and come thwart a settled devotion, worse than the din of bells and rattles.

It is a work good and prudent to be able to guide one man; of larger extended virtue to order well one house; but to govern a nation piously and justly, which only is to say happily, is for a spirit of the greatest size, and divinest mettle. And certainly of no less a mind, nor of less excellence in another way, were they who, by writing, laid the solid and true foundations of this science, which being of greatest importance to the life of man, yet there is no art that hath been more cankered in her principles, more soiled and slubbered with aphorisming pedantry than the art of policy; and that most, where a man would think should least be, in Christian commonwealths. They teach not, that to govern well, is to train up a nation in true wisdom and virtue, and that which springs from thence, magnanimity (take heed of that), and that which is our beginning, regeneration, and happiest end, likeness to God, which in one word we call godliness; and that this is the true flourishing of a land, other things follow as the shadow does the substance: to teach thus were mere pulpitry to them. This is the masterpiece of a modern politician, how to qualify and mould the sufferance and subjection of the people to the length of that foot that is to tread on their necks; how rapine may serve itself with the fair and honorable pretences of public good; how the puny law may be brought under the wardship and control of lust and will; in which attempt, if they fall short, then must a superficial color of reputation, by all means, direct or indirect, be gotten to wash over the unsightly bruise of honor. To make men governable in this manner, their precepts mainly tend to break a national spirit and courage, by countenancing open riot, luxury, and ignorance, till, having thus disfigured and made men beneath men, as Juno in the fable of Io, they deliver up the poor transformed heifer of the commonwealth to be stung and vexed with the breeze and goad of oppression, under the custody of some Argus with a hundred eyes of jealousy. To be plainer, sir, how to solder, how to stop a leak, how to keep up the floating carcass of a crazy and diseased monarchy or state, betwixt wind and water, swimming still upon her own dead lees, that now is the deep design of a politician.

A COMMONWEALTH ought to be but as one huge Christian personage, one mighty growth and stature of an honest man, as big and compact in virtue as in body; for look what the grounds and causes are of single happiness to one man, the same ye shall find them to a whole state, as Aristotle, both in his Ethics and Politics, from the principles of reason, lays down: by consequence, therefore, that which is good and agreeable to monarchy will appear soonest to be so, by being good and agreeable to the true welfare of every Christian; and that which can be justly proved hurtful and offensive to every true Christian will be evinced to be alike hurtful to monarchy: for God forbid that we should separate and distinguish the end and good of a monarch from the end and good of the monarchy, or of that from Christianity. . . . .

Seeing that the churchman's office is only to teach men the Christian faith, to exhort all, to encourage the good, to admonish the bad, privately the less offender, publicly the scandalous and stubborn; to censure and separate, from the communion of Christ's flock, the contagious and incorrigible, to receive with joy and fatherly compassion the penitent: all this must be done, and more than this is beyond any church-authority. What is all this, either here or there, to the temporal regiment of weal public, whether it be popular, princely, or monarchical? Where doth it entrench upon the temporal governor? where does it come in his walk? where doth it make inroad upon his jurisdiction? Indeed, if the minister's part be rightly discharged, it renders him the people more conscionable, quiet, and easy to be governed; if otherwise, his life and doctrine will declare him. If, therefore, the constitution of the Church be already set down by divine prescript, as all sides confess, then can she not be a handmaid to wait on civil commodities and respects; and if the nature and limits of church-discipline be such as are either helpful to all political estates indifferently, or have no particular relation to any, then is there no necessity, nor indeed possibility, of linking the one with the other in a special conformation. . . . .

Well knows every wise nation that their liberty consists in manly and honest labors, in sobriety and rigorous honor to the marriage-bed, which in both sexes should be bred up from chaste hopes to loyal enjoyments; and when the people slacken, and fall to looseness and riot, then do they as much as if they laid down their necks for some wild tyrant to get up and ride. Thus learnt Cyrus to tame the Lydians, whom by arms he could not whilst they kept themselves from luxury; with one easy proclamation to set up stews, dancing, feasting, and dicing, he made them soon his slaves.

I know not what drift the prelates had, whose brokers they were to prepare, and supple us either for a foreign invasion or domestic oppression: but this I am sure, they took the ready way to despoil us both of manhood and grace at once, and that in the shamefullest and ungodliest manner, upon that day which God's law, and even our own reason, hath consecrated, that we might have one day at least of seven set apart wherein to examine and increase our knowledge of God, to meditate and commune of our faith, our hope, our eternal city in heaven, and to quicken withal the study and exercise of charity; at such a time that men should be plucked from their soberest and saddest thoughts, and by bishops, the pretended fathers of the Church, instigated, by public edict, and with earnest endeavor pushed forward to gaming, jigging, wassailing, and mixed dancing, is a horror to think! Thus did the reprobate hireling priest Balaam seek to subdue the Israelites to Moab, if not by force, then by this devilish policy, to draw them from the sanctuary of God to the luxurious and ribald feasts of Baal-peor. Thus have they trespassed not only against the monarchy of England, but of Heaven also, as others, I doubt not, can prosecute against them.

THE emulation that under the old law was in the king towards the priest is now so come about in the gospel, that all the danger is to be feared from the priest to the king. Whilst the priest's office in the law was set out with an exterior lustre of pomp and glory, kings were ambitious to be priests; now priests, not perceiving the heavenly brightness and inward splendor of their more glorious evangelic ministry, with as great ambition affect to be kings, as in all their courses is easy to be observed. Their eyes ever eminent upon worldly matters, their desires ever thirsting after worldly employments, instead of diligent and fervent study in the Bible, they covet to be expert in canons and decretals, which may enable them to judge and interpose in temporal causes, however pretended ecclesiastical. Do they not hoard up pelf, seek to be potent in secular strength, in state affairs, in lands, lordships, and domains, to sway and carry all before them in high courts and privy-councils, to bring into their grasp the high and principal offices of the kingdom? . . . .

But ever blessed be He, and ever glorified, that from his high watch-tower in the heavens, discerning the crooked ways of perverse and cruel men, hath hitherto maimed and infatuated all their damnable inventions, and deluded their great wizards with a delusion fit for fools and children: had God been so minded, he could have sent a spirit of mutiny amongst us, as he did between Abimelech and the Sechemites, to have made our funerals, and slain heaps more in number than the miserable surviving remnant; but he, when we least deserved, sent out a gentle gale and message of peace from the wings of those his cherubims that fan his mercy-seat. Nor shall the wisdom, the moderation, the Christian piety, the constancy, of our nobility and commons of England, be ever forgotten, whose calm and temperate connivance could sit still and smile out the stormy bluster of men more audacious and precipitant than of solid and deep reach, until their own fury had run itself out of breath, assailing by rash and heady approaches the impregnable situation of our liberty and safety, that laughed such weak enginery to scorn, such poor drifts to make a national war of a surplice brabble, a tippet scuffle, and engage the untainted honor of English knighthood to unfurl the streaming red cross, or to rear the horrid standard of those fatal guly dragons, for so unworthy a purpose as to force upon their fellow-subjects that which themselves are weary of, the skeleton of a mass-book. Nor must the patience, the fortitude, the firm obedience, of the nobles and people of Scotland, striving against manifold provocations, nor must their sincere and moderate proceedings hitherto, be unremembered, to the shameful conviction of all their detractors.

Go on both hand in hand, O nations, never to be disunited; be the praise and the heroic song of all posterity; merit this, but seek only virtue, not to extend your limits, (for what needs to win a fading triumphant laurel out of the tears of wretched men?) but to settle the pure worship of God in his Church, and justice in the state: then shall the hardest difficulties smooth out themselves before ye; envy shall sink to hell, craft and malice be confounded, whether it be homebred mischief or outlandish cunning: yea, other nations will then covet to serve ye, for lordship and victory are but the pages of justice and virtue. Commit securely to true wisdom the vanquishing and uncasing of craft and subtlety, which are but her two runagates: join your invincible might to do worthy and godlike deeds; and then he that seeks to break your union, a cleaving curse be his inheritance to all generations. . . . .

Thus then we see that our ecclesiastical and political choices may consent and sort as well together without any rupture in the state, as Christians and freeholders. But as for honor, that ought indeed to be different and distinct, as either office looks a several way; the minister whose calling and end is spiritual ought to be honored as a father and physician to the soul (if he be found to be so), with a son-like and disciple-like reverence, which is indeed the dearest and most affectionate honor, most to be desired by a wise man, and such as will easily command a free and plentiful provision of outward necessaries, without his further care of this world.

The magistrate, whose charge is to see to our persons and estates, is to be honored with a more elaborate and personal courtship, with large salaries and stipends, that he himself may abound in those things whereof his legal justice and watchful care give us the quiet enjoyment. And this distinction of honor will bring forth a seemly and graceful uniformity over all the kingdom.

Then shall the nobles possess all the dignities and offices of temporal honor to themselves, sole lords without the improper mixture of scholastic and pusillanimous upstarts; the Parliament shall void her upper house of the same annoyances; the common and civil laws shall be both set free, the former from the control, the other from the mere vassalage and copyhold of the clergy.

And whereas temporal laws rather punish men when they have transgressed than form them to be such as should transgress seldomest, we may conceive great hopes, through the showers of divine benediction watering the unmolested and watchful pains of the ministry, that the whole inheritance of God will grow up so straight and blameless, that the civil magistrate may with far less toil and difficulty, and far more ease and delight, steer the tall and goodly vessel of the commonwealth through all the gusts and tides of the world's mutability.

We must not run, they say, into sudden extremes. This is a fallacious rule, unless understood only of the actions of virtue about things indifferent: for if it be found that those two extremes be vice and virtue, falsehood and truth, the greater extremity of virtue and superlative truth we run into, the more virtuous and the more wise we become; and he that, flying from degenerate and traditional corruption, fears to shoot himself too far into the meeting embrace of a divinely warranted reformation, had better not have run at all. . . . .

Let us not dally with God when he offers us a full blessing, to take as much of it as we think will serve our ends, and turn him back the rest upon his hands, lest in his anger he snatch all from us again. . . . .

But in the evangelical and reformed use of this sacred censure,* no such prostitution, no such Iscariotical drifts, are to be doubted, as that spiritual doom and sentence should invade worldly possession, which is the rightful lot and portion even of the wickedest men, as frankly bestowed upon them by the all-dispensing bounty as rain and sunshine. No, no, it seeks not to bereave or destroy the body; it seeks to save the soul by humbling the body, not by imprisonment, or pecuniary mulct, much less by stripes, or bonds, or disinheritance, but by fatherly admonishment and Christian rebuke, to cast it into godly sorrow, whose end is joy, and ingenuous bashfulness to sin: if that can-

* Excommunication.

not be wrought, then as a tender mother takes her child and holds it over the pit with scaring words, that it may learn to fear where danger is; so doth excommunication as dearly and as freely, without money, use her wholesome and saving terrors: she is instant, she beseeches, by all the dear and sweet promises of salvation she entices and wooes; by all the threatenings and thunders of the law, and rejected gospel, she charges and adjures: this is all her armory, her munition, her artillery; then she awaits with long-sufferance, and yet ardent zeal. In brief, there is no act in all the errand of God's ministers to mankind wherein passes more lover-like contestation between Christ and the soul of a regenerate man lapsing, than before, and in, and after the sentence of excommunication. As for the fogging proctorage of money, with such an eye as struck Gehazi with leprosy and Simon Magus with a curse, so does she look, and so threaten her fiery whip against that banking den of thieves that dare thus baffle, and buy and sell the awful and majestic wrinkles of her brow. He that is rightly and apostolically sped with her invisible arrow, if he can be at peace in his soul, and not smell within him the brimstone of hell, may have fair leave to tell all his bags over undiminished of the least farthing, may eat his dainties, drink his wine, use his delights, enjoy his lands and liberties, not the least skin raised, not the least hair misplaced, for all that excommunication has done: much more may a king enjoy his rights and prerogatives undeflowered, untouched, and be as absolute and complete a king as all his royalties and revenues can make him. . . . .

O sir, I do now feel myself inwrapped on the sudden into those mazes and labyrinths of dreadful and hideous thoughts, that which way to get out, or which way to end, I know not, unless I turn mine eyes, and with your help lift up my hands to that eternal and propitious throne, where nothing is readier than grace and refuge to the distresses of mortal suppliants: and it were a shame to leave these serious thoughts less piously than the heathen were wont to conclude their graver discourses.

Thou, therefore, that sittest in light and glory unapproachable, Parent of angels and men! next, thee I implore, Omnipotent King, Redeemer of that lost remnant, whose nature thou didst assume, ineffable and everlasting Love! and thou, the third subsistence of Divine infinitude, illumining Spirit, the joy and solace of created things! one Tripersonal Godhead! look upon this thy poor and almost spent and expiring Church, leave her not thus a prey to these importunate wolves that wait and think long till they devour thy tender flock; these wild boars that have broke into thy vineyard, and left the print of their polluting hoofs on the souls of thy servants. O, let them not bring about their damned designs, that stand now at the entrance of the bottomless pit, expecting the watchword to open and let out those dreadful locusts and scorpions, to reinvolve us in that pitchy cloud of infernal darkness, where we shall never more see the sun of thy truth again, never hope for the cheerful dawn, never more hear the bird of morning sing! Be moved with pity at the afflicted state of this our shaken monarchy, that now lies laboring under her throes and struggling against the grudges of more dreaded calamities.

O thou, that, after the impetuous rage of five bloody inundations, and the succeeding sword of intestine war, soaking the land in her own gore, didst pity the sad and ceaseless revolution of our swift and thick-coming sorrows; when we were quite breathless, of thy free grace didst motion peace and terms of covenant with us; and, having first wellnigh freed us from Antichristian thraldom, didst build up this Britannic empire to a glorious and enviable height, with all her daughter-islands about her; stay us in this felicity, let not the obstinacy of our half-obedience and will-worship bring forth that viper of sedition, that for these fourscore years hath been breeding to eat through the entrails of our peace; but let her cast her abortive spawn without the danger of this travailing and throbbing kingdom: that we may still remember, in our solemn thanksgivings, how for us the Northern Ocean even to the frozen Thule was scattered with the proud shipwrecks of the Spanish Armada, and the very maw of hell ransacked, and made to give up her concealed destruction, ere she could vent it in that horrible and damned blast.

O, how much more glorious will those former deliverances appear, when we shall know them not only to have saved us from greatest miseries past, but to have reserved us for greatest happiness to come! Hitherto thou hast but freed us, and that not fully, from the unjust and tyrannous claim of thy foes; now unite us entirely, and appropriate us to thyself; tie us everlastingly in willing homage to the prerogative of thy eternal throne.

And now we know, O thou our most certain hope and defence, that thine enemies have been consulting all the sorceries of the great whore, and have joined their plots with that sad intelligencing tyrant that mischiefs the world with his mines of Ophir, and lies thirsting to revenge his naval ruins that have larded our seas: but let them all take counsel together, and let it come to naught; let them decree, and do thou cancel it; let them gather themselves, and be scattered; let them embattle themselves, and be broken; let them embattle, and be broken, for thou art with us.

Then, amidst the hymns and hallelujahs of saints, some one may perhaps be heard offering at high strains in new and lofty measure to sing and celebrate thy divine mercies and marvellous judgments in this land throughout all ages; whereby this great and warlike nation, instructed and inured to the fervent and continual practice of truth and righteousness, and casting far from her the rags of her whole vices, may press on hard to that high and happy emulation to be found the soberest, wisest, and most Christian people at that day when thou, the eternal and shortly expected King, shalt open the clouds to judge the several kingdoms of the world, and, distributing national honors and rewards to religious and just commonwealths, shalt put an end to all earthly tyrannies, proclaiming thy universal and mild monarchy through heaven and earth, where they undoubtedly, that by their labors, counsels, and prayers have been earnest for the common good of religion and their country, shall receive, above the inferior orders of the blessed, the regal addition of principalities, legions, and thrones into their glorious titles, and in supereminence of beatific vision, progressing the dateless and irrevoluble circle of eternity, shall clasp inseparable hands with joy and bliss, in overmeasure forever.

But they contrary, that by the impairing and diminution of the true faith, the distresses and servitude of their country, aspire to high dignity, rule, and promotion here, after a shameful end in this life (which God grant them) shall be thrown down eternally into the darkest and deepest gulf of hell, where, under the despiteful control, the trample and spurn of all the other damned, that in the anguish of their torture shall have no other ease than to exercise a raving and bestial tyranny over them as their slaves and negroes, they shall remain in that plight forever, the basest, the lowermost, the most dejected, most underfoot, and down-trodden vassals of perdition.

FROM THE TREATISE

OF PRELATICAL EPISCOPACY.

IF it be of divine constitution, to satisfy us fully in that, the Scripture only is able, it being the only book left us of divine authority, not in anything more divine than in the all-sufficiency it hath to furnish us, as with all other spiritual knowledge, so with this in particular, setting out to us a perfect man of God, accomplished to all the good works of his charge. .... To verify that which St. Paul foretold of succeeding times, when men began to have itching ears, then, not contented with the plentiful and wholesome fountains of the Gospel, they began after their own lusts to heap to themselves teachers, and as if the Divine Scripture wanted a supplement, and were to be eked out, they cannot think any doubt resolved, and any doctrine confirmed, unless they run to that indigested heap and fry of authors which they call antiquity. Whatsoever time, or the heedless hand of blind chance, hath drawn down from of old to this present, in her huge drag-net, whether fish or sea-weed, shells or shrubs, unpicked, unchosen, those are the fathers. . . . .

How can they bring satisfaction from such an author, to whose every essence the reader must be fain to contribute his own understanding? Had God ever intended that we should have sought any part of useful instruction from Ignatius, doubtless he would not have so ill provided for our knowledge as to send him to our hands in this broken and disjointed plight; and if he intended no such thing, we do injuriously in thinking to taste better the pure evangelic manna, by seasoning our mouths with the tainted scraps and fragments of an unknown table, and searching among the verminous and polluted rags dropped overworn from the toiling shoulders of time, with these deformedly to quilt and interlace the entire, the spotless, and undecaying robe of truth, the daughter not of time, but of Heaven, only bred up here below in Christian hearts, between two grave and holy nurses, the doctrine and discipline of the Gospel. . . . .

He that thinks it the part of a well-learned man to have read diligently the ancient stories of the Church, and to be no stranger in the volumes of the fathers, shall have all judicious men consenting with him; not hereby to control and new-fangle the Scripture, God forbid! but to mark how corruption and apostasy crept in by degrees, and to gather up wherever we find the remaining sparks of original truth, wherewith to stop the mouths of our adversaries, and to bridle them with their own curb, who willingly pass by that which is orthodoxal in them, and studiously cull out that which is commentitious, and best for their turns, not weighing the fathers in the balance of Scripture, but Scripture in the balance of the fathers. If we, therefore, making first the Gospel our rule and oracle, shall take the good which we light on in the fathers, and set it to oppose the evil which other men seek from them, in this way of skirmish we shall easily master all superstition and false doctrine; but if we turn this our discreet and wary usage of them into a blind devotion towards them, and whatsoever we find written by them, we both forsake our own grounds and reasons which led us at first to part from Rome, that is, to hold to the Scriptures against all antiquity; we remove our cause into our adversaries' own court, and take up there those cast principles which will soon cause us to solder up with them again; inasmuch as, believing antiquity for itself in any one point, we bring an engagement upon ourselves of assenting to all that it charges upon us.

FROM THE

REASON OF CHURCH GOVERNMENT URGED AGAINST PRELATY.

IN the publishing of human laws, which for the most part aim not beyond the good of civil society, to set them barely forth to the people without reason or preface, like a physical prescript, or only with threatenings, as it were a lordly command, in the judgment of Plato was thought to be done neither generously nor wisely. His advice was, seeing that persuasion certainly is a more winning and more manlike way to keep men in obedience than fear, that to such laws as were of principal moment, there should be used as an induction some well-tempered discourse, showing how good, how gainful, how happy it must needs be to live according to honesty and justice; which being uttered with those native colors and graces of speech, as true eloquence, the daughter of virtue, can best bestow upon her mother's praises, would so incite, and in a manner charm, the multitude into the love of that which is really good, as to embrace it ever after, not of custom and awe, which most men do, but of choice and purpose, with true and constant delight. But this practice we may learn from a better and more ancient authority than any heathen writer hath to give us; and, indeed, being a point of so high wisdom and worth, how could it be but we should find it in that book within whose sacred context all wisdom is unfolded? Moses, therefore, the only lawgiver that we can believe to have been visibly taught of God, knowing how vain it was to write laws to men whose hearts were not first seasoned with the knowledge of God and of his works, began from the book of Genesis, as a prologue to his laws; which Josephus right well hath noted: that the nation of the Jews, reading therein the universal goodness of God to all creatures in the creation, and his peculiar favor to them in his election of Abraham, their ancestor, from whom they could derive so many blessings upon themselves, might be moved to obey sincerely, by knowing so good a reason of their obedience. If, then, in the administration of civil justice, and under the obscurity of ceremonial rites, such care was had by the wisest of the heathen, and by Moses among the Jews, to instruct them at least in a general reason of that government to which their subjection was required, how much more ought the members of the Church, under the

Gospel, seek to inform their understanding in the reason of that government which the Church claims to have over them! Especially for that Church hath in her immediate cure those inner parts and affections of the mind, where the seat of reason is having power to examine our spiritual knowledge, and to demand from us, in God's behalf, a service entirely reasonable.

THERE is not that thing in the world of more grave and urgent importance throughout the whole life of man than is discipline. What need I instance! He that hath read with judgment of nations and commonwealths, of cities and camps, of peace and war, sea and land, will readily agree that the flourishing and decaying of all civil societies, all the moments and turnings of human occasions, are moved to and fro as upon the axle of discipline. So that whatsoever power or sway in mortal things weaker men have attributed to fortune, I durst with more confidence (the honor of Divine Providence ever saved) ascribe either to the vigor or the slackness of discipline. Nor is there any sociable perfection in this life, civil or sacred, that can be above discipline; but she is that which with her musical cords preserves and holds all the parts thereof together. Hence in those perfect armies of Cyrus in Xenophon, and Scipio in the Roman stories, the excellence of military skill was esteemed, not by the not needing, but by the readiest submitting to the edicts of their commander. And certainly discipline is not only the removal of disorder; but if any visible shape can be given to divine things, the very visible shape and image of virtue, whereby she is not only seen in the regular gestures and motions of her heavenly paces as she walks, but also makes the harmony of her voice audible to mortal ears. Yea, the angels themselves, in whom no disorder is feared, as the apostle that saw them in his rapture describes, are distinguished and quaternioned into their celestial princedoms and satrapies, according as God himself has writ his imperial decrees through the great provinces of heaven. The state also of the blessed in paradise, though never so perfect, is not therefore left without discipline, whose golden surveying-reed marks out and measures every quarter and circuit of New Jerusalem. Yet is it not to be conceived that those eternal effluences of sanctity and love in the glorified saints should by this means be confined and cloyed with repetition of that which is prescribed, but that our happiness may orb itself into a thousand vagancies of glory and delight, and with a kind of eccentrical equation be, as it were, an invariable planet of joy and felicity; how much less can we believe that God would leave his frail and feeble, though not less beloved Church here below, to the perpetual stumble of conjecture and disturbance in this our dark voyage, without the card and compass of discipline? Which is so hard to be of man's making, that we may see even in the guidance of a civil state to worldly happiness, it is not for every learned or every wise man, though many of them consult in common, to invent or frame a discipline: but if it be at all the work of man, it must be of such a one as is a true knower of himself, and in whom contemplation and practice, wit, prudence, fortitude, and eloquence, must be rarely met, both to comprehend the hidden causes of things, and span in his thoughts all the various effects that passion or complexion can work in man's nature; and hereto must his hand be at defiance with gain, and his heart in all virtues heroic; so far is it from the ken of these wretched projectors of ours, that bescrawl their pamphlets every day with new forms of government for our Church. And therefore all the ancient lawgivers were either truly inspired, as Moses, or were such men as with authority enough might give it out to be so, as Minos, Lycurgus, Numa, because they wisely forethought that men would never quietly submit to such a discipline as had not more of God's hand in it than man's. . . .

Public preaching indeed is the gift of the Spirit, working as best seems to his secret will; but discipline is the practic work of preaching directed and applied, as is most requisite, to particular duty; without which it were all one to the benefit of souls, as it would be to the cure of bodies, if all the physicians in London should get into the several pulpits of the city, and, assembling all the diseased in every parish, should begin a learned lecture of pleurisies, palsies, lethargies, to which perhaps none there present were inclined; and so, without so much as feeling one pulse, or giving the least order to any skilful apothecary, should dismiss them from time to time, some groaning, some languishing, some expiring, with this only charge, to look well to themselves, and do as they hear. . . . .

Did God take such delight in measuring out the pillars, arches, and doors of a material temple? Was he so punctual and circumspect in lavers, altars, and sacrifices soon after to be abrogated, lest any of these should have been made contrary to his mind? Is not a far more perfect work more agreeable to his perfections in the most perfect state of the Church Militant, the new alliance of God to man? Should not he rather now by his own prescribed discipline have cast his line and level upon the soul of man, which is his rational temple, and, by the divine square and compass thereof, form and regenerate in us the lovely shapes of virtues and graces, the sooner to edify and accomplish that immortal stature of Christ's body, which is his Church, in all her glorious lineaments and proportions? And that this indeed God hath done for us in the Gospel we shall see with open eyes, not under a veil. We may pass over the history of the Acts and other places, turning only to those epistles of St. Paul to Timothy and Titus; where the spiritual eye may discern more goodly and gracefully erected, than all the magnificence of temple or tabernacle, such a heavenly structure of evangelical discipline, so diffusive of knowledge and charity to the prosperous increase and growth of the Church, that it cannot be wondered if that elegant and artful symmetry of the promised new temple in Ezekiel, and all those sumptuous things under the law, were made to signify the inward beauty and splendor of the Christian Church thus governed. . . . .

And therefore, if God afterward gave or permitted this insurrection of episcopacy, it is to be feared he did it in his wrath, as he gave the Israelites a king. With so good a will doth he use to alter his own chosen government once established. For mark whether this rare device of man's brain, thus preferred before the ordinance of God, had better success than fleshly wisdom, not counselling with God, is wont to have. So far was it from removing schism, that, if schism parted the congregations before, now it rent and mangled, now it raged. Heresy begat heresy with a certain monstrous haste of pregnancy in her birth, at once born and bringing forth. Contentions, before brotherly, were now hostile. Men went to choose their bishop as they went to a pitched field, and the day of his election was, like the sacking of a city, sometimes ended with the blood of thousands. Nor this among heretics only, but men of the same belief, yea, confessors; and that with such odious ambition, that Eusebius, in his eighth book, testifies he abhorred to write. And the reason is not obscure, for the poor dignity, or rather burden, of a parochial presbyter could not engage any great party, nor that to any deadly feud: but prelaty was a power of that extent and sway, that, if her election were popular, it was seldom not the cause of some faction or broil in the church. But if her dignity came by favor of some prince, she was from that time his creature, and obnoxious to comply with his ends in state, were they right or wrong. So that, instead of finding prelaty an impeacher of schism or faction, the more I search, the more I grow into all persuasion to think rather that faction and she, as with a spousal ring, are wedded together, never to be divorced. . . . .

Do they keep away schism? If to bring a numb and chill stupidity of soul, an unactive blindness of mind, upon the people by their leaden doctrine, or no doctrine at all, if to persecute all knowing and zealous Christians by the violence of their courts, be to keep away schism, they keep schism away indeed; and by this kind of discipline all Italy and Spain is as purely and politicly kept from schism as England hath been by them.

With as good a plea might the dead-palsy boast to a man, It is I that free you from stitches and pains, and the troublesome feeling of cold and heat, of wounds and strokes: if I were gone, all these would molest you. The winter might as well vaunt itself against the spring, I destroy all noisome and rank weeds, I keep down all pestilent vapors; yes, and all wholesome herbs, and all fresh dews, by your violent and hide-bound frost: but when the gentle west winds shall open the fruitful bosom of the earth, thus overgirded by your imprisonment, then the flowers put forth and spring, and then the sun shall scatter the mists, and the manuring hand of the tiller shall root up all that burdens the soil without thank to your bondage. . . . .

It may suffice us to be taught by St. Paul, that there must be sects for the manifesting of those that are sound-hearted. These are but winds and flaws to try the floating vessel of our faith, whether it be stanch and sail well, whether our ballast be just, our anchorage and cable strong. By this is seen who lives by faith and certain knowledge, and who by credulity and the prevailing opinion of the age; whose virtue is of an unchangeable grain, and whose of a slight wash. If God come to try our constancy, we ought not to shrink or stand the less firmly for that, but pass on with more steadfast resolution to establish the truth, though it were through a lane of sects and heresies on each side. Other things men do to the glory of God: but sects and errors, it seems, God suffers to be for the glory of good men, that the world may know and reverence their true fortitude and undaunted constancy in the truth. Let us not therefore make these things an incumbrance, or an excuse of our delay in reforming, which God sends as us an incitement to proceed with more honor and alacrity: for if there were no opposition, where were the trial of an unfeigned goodness and magnanimity? Virtue that wavers is not virtue, but vice revolted from itself, and after a while returning. The actions of just and pious men do not darken in their middle course; but Solomon tells us, they are as the shining light, that shineth more and more unto the perfect day. But if we shall suffer the trifling doubts and jealousies of future sects to overcloud the fair beginnings of purposed reformation, let us rather fear that another proverb of the same wise man be not upbraided to us, that "the way of the wicked is as darkness; they stumble at they know not what." If sects and schisms be turbulent in the unsettled estate of a church, while it lies under the amending hand, it best beseems our Christian courage to think they are but as the throes and pangs that go before the birth of reformation, and that the work itself is now in doing. For if we look but on the nature of elemental and mixed things, we know they cannot suffer any change of one kind or quality into another, without the struggle of contrarieties. And in things artificial, seldom any elegance is wrought without a superfluous waste and refuse in the transaction. No marble statue can be politely carved, no fair edifice built, without almost as much rubbish and sweeping. Insomuch that even in the spiritual conflict of St. Paul's conversion, there fell scales from his eyes, that were not perceived before. No wonder, then, in the reforming of a church, which is never brought to effect without the fierce encounter of truth and falsehood together, if, as it were, the splinters and shards of so violent a jousting, there fall from between the shock many fond errors and fanatic opinions, which, when truth has the upper hand, and the reformation shall be perfected, will easily be rid out of the way, or kept so low, as that they shall be only the exercise of our knowledge, not the disturbance or interruption of our faith.....

In state many things at first are crude and hard to digest, which only time and deliberation can supple and concoct. But in religion, wherein is no immaturity, nothing out of season, it goes far otherwise. The door of grace turns upon smooth hinges, wide opening to send out, but soon shutting to recall the precious offers of mercy to a nation: which, unless watchfulness and zeal, two quicksighted and ready-handed virgins, be there in our behalf to receive, we lose; and still the oftener we lose, the straiter the door opens, and the less is offered. This is all we get by demurring in God's service.

How happy were it for this frail, and as it may be called mortal life of man, since all earthly things which have the name of good and convenient in our daily use, are withal so cumbersome and full of trouble, if knowledge, yet which is the best and lightsomest possession of the mind, were, as the common saying is, no burden; and that what it wanted of being a load to any part of the body, it did not with a heavy advantage overlay upon the spirit! For not to speak of that knowledge that rests in the contemplation of natural causes and dimensions, which must needs be a lower wisdom, as the object is low, certain it is, that he who hath obtained in more than the scantiest measure to know anything distinctly of God, and of his true worship, and what is infallibly good and happy in the state of man's life, what in itself evil and miserable, though vulgarly not so esteemed, — he that hath obtained to know this, the only high valuable wisdom indeed, remembering also that God, even to a strictness, requires the improvement of those his intrusted gifts, cannot but sustain a sorer burden of mind, and more pressing than any supportable toil or weight which the body can labor under, how and in what manner he shall dispose and employ these sums of knowledge and illumination, which God hath sent him into this world to trade with. And that which aggravates the burden more is, that, having received amongst his allotted parcels certain precious truths, of such an orient lustre as no diamond can equal, which nevertheless he has in charge to put off at any cheap rate, yea, for nothing to them that will, the great merchants of this world, fearing that this course would soon discover and disgrace the false glitter of their deceitful wares, wherewith they abuse the people, like poor Indians with beads and glasses, practise by all means how they may suppress the vending of such rarities, and at such a cheapness as would undo them, and turn their trash upon their hands. Therefore, by gratifying the corrupt desires of men in fleshly doctrines, they stir them up to persecute with hatred and contempt all those that seek to bear themselves uprightly in this their spiritual factory: which they foreseeing, though they cannot but testify of truth, and the excellency of that heavenly traffic which they bring, against what opposition or danger soever, yet needs must it sit heavily upon their spirits, that being, in God's prime intention and their own, selected heralds of peace, and dispensers of treasure inestimable, without price, to them that have no peace, they find in the discharge of their commission that they are made the greatest variance and offence, a very sword and fire, both in house and city, over the whole earth. This is that which the sad prophet Jeremiah laments: "Woe is me, my mother, that thou hast borne me a man of strife and contention!" And although divine inspiration must certainly have been sweet to those ancient prophets, yet the irksomeness of that truth which they brought was so unpleasant unto them, that everywhere they call it a burden. Yea, that mysterious book of revelation which the great Evangelist was bid to eat, as it had been some eye-brightening electuary of knowledge and foresight, though it were sweet in his mouth, and in the learning, it was bitter in his belly, bitter in the denouncing. Nor was this hid from the wise poet Sophocles, who in that place of his tragedy where Tiresias is called to resolve King Œdipus in a matter which he knew would be grievous, brings him in bemoaning his lot, that he knew more than other men. For surely to every good and peaceable man it must in nature needs be a hateful thing to be the displeaser and molester of thousands; much better would it like him doubtless to be the messenger of gladness and contentment which is his chief intended business to all mankind, but that they resist and oppose their own true happiness. But when God commands to take the trumpet, and blow a dolorous or a jarring blast, it lies not in man's will, what he shall say, or what he shall conceal. If he shall think to be silent as Jeremiah did, because of the reproach and derision he met with daily,—"And all his familiar friends watched for his halting," to be revenged on him for speaking the truth, — he would be forced to confess as he confessed: "His word was in my heart as a burning fire shut up in my bones; I was weary with forbearing, and could not stay." Which might teach these times not suddenly to condemn all things that are sharply spoken or vehemently written as proceeding out of stomach, virulence, or ill-nature, but to consider rather, that, if the prelates have leave to say the worst that can be said, or do the worst that can be done, while they strive to keep to themselves, to their great pleasure and commodity, those things which they ought to render up, no man can be justly offended with him that shall endeavor to impart and bestow, without any gain to himself, those sharp but saving words which would be a terror and a torment in him to keep back.

For me, I have determined to lay up as the best treasure and solace of a good old age, if God vouchsafe it me, the honest liberty of free speech from my youth, where I shall think it available in so dear a concernment as the Church's good. For if I be, either by disposition or what other cause, too inquisitive, or suspicious of myself and mine own doings, who can help it? But this I foresee, that should the Church be brought under heavy oppression, and God have given me ability the while to reason against that man that should be the author of so foul a deed, — or should she, by blessing from above on the industry and courage of faithful men, change this her distracted estate into better days without the least furtherance or contribution of those few talents which God at that present had lent me, — I foresee what stories I should hear within myself, all my life after, of discourage and reproach. Timorous and ungrateful, the Church of God is now again at the foot of her insulting enemies, and thou bewailest. What matters it for thee, or thy bewailing? When time was, thou couldst not find a syllable of all that thou hast read, or studied, to utter in her behalf. Yet ease and leisure was given thee for thy retired thoughts, out of the sweat of other men. Thou hast the diligence, the parts, the language of a man, if a vain subject were to be adorned or beautified; but when the cause of God and his Church was to be pleaded, for which purpose that tongue was given thee which thou hast, God listened if he could hear thy voice among his zealous servants, but thou wert dumb as a beast; from henceforward be that which thine own brutish silence hath made thee. Or else I should have heard on the other ear: Slothful, and ever to be set light by, the Church hath now overcome her late distresses after the unwearied labors of many her true servants that stood up in her defence; thou also wouldst take upon thee to share amongst them of their joy: but wherefore thou? Where canst thou show any word or deed of thine which might have hastened her peace? Whatever thou dost now talk, or write, or look, is the alms of other men's active prudence and zeal. Dare not now to say or do anything better than thy former sloth and infancy; or if thou darest, thou dost impudently to make a thrifty purchase of boldness to thyself, out of the painful merits of other men; what before was thy sin is now thy duty, to be abject and worthless. These, and such like lessons as these, I know would have been my matins duly and my even-song. But now, by this little diligence, mark what a privilege I have gained with good men and saints to claim my right of lamenting the tribulations of the Church, if she should suffer when others, that have ventured nothing for her sake, have not the honor to be admitted mourners. But if she lift up her drooping head and prosper, among those that have something more than wished her welfare, I have my charter and freehold of rejoicing to me and my heirs. Concerning, therefore, this wayward subject, against prelaty, the touching whereof is so distasteful and disquietous to a number of men, as by what hath been said I may deserve of charitable readers to be credited, that neither envy nor gall hath entered me upon this controversy, but the enforcement of conscience only, and a preventive fear lest the omitting of this duty should be against me, when I would store up to myself the good provision of peaceful hours: so, lest it should be still imputed to me, as I have found it hath been, that some self-pleasing humor of vainglory hath incited me to contest with men of high estimation, now while green years are upon my head, from this needless surmisal I shall hope to dissuade the intelligent and equal auditor, if I can but say successfully that which in this exigent behoves me; although I would be heard only, if it might be, by the elegant and learned reader, to whom principally for a while I shall beg leave I may address myself. To him it will be no new thing, though I tell him that if I hunted after praise, by the ostentation of wit and learning, I should not write thus out of mine own season, when I have neither yet completed to my mind the full circle of my private studies, although I complain not of any insufficiency to the matter in hand; or were I ready to my wishes, it were a folly to commit anything elaborately composed to the careless and interrupted listening of these tumultuous times. Next, if I were wise only to my own ends, I would certainly take such a subject as of itself might catch applause, whereas this hath all the disadvantages on the contrary, and such a subject as the publishing whereof might be delayed at pleasure, and time enough to pencil it over with all the curious touches of art, even to the perfection of a faultless picture; whereas in this argument the not deferring is of great moment to the good speeding, that if solidity have leisure to do her office, art cannot have much. Lastly, I should not choose this manner of writing, wherein knowing myself inferior to myself, led by the genial power of nature to another task, I have the use, as I may account, but of my left hand. And though I shall be foolish in saying more to this purpose, yet, since it will be such a folly as wisest men go about to commit, having only confessed and so committed, I may trust with more reason, because with more folly, to have courteous pardon. For although a poet, soaring in the high reason of his fancies, with his garland and singing-robes about him, might, without apology, speak more of himself than I mean to do; yet for me, sitting here below in the cool element of prose, a mortal thing among many readers of no empyreal conceit, to venture and divulge unusual things of myself, I shall petition to the gentler sort, it may not be envy to me. I must say, therefore, that after I had for my first years, by the ceaseless diligence and care of my father, (whom God recompense!) been exercised to the tongues, and some sciences, as my age would suffer, by sundry masters and teachers, both at home and at the schools, it was found that whether aught was imposed me by them that had the overlooking, or betaken to of mine own choice in English, or other tongue, prosing or versing, but chiefly by this latter, the style, by certain vital signs it had, was likely to live. But much latelier in the private academies of Italy, whither I was favored to resort, perceiving that some trifles which I had in memory, composed at under twenty or thereabout, (for the manner is, that every one must give some proof of his wit and reading there,) met with acceptance above what was looked for; and other things, which I had shifted in scarcity of books and conveniences to patch up amongst them, were received with written encomiums, which the Italian is not forward to bestow on men of this side the Alps; I began thus far to assent both to them and divers of my friends here at home, and not less to an inward prompting which now grew daily upon me, that by labor and intense study, (which I take to be my portion in this life,) joined with the strong propensity of nature, I might perhaps leave something so written to after-times, as they should not willingly let it die. These thoughts at once possessed me, and these other; that if I were certain to write as men buy leases, for three lives and downward, there ought no regard be sooner had than to God's glory by the honor and instruction of my country. For which cause, and not only for that I knew it would be hard to arrive at the second rank among the Latins, I applied myself to that resolution, which Ariosto followed against the persuasions of Bembo, to fix all the industry and art I could unite to the adorning of my native tongue; not to make verbal curiosities the end, (that were a toilsome vanity,) but to be an interpreter and relater of the best and sagest things among mine own citizens throughout this island in the mother dialect. That what the greatest and choicest wits of Athens, Rome, or modern Italy, and those Hebrews of old did for their country, I, in my proportion, with this over and above of being a Christian, might do for mine; not caring to be once named abroad, though perhaps I could attain to that, but content with these British islands as my world; whose fortune hath hitherto been, that if the Athenians, as some say, made their small deeds great and renowned by their eloquent writers, England hath had her noble achievements made small by the unskilful handling of monks and mechanics.

Time serves not now, and perhaps I might seem too profuse to give any certain account of what the mind at home, in the spacious circuits of her musing, hath liberty to propose to herself, though of highest hope and hardest attempting; whether that epic form whereof the two poems of Homer, and those other two of Virgil and Tasso, are a diffuse, and the book of Job a brief model: or whether the rules of Aristotle herein are strictly to be kept, or nature to be followed, which in them that know art, and use judgment, is no transgression, but an enriching of art: and, lastly, what king or knight before the Conquest might be chosen in whom to lay the pattern of a Christian hero. And as Tasso gave to a prince of Italy his choice whether he would command him to write of Godfrey's expedition against the Infidels, or Belisarius against the Goths, or Charlemain against the Lombards; if to the instinct of nature and the emboldening of art aught may be trusted, and that there be nothing adverse in our climate, or the fate of this age, it haply would be no rashness, from an equal diligence and inclination, to present the like offer in our own ancient stories; or whether those dramatic constitutions, wherein Sophocles and Euripides reign, shall be found more doctrinal and exemplary to a nation. The Scripture also affords us a divine pastoral drama in the Song of Solomon, consisting of two persons, and a double chorus, as Origen rightly judges. And the Apocalypse of St. John is the majestic image of a high and stately tragedy, shutting up and intermingling her solemn scenes and acts with a sevenfold chorus of hallelujahs and harping symphonies: and this my opinion the grave authority of Pareus, commenting that book, is sufficient to confirm. Or if occasion shall lead, to imitate those magnific odes and hymns, wherein Pindarus and Callimachus are in most things worthy, some others in their frame judicious, in their matter most an end faulty. But those frequent songs throughout the law and prophets beyond all these, not in their divine argument alone, but in the very critical art of composition, may be easily made appear over all the kinds of lyric poesy to be incomparable.

These abilities, wheresoever they be found, are the inspired gift of God, rarely bestowed, but yet to some (though most abuse) in every nation; and are of power, beside the office of a pulpit, to imbreed and cherish in a great people the seeds of virtue and public civility, to allay the perturbations of the mind, and set the affections in right tune; to celebrate in glorious and lofty hymns the throne and equipage of God's almightiness, and what he works, and what he suffers to be wrought with high providence in his Church; to sing victorious agonies of martyrs and saints, the deeds and triumphs of just and pious nations, doing valiantly through faith against the enemies of Christ; to deplore the general relapses of kingdoms and states from justice and God's true worship. Lastly, whatsoever in religion is holy and sublime, in virtue amiable or grave, whatsoever hath passion or admiration in all the changes of that which is called fortune from without, or the wily subtleties and refluxes of man's thoughts from within; all these things with a solid and treatable smoothness to paint out and describe: teaching over the whole book of sanctity and virtue, through all the instances of example, with such delight to those especially of soft and delicious temper, who will not so much as look upon truth herself unless they see her elegantly dressed; that whereas the paths of honesty and good life appear now rugged and difficult, though they be indeed easy and pleasant, they will then appear to all men both easy and pleasant, though they were rugged and difficult indeed. And what a benefit this would be to our youth and gentry, may be soon guessed by what we know of the corruption and bane which they suck in daily from the writings and interludes of libidinous and ignorant poetasters, who, having scarce ever heard of that which is the main consistence of a true poem, the choice of such persons as they ought to introduce, and what is moral and decent to each one, do for the most part lay up vicious principles in sweet pills to be swallowed down, and make the taste of virtuous documents harsh and sour. But because the spirit of man cannot demean itself lively in this body, without some recreating intermission of labor and serious things, it were happy for the commonwealth, if our magistrates, as in those famous governments of old, would take into their care, not only the deciding of our contentious law-cases and brawls, but the managing of our public sports and festival pastimes; that they might be, not such as were authorized a while since, the provocations of drunkenness and lust, but such as may inure and harden our bodies by martial exercises to all warlike skill and performance; and may civilize, adorn, and make discreet our minds by the learned and affable meeting of frequent academies, and the procurement of wise and artful recitations, sweetened with eloquent and graceful enticements to the love and practice of justice, temperance, and fortitude, instructing and bettering the nation at all opportunities, that the call of wisdom and virtue may be heard everywhere, as Solomon saith: "She crieth without, she uttereth her voice in the streets, in the top of high places, in the chief concourse, and in the openings of the gates." Whether this may not be, not only in pulpits, but after another persuasive method, at set and solemn paneguries, in theatres, porches, or what other place or way may win most upon the people to receive at once both recreation and instruction, let them in authority consult. The thing which I had to say, and those intentions which have lived within me ever since I could conceive myself anything worth to my country, I return to crave excuse that urgent reason hath plucked from me, by an abortive and foredated discovery. And the accomplishment of them lies not but in a power above man's to promise; but that none hath by more studious ways endeavored, and with more unwearied spirit that none shall, that I dare almost aver of myself, as far as life and free leisure will extend; and that the land had once enfranchised herself from this impertinent yoke of prelaty, under whose inquisitorious and tyrannical duncery no free and splendid wit can flourish. Neither do I think it shame to covenant with any knowing reader, that for some few years yet I may go on trust with him toward the payment of what I am now indebted, as being a work not to be raised from the heat of youth, or the vapors of wine; like that which flows at waste from the pen of some vulgar amourist, or the trencher fury of a rhyming parasite; nor to be obtained by the invocation of Dame Memory and her siren daughters, but by devout prayer to that Eternal Spirit, who can enrich with all utterance and knowledge, and sends out his seraphim, with the hallowed fire of his altar, to touch and purify the lips of whom he pleases: to this must be added industrious and select reading, steady observation, insight into all seemly and generous arts and affairs; till which in some measure be compassed, at mine own peril and cost, I refuse not to sustain this expectation from as many as are not loath to hazard so much credulity upon the best pledges that I can give them. Although it nothing content me to have disclosed thus much beforehand, but that I trust hereby to make it manifest with what small willingness I endure to interrupt the pursuit of no less hopes than these, and leave a calm and pleasing solitariness, fed with cheerful and confident thoughts, to embark in a troubled sea of noises and hoarse disputes, put from beholding the bright countenance of truth in the quiet and still air of delightful studies, to come into the dim reflection of hollow antiquities sold by the seeming bulk, and there be fain to club quotations with men whose learning and belief lies in marginal stuffings, who, when they have, like good sumpters, laid ye down their horse-loads of citations and fathers at your door, with a rhapsody of who and who were bishops here or there, ye may take off their packsaddles, their day's work is done, and episcopacy, as they think, stoutly vindicated. Let any gentle apprehension, that can distinguish learned pains from unlearned drudgery, imagine what pleasure or profoundness can be in this, or what honor to deal against such adversaries. But were it the meanest under-service, if God by his secretary Conscience enjoin it, it were sad for me if I should draw back; for me especially, now when all men offer their aid to help, ease, and lighten the difficult labors of the Church, to whose service, by the intentions of my parents and friends, I was destined of a child, and in mine own resolutions: till coming to some maturity of years, and perceiving what tyranny had invaded the Church, that he who would take orders must subscribe slave, and take an oath withal, which, unless he took with a conscience that would retch, he must either straight perjure, or split his faith; I thought it better to prefer a blameless silence before the sacred office of speaking, bought and begun with servitude and forswearing. Howsoever, thus church-outed by the prelates, hence may appear the right I have to meddle in these matters, as before the necessity and constraint appeared. . . . .

Who is there almost that measures wisdom by simplicity, strength by suffering, dignity by lowliness? Who is there that counts it first to be last, something to be nothing, and reckons himself of great command in that he is a servant? Yet God, when he meant to subdue the world and hell at once, part of that to salvation, and this wholly to perdition, made choice of no other weapons or auxiliaries than these, whether to save or to destroy. It had been a small mastery for him to have drawn out his legions into array, and flanked them with his thunder; therefore he sent foolishness to confute wisdom, weakness to bind strength, despisedness to vanquish pride: and this is the great mystery of the Gospel made good in Christ himself, who, as he testifies, came not to be ministered to, but to minister; and must be fulfilled in all his ministers till his second coming. . . .

For truth, I know not how, hath this unhappiness fatal to her, ere she can come to the trial and inspection of the understanding; being to pass through many little wards and limits of the several affections and desires, she cannot shift it, but must put on such colors and attire as those pathetic handmaids of the soul please to lead her in to their queen: and if she find so much favor with them, they let her pass in her own likeness; if not, they bring her into the presence habited and colored like a notorious falsehood. And contrary, when any falsehood comes that way, if they like the errand she brings, they are so artful to counterfeit the very shape and visage of truth, that the understanding not being able to discern the fucus which these enchantresses with such cunning have laid upon the feature sometimes of truth, sometimes of falsehood interchangeably, sentences for the most part one for the other at the first blush, according to the subtle imposture of these sensual mistresses, that keep the ports and passages between her and the object. . . . .

But there is yet a more ingenuous and noble degree of honest shame, or, call it, if you will, an esteem, whereby men bear an inward reverence toward their own persons. And if the love of God, as a fire sent from heaven to be ever kept alive upon the altars of our hearts, be the first principle of all godly and virtuous actions in men, this pious and just honoring of ourselves is the second, and may be thought as the radical moisture and fountain-head, whence every laudable and worthy enterprise issues forth. And although I have given it the name of a liquid thing, yet it is not incontinent to bound itself, as humid things are, but hath in it a most restraining and powerful abstinence to start back, and glob itself upward from the mixture of any ungenerous and unbeseeming motion, or any soil wherewith it may peril to stain itself. Something I confess it is to be ashamed of evil-doing in the presence of any; and to reverence the opinion and the countenance of a good man rather than a bad, fearing most in his sight to offend, goes so far as almost to be virtuous; yet this is but still the fear of infamy, and many such, when they find themselves alone, saving their reputation, will compound with other scruples, and come to a close treaty with their dearer vices in secret. But he that holds himself in reverence and due esteem, both for the dignity of God's image upon him, and for the price of his redemption, which he thinks is visibly marked upon his forehead, accounts himself both a fit person to do the noblest and godliest deeds, and much better worth than to deject and defile, with such a debasement, and such a pollution as sin is, himself so highly ransomed and ennobled to a new friendship and filial relation with God. Nor can he fear so much the offence and reproach of others, as he dreads and would blush at the reflection of his own severe and modest eye upon himself, if it should see him doing or imagining that which is sinful, though in the deepest secrecy. . . . .

Thus therefore the minister assisted attends his heavenly and spiritual cure: where we shall see him both in the course of his proceeding, and first in the excellency of his end, from the magistrate far different, and not more different than excelling. His end is to recover all that is of man, both soul and body, to an everlasting health; and yet as for worldly happiness, which is the proper sphere wherein the magistrate cannot but confine his motion, without a hideous exorbitancy from law, so little aims the minister, as his intended scope, to procure the much prosperity of this life, that ofttimes he may have cause to wish much of it away, as a diet puffing up the soul with a slimy fleshiness, and weakening her principal organic parts. Two heads of evil he has to cope with, ignorance and malice. Against the former he provides the daily manna of incorruptible doctrine, not at those set meals only in public, but as oft as he shall know that each infirmity or constitution requires. Against the latter with all the branches thereof, not meddling with that restraining and styptic surgery, which the law uses, not indeed against the malady, but against the eruptions, and outermost effects thereof; he, on the contrary, beginning at the prime causes and roots of the disease, sends in those two divine ingredients of most cleansing power to the soul, admonition and reproof; besides which two, there is no drug or antidote that can reach to purge the mind, and without which all other experiments are but vain, unless by accident. And he that will not let these pass into him, though he be the greatest king, as Plato affirms, must be thought to remain impure within, and unknowing of those things wherein his pureness and his knowledge should most appear. As soon therefore as it may be discerned that the Christian patient, by feeding otherwhere on meats not allowable, but of evil juice, hath disordered his diet, and spread an ill-humor through his veins, immediately disposing to a sickness, the minister, as being much nearer both in eye and duty than the magistrate, speeds him betimes to overtake that diffused malignance with some gentle potion of admonishment; or if aught be obstructed, puts in his opening and discussive confections. This not succeeding after once or twice, or oftener, in the presence of two or three his faithful brethren appointed thereto, he advises him to be more careful of his dearest health, and what it is that he so rashly hath let down into the divine vessel of his soul, God's temple. If this obtain not, he then, with the counsel of more assistants, who are informed of what diligence hath been already used, with more speedy remedies lays nearer siege to the entrenched causes of his distemper, not sparing such fervent and well-aimed reproofs as may best give him to see the dangerous estate wherein he is. To this also his brethren and friends entreat, exhort, adjure; and all these endeavors, as there is hope left, are more or less repeated. But if neither the regard of himself, nor the reverence of his elders and friends prevail with him to leave his vicious appetite, then as the time urges, such engines of terror God hath given into the hand of his minister, as to search the tenderest angles of the heart: one while he shakes his stubbornness with racking convulsions nigh despair; otherwhiles with deadly corrosives he gripes the very roots of his faulty liver to bring him to life through the entry of death. Hereto the whole Church beseech him, beg of him, deplore him, pray for him. After all this, performed with what patience and attendance is possible, and no relenting on his part, having done the utmost of their cure, in the name of God and of the Church they dissolve their fellowship with him, and, holding forth the dreadful sponge of excommunion, pronounce him wiped out of the list of God's inheritance, and in the custody of Satan till he repent. Which horrid sentence, though it touch neither life nor limb, nor any worldly possession, yet has it such a penetrating force, that swifter than any chemical sulphur, or that lightning which harms not the skin, and rifles the entrails, it scorches the inmost soul. Yet even this terrible denouncement is left to the Church for no other cause but to be as a rough and vehement cleansing medicine, where the malady is obdurate, a mortifying to life, a kind of saving by undoing. And it may be truly said, that as the mercies of wicked men are cruelties, so the cruelties of the Church are mercies. For if repentance sent from Heaven meet this lost wanderer, and draw him out of that steep journey wherein he was hasting towards destruction, to come and reconcile to the Church, if he bring with him his bill of health, and that he is now clear of infection, and of no danger to the other sheep; then with incredible expressions of joy all his brethren receive him, and set before him those perfumed banquets of Christian consolation; with precious ointments bathing and fomenting the old, and now to be forgotten stripes, which terror and shame had inflicted; and thus with heavenly solaces they cheer up his humble remorse, till he regain his first health and felicity. . . . .

I cannot better liken the state and person of a king than to that mighty Nazarite Samson; who being disciplined from his birth in the precepts and the practice of temperance and sobriety, without the strong drink of injurious and excessive desires, grows up to a noble strength and perfection with those his illustrious and sunny locks, the laws, waving and curling about his godlike shoulders. And while he keeps them about him undiminished and unshorn, he may with the jawbone of an ass, that is, with the word of his meanest officer, suppress and put to confusion thousands of those that rise against his just power. But laying down his head among the strumpet flatteries of prelates, while he sleeps and thinks no harm, they wickedly shaving off all those bright and weighty tresses of his law, and just prerogatives, which were his ornament and strength, deliver him over to indirect and violent counsels, which, as those Philistines, put out the fair and far-sighted eyes of his natural discerning, and make him grind in the prison-house of their sinister ends and practices upon him; till he, knowing this prelatical razor to have bereft him of his wonted might, nourish again his puissant hair, the golden beams of law and right; and they sternly shook thunder with ruin upon the heads of those his evil counsellors, but not without great affliction to himself. . . . .

Though God for less than ten just persons would not spare Sodom, yet if you can find, after due search, but only one good thing in prelaty, either to religion or civil government, to King or Parliament, to prince or people, to law, liberty, wealth, or learning, spare her, let her live, let her spread among ye, till with her shadow all your dignities and honors, and all the glory of the land be darkened and obscured. But on the contrary, if she be found to be malignant, hostile, destructive to all these, as nothing can be surer, then let your severe and impartial doom imitate the divine vengeance; rain down your punishing force upon this godless and oppressing government, and bring such a dead sea of subversion upon her, that she may never in this land rise more to afflict the holy reformed Church, and the elect people of God.

FROM

ANIMADVERSIONS UPON THE REMONSTRANT'S DEFENCE AGAINST SMECTYMNUUS.

WE all know that in private or personal injuries, yea, in public sufferings for the cause of Christ, his rule and example teaches us to be so far from a readiness to speak evil, as not to answer the reviler in his language, though never so much provoked: yet in the detecting and convincing of any notorious enemy to truth and his country's peace, especially that is conceited to have a voluble and smart fluence of tongue, and in the vain confidence of that, and out of a more tenacious cling to worldly respects, stands up for all the rest to justify a long usurpation and convicted pseudepiscopy of prelates, with all their ceremonies, liturgies, and tyrannies, which God and man are now ready to explode and hiss out of the land; I suppose, and more than suppose, it will be nothing disagreeing from Christian meekness to handle such a one in a rougher accent, and to send home his haughtiness well bespurted with his own holy water. Nor to do thus are we unautoritied either from the moral precept of Solomon, to answer him thereafter that prides him in his folly; nor from the example of Christ, and all his followers in all ages, who, in the refuting of those that resisted sound doctrine, and by subtile dissimulations corrupted the minds of men, have wrought up their zealous souls into such vehemencies, as nothing could be more killingly spoken: for who can be a greater enemy to mankind, who a more dangerous deceiver, than he who, defending a traditional corruption, uses no common arts, but with a wily stratagem of yielding to the time a greater part of his cause, seeming to forego all that man's invention hath done therein, and driven from much of his hold in Scripture; yet leaving it hanging by a twined thread, not from divine command, but from apostolical prudence or assent; as if he had the surety of some rolling trench, creeps up by this mean to his relinquished fortress of divine authority again, and still hovering between the confines of that which he dares not be openly, and that which he will not be sincerely, trains on the easy Christian insensibly within the close ambushment of worst errors, and with a sly shuffle of counterfeit principles, chopping and changing till he have gleaned all the good ones out of their minds, leaves them at last, after a slight resemblance of sweeping and garnishing, under the sevenfold possession of a desperate stupidity? And, therefore, they that love the souls of men, which is the dearest love, and stirs up the noblest jealousy, when they meet with such collusion, cannot be blamed though they be transported with the zeal of truth to a well-heated fervency; especially, seeing they which thus offend against the souls of their brethren, do it with delight to their great gain, ease, and advancement in this world; but they that seek to discover and oppose their false trade of deceiving, do it not without a sad and unwilling anger, not without many hazards; but without all private and personal spleen, and without any thought of earthly reward, whenas this very course they take stops their hopes of ascending above a lowly and unenviable pitch in this life. And although in the serious uncasing of a grand imposture (for to deal plainly with you, readers, prelaty is no better) there be mixed here and there such a grim laughter as may appear at the same time in an austere visage, it cannot be taxed of levity or insolence, for even this vein of laughing (as I could produce out of grave authors) hath ofttimes a strong and sinewy force in teaching and confuting; nor can there be a more proper object of indignation and scorn together, than a false prophet taken in the greatest, dearest, and most dangerous cheat, the cheat of souls: in the disclosing whereof, if it be harmful to be angry, and withal to cast a lowering smile, when the properest object calls for both, it will be long enough ere any be able to say, why those two most rational faculties of human intellect, anger and laughter, were first seated in the breast of man.....

The Romans had a time, once every year, when their slaves might freely speak their minds; it were hard if the freeborn people of England, with whom the voice of truth for these many years, even against the proverb, hath not been heard but in corners, after all your monkish prohibitions, and expurgatorious indexes, your gags and snaffles, your proud Imprimaturs not to be obtained without the shallow surview, but not shallow hand of some mercenary, narrow-souled, and illiterate chaplain; when liberty of speaking, than which nothing is more sweet to man, was girded and strait-laced almost to a broken-winded phthisic, if now at a good time, our time of parliament, the very jubilee and resurrection of the state, if now the concealed, the aggrieved, and long-persecuted truth, could not be suffered to speak; and though she burst out with some efficacy of words, could not be excused after such an injurious strangle of silence, nor avoid the censure of libelling, it were hard, it were something pinching in a kingdom of free spirits. Some princes and great statists have thought it a prime piece of necessary policy to thrust themselves under disguise into a popular throng, to stand the night long under eaves of houses, and low windows, that they might hear everywhere the utterances of private breasts, and amongst them find out the precious gem of truth, as amongst the numberless pebbles of the shore; whereby they might be the abler to discover, and avoid, that deceitful and close-couched evil of flattery that ever attends them, and misleads them, and might skilfully know how to apply the several redresses to each malady of state, without trusting the disloyal information of parasites and sycophants: whereas now this permission of free writing, were there no good else in it, yet at some times thus licensed, is such an unripping, such an anatomy of the shyest and tenderest particular truths, as makes not only the whole nation in many points the wiser, but also presents and carries home to princes, men most remote from vulgar concourse, such a full insight of every lurking evil, or restrained good among the commons, as that they shall not need hereafter, in old cloaks and false beards, to stand to the courtesy of a night-walking cudgeller for eaves-dropping. . . . . Who could be angry, therefore, but those that are guilty, with these free-spoken and plain-hearted men, that are the eyes of their country, and the prospective glasses of their prince? . . . .

But he that shall bind himself to make antiquity his rule, if he read but part, besides the difficulty of choice, his rule is deficient, and utterly unsatisfying; for there may be other writers of another mind which he hath not seen; and if he undertake all, the length of man's life cannot extend to give him a full and requisite knowledge of what was done in antiquity. Why do we therefore stand worshipping and admiring this unactive and lifeless Colossus, that, like a carved giant terribly menacing to children and weaklings, lifts up his club, but strikes not, and is subject to the muting of every sparrow? If you let him rest upon his basis, he may perhaps delight the eyes of some with his huge and mountainous bulk, and the quaint workmanship of his massy limbs; but if ye go about to take him in pieces, ye mar him; and if you think, like pigmies, to turn and wind him whole as he is, besides your vain toil and sweat, he may chance to fall upon your own heads. . . . .

We shall adhere close to the Scriptures of God, which he hath left us as the just and adequate measure of truth, fitted and proportioned to the diligent study, memory, and use of every faithful man, whose every part consenting, and making up the harmonious symmetry of complete instruction, is able to set out to us a perfect man of God, or bishop thoroughly furnished to all the good works of his charge: and with this weapon, without stepping a foot farther, we shall not doubt to batter and throw down your Nebuchadnezzar's image, and crumble it like the chaff of the summer threshing-floors, as well the gold of those apostolic successors that you boast of, as your Constantinian silver, together with the iron, the brass, and the clay of those muddy and strawy ages that follow. . . . .

"They cannot name any man in this nation, that ever contradicted episcopacy, till this present age." What an overworn and bedridden argument is this! the last refuge ever of old falsehood, and therefore a good sign, I trust, that your castle cannot hold out long. This was the plea of Judaism and idolatry against Christ and his Apostles, of Papacy against Reformation; and perhaps to the frailty of flesh and blood in a man destitute of better enlightening may for some while be pardonable: for what has fleshly apprehension other to subsist by than succession, custom, and visibility; which only hold, if in his weakness and blindness he be loath to lose, who can blame? But in a Protestant nation, that should have thrown off these tattered rudiments long ago, after the many strivings of God's Spirit, and our fourscore years' vexation of him in this our wilderness since Reformation began to urge these rotten principles, and twit us with the present age, which is to us an age of ages wherein God is manifestly come down among us to do some remarkable good to our church or state, is as if a man should tax the renovating and reingendering Spirit of God with innovation, and that new creature for an upstart novelty; yea, the New Jerusalem, which, without your admired link of succession, descends from heaven, could not escape some such like censure. If you require a further answer, it will not misbecome a Christian to be either more magnanimous or more devout than Scipio was, who, instead of other answer to the frivolous accusations of Petilius the Tribune, "This day, Romans," saith he, "I fought with Hannibal prosperously; let us all go and thank the gods that gave us so great a victory"; in like manner will we now say, not caring otherwise to answer this unprotestantlike objection: In this age, Britons, God hath reformed his Church after many hundred years of Popish corruption; in this age he hath freed us from the intolerable yoke of prelates and papal discipline; in this age he hath renewed our protestation against all those yet remaining dregs of superstition. Let us all go, every true protested Briton, throughout the three kingdoms, and render thanks to God the Father of light, and Fountain of heavenly grace, and to His Son Christ our Lord, leaving this remonstrant and his adherents to their own designs; and let us recount, even here without delay, the patience and long-suffering that God hath used towards our blindness and hardness time after time. For he being equally near to his whole creation of mankind, and of free power to turn his beneficent and fatherly regard to what region or kingdom he pleases, hath yet ever had this island under the special indulgent eye of his providence, and pity ing us the first of all other nations, after he had decreed to purify and renew his Church that lay wallowing in idolatrous pollutions, sent first to us a healing messenger to touch softly our sores, and carry a gentle hand over our wounds: he knocked once and twice, and came again opening our drowsy eyelids leisurely by that glimmering light which Wickliff and his followers dispersed; and still taking off by degrees the inveterate scales from our nigh perished sight, purged also our deaf ears, and prepared them to attend his second warning trumpet in our grandsire's days. How else could they have been able to have received the sudden assault of his reforming Spirit, warring against human principles, and carnal sense, the pride of flesh, that still cried up antiquity, custom, canons, councils, and laws; and cried down the truth for novelty, schism, profaneness, and sacrilege? whenas we that have lived so long in abundant light, besides the sunny reflection of all the neighboring churches, have yet our hearts riveted with those old opinions, and so obstructed and benumbed with the same fleshy reasonings, which in our forefathers soon melted and gave way, against the morning beam of Reformation. If God had left undone this whole work, so contrary to flesh and blood, till these times, how should we have yielded to his heavenly call, had we been taken, as they were, in the starkness of our ignorance; that yet, after all these spiritual preparatives and purgations, have our earthly apprehensions so clammed and furred with the old leaven? O if we freeze at noon after their early thaw, let us fear lest the sun forever hide himself, and turn his orient steps from our ingrateful horizon, justly condemned to be eternally benighted. Which dreadful judgment, O Thou the ever-begotten Light and perfect Image of the Father! intercede, may never come upon us, as we trust thou hast; for thou hast opened our difficult and sad times, and given us an unexpected breathing after our long oppressions: thou hast done justice upon those that tyrannized over us, while some men wavered and admired a vain shadow of wisdom in a tongue nothing slow to utter guile, though thou hast taught us to admire only that which is good, and to count that only praiseworthy, which is grounded upon thy divine precepts. Thou hast discovered the plots, and frustrated the hopes, of all the wicked in the land, and put to shame the persecutors of thy Church: thou hast made our false prophets to be found a lie in the sight of all the people, and chased them with sudden confusion and amazement before the redoubled brightness of thy descending cloud, that now covers thy tabernacle. Who is there that cannot trace thee now in thy beamy walk through the midst of thy sanctuary, amidst those golden candlesticks, which have long suffered a dimness amongst us through the violence of those that had seized them, and were more taken with the mention of their gold than of their starry light; teaching the doctrine of Balaam, to cast a stumbling-block before thy servants, commanding them to eat things sacrificed to idols, and forcing them to fornication? Come therefore, O Thou that hast the seven stars in thy right hand, appoint thy chosen priests according to their orders and courses of old, to minister before thee, and duly to press and pour out the consecrated oil into thy holy and ever-burning lamps. Thou hast sent out the spirit of prayer upon thy servants over all the land to this effect, and stirred up their vows as the sound of many waters about thy throne. Every one can say, that now certainly thou hast visited this land, and hast not forgotten the utmost corners of the earth, in a time when men had thought that thou wast gone up from us to the furthest end of the heavens, and hadst left to do marvellously among the sons of these last ages. O perfect and accomplish thy glorious acts! for men may leave their works unfinished, but thou art a God, thy nature is perfection: shouldst thou bring us thus far onward from Egypt to destroy us in this wilderness, though we deserve, yet thy great name would suffer in the rejoicing of thine enemies and the deluded hope of all thy servants. When thou hast settled peace in the Church, and righteous judgment in the kingdom, then shall all thy saints address their voices of joy and triumph to thee, standing on the shore of that Red Sea into which our enemies had almost driven us. And he that now for haste snatches up a plain ungarnished present as a thank-offering to thee, which could not be deferred in regard of thy so many late deliverances wrought for us one upon another, may then perhaps take up a harp and sing thee an elaborate song to generations. In that day it shall no more be said, as in scorn, this or that was never held so till this present age, when men have better learnt that the times and seasons pass along under thy feet, to go and come at thy bidding: and as thou didst dignify our fathers' days with many revelations above all the foregoing ages, since thou tookest the flesh, so thou canst vouchsafe to us (though unworthy) as large a portion of thy Spirit as thou pleasest: for who shall prejudice thy all-governing will? seeing the power of thy grace is not passed away with the primitive times, as fond and faithless men imagine, but thy kingdom is now at hand, and thou standing at the door. Come forth out of thy royal chambers, O Prince of all the kings of the earth! put on the visible robes of thy imperial majesty, take up that unlimited sceptre which thy Almighty Father hath bequeathed thee; for now the voice of thy bride calls thee, and all creatures sigh to be renewed. . . . .

As for ordination, what is it, but the laying on of hands, an outward sign or symbol of admission?

It creates nothing, it confers nothing; it is the inward calling of God that makes a minister, and his own painful study and diligence that manures and improves his ministerial gifts. . . . .

We cannot therefore do better than to leave this care of ours to God: he can easily send laborers into his harvest, that shall not cry, Give, give, but be contented with a moderate and beseeming allowance; nor will he suffer true learning to be wanting, where true grace and our obedience to him abounds: for if he give us to know him aright, and to practise this our knowledge in right-established discipline, how much more will he replenish us with all abilities in tongues and arts, that may conduce to his glory and our good! He can stir up rich fathers to bestow exquisite education upon their children, and so dedicate them to the service of the Gospel; he can make the sons of nobles his ministers, and princes to be his Nazarites; for certainly there is no employment more honorable, more worthy to take up a great spirit, more requiring a generous and free nurture, than to be the messenger and herald of heavenly truth from God to man, and, by the faithful work of holy doctrine, to procreate a number of faithful men, making a kind of creation like to God's, by infusing his spirit and likeness into them, to their salvation, as God did into him; arising to what climate soever he turn him, like that Sun of Righteousness that sent him, with healing in his wings, and new light to break in upon the chill and gloomy hearts of his hearers, raising out of darksome barrenness a delicious and fragrant spring of saving knowledge, and good works.

FROM

AN APOLOGY FOR SMECTYMNUUS.

FOR doubtless that indeed according to art is most eloquent, which turns and approaches nearest to nature, from whence it came; and they express nature best, who in their lives least wander from her safe leading, which may be called regenerate reason. So that how he should be truly eloquent who is not withal a good man, I see not. . . . .

For as in teaching, doubtless, the spirit of meekness is most powerful, so are the meek only fit persons to be taught: as for the proud, the obstinate, and false doctors of men's devices, be taught they will not, but discovered and laid open they must be.

For how can they admit of teaching, who have the condemnation of God already upon them for refusing divine instruction? That is, to be filled with their own devices, as in the Proverbs we may read: therefore we may safely imitate the method that God uses, "with the froward to be froward, and to throw scorn upon the scorner," whom if anything, nothing else will heal. . . . .

Those morning haunts are where they should be, at home; not sleeping, or concocting the surfeits of an irregular feast, but up and stirring, in winter often ere the sound of any bell awake men to labor, or to devotion; in summer as oft with the bird that first rouses, or not much tardier, to read good authors, or cause them to be read, till the attention be weary, or memory have its full fraught: then, with useful and generous labors preserving the body's health and hardiness to render lightsome, clear, and not lumpish obedience to the mind, to the cause of religion, and our country's liberty, when it shall require firm hearts in sound bodies to stand and cover their stations, rather than to see the ruin of our protestation, and the enforcement of a slavish life. . . . .

But because as well by this upbraiding to me the bordelloes, as by other suspicious glancings in his book, he would seem privily to point me out to his readers, as one whose custom of life were not honest, but licentious, I shall entreat to be borne with though I digress; and in a way not often trod, acquaint ye with the sum of my thoughts in this matter, through the course of my years and studies: although I am not ignorant how hazardous it will be to do this under the nose of the envious, as it were in skirmish to change the compact order, and instead of outward actions, to bring inmost thoughts into front. . . . .

I had my time, readers, as others have, who have good learning bestowed upon them, to be sent to those places where the opinion was, it might be soonest attained; and as the manner is, was not unstudied in those authors which are most commended. Whereof some were grave orators and historians, whose matter methought I loved indeed, but as my age then was, so I understood them; others were the smooth elegiac poets, whereof the schools are not scarce, whom both for the pleasing sound of their numerous writing, which in imitation I found most easy, and most agreeable to nature's part in me, and for their matter, which what it is, there be few who know not, I was so allured to read, that no recreation came to me better welcome. For that it was then those years with me which are excused, though they be least severe, I may be saved the labor to remember ye. Whence having observed them to account it the chief glory of their wit, in that they were ablest to judge, to praise, and by that could esteem themselves worthiest to love those high perfections, which under one or other name they took to celebrate; I thought with myself by every instinct and presage of nature, which is not wont to be false, that what emboldened them to this task, might with such diligence as they used embolden me; and that what judgment, wit, or elegance was my share, would herein best appear, and best value itself, by how much more wisely, and with more love of virtue I should choose (let rude ears be absent) the object of not unlike praises. . . . By the firm settling of these persuasions, I became, to my best memory, so much a proficient, that if I found those authors anywhere speaking unworthy things of themselves, or unchaste of those names which before they had extolled; this effect it wrought with me, from that time forward their art I still applauded, but the men I deplored; and above them all, preferred the two famous renowners of Beatrice and Laura, who never write but honor of them to whom they devote their verse, displaying sublime and pure thoughts, without transgression. And long it was not after, when I was confirmed in this opinion, that he who would not be frustrate of his hope to write well hereafter in laudable things, ought himself to be a true poem; that is, a composition and pattern of the best and honorablest things; not presuming to sing high praises of heroic men, or famous cities, unless he have in himself the experience and the practice of all that which is praiseworthy. These reasonings, together with a certain niceness of nature, an honest haughtiness and self-esteem, either of what I was or what I might be (which let envy call pride), and lastly that modesty, whereof, though not in the title-page, yet here I may be excused to make some beseeming profession; all these uniting the supply of their natural aid together, kept me still above those low descents of mind, beneath which he must deject and plunge himself, that can agree to salable and unlawful prostitutions.

Next (for hear me out now, readers), that I may tell ye whither my younger feet wandered; I betook me among those lofty fables and romances which recount in solemn cantos the deeds of knighthood founded by our victorious kings, and from hence had in renown over all Christendom. There I read it in the oath of every knight, that he should defend, to the expense of his best blood, or of his life, if it so befell him, the honor and chastity of virgin or matron; from whence even then I learned what a noble virtue chastity sure must be, to the defence of which so many worthies, by such a dear adventure of themselves, had sworn. And if I found in the story afterward, any of them, by word or deed, breaking that oath, I judged it the same fault of the poet, as that which is attributed to Homer, to have written indecent things of the gods. Only this my mind gave me, that every free and gentle spirit, without that oath, ought to be born a knight, nor needed to expect a gilt spur, or the laying of a sword upon his shoulder to stir him up both by his counsel and his arms, to secure and protect the weakness of any attempted chastity. So that even these books, which to many others have been the fuel of wantonness and loose living, I cannot think how, unless by divine indulgence, proved to me so many incitements, as you have heard, to the love and steadfast observation of that virtue which abhors the society of bordelloes.

Thus, from the laureat fraternity of poets, riper years and the ceaseless round of study and reading led me to the shady spaces of philosophy; but chiefly to the divine volumes of Plato, and his equal Xenophon: where, if I should tell ye what I learnt of chastity and love, — I mean that which is truly so, — whose charming cup is only virtue, which she bears in her hand to those who are worthy (the rest are cheated with a thick intoxicating potion, which a certain sorceress, the abuser of love's name, carries about); and how the first and chiefest office of love begins and ends in the soul, producing those happy twins of her divine generation, knowledge and virtue. With such abstracted sublimities as these, it might be worth your listening, readers, as I may one day hope to have ye in a still time, when there shall be no chiding. . . . .

Last of all, not in time, but as perfection is last, that care was ever had of me, with my earliest capacity, not to be negligently trained in the precepts of the Christian religion: this that I have hitherto related, hath been to show, that though Christianity had been but slightly taught me, yet a certain reservedness of natural disposition, and moral discipline, learnt out of the noblest philosophy, was enough to keep me in disdain of far less incontinences than this of the bordello. But having had the doctrine of Holy Scripture unfolding those chaste and high mysteries, with timeliest care infused, that "the body is for the Lord, and the Lord for the body"; thus also I argued to myself, that if unchastity in a woman, whom St. Paul terms the glory of man, be such a scandal and dishonor, then certainly in a man, who is both the image and glory of God, it must, though commonly not so thought, be much more deflouring and dishonorable; in that he sins both against his own body, which is the perfecter sex, and his own glory, which is in the woman; and, that which is worst, against the image and glory of God, which is in himself. Nor did I slumber over that place expressing such high rewards of ever accompanying the Lamb, with those celestial songs to others inapprehensible, but not to those who were not defiled with women, which doubtless means fornication; for marriage must not be called a defilement.

Thus large I have purposely been, that if I have been justly taxed with this crime, it may come upon me, after all this my confession, with a tenfold shame: but if I have hitherto deserved no such opprobrious word, or suspicion, I may hereby engage myself now openly to the faithful observation of what I have professed. . . . .

If therefore the question were in oratory, whether a vehement vein throwing out indignation or scorn upon an object that merits it, were among the aptest *ideas* of speech to be allowed, it were my work, and that an easy one, to make it clear both by the rules of best rhetoricians, and the famousest examples of the Greek and Roman orations. But since the religion of it is disputed, and not the art, I shall make use only of such reasons and authorities as religion cannot except against. It will be harder to gainsay, than for me to evince, that in the teaching of men diversely tempered, different ways are to be tried. The Baptist, we know, was a strict man, remarkable for austerity and set order of life. Our Saviour, who had all gifts in him, was Lord to express his indoctrinating power in what sort him best seemed; sometimes by a mild and familiar converse; sometimes with plain and impartial home-speaking, regardless of those whom the auditors might think he should have had in more respect; otherwhile, with bitter and ireful rebukes, if not teaching, yet leaving excuseless those his wilful impugners.

What was all in him, was divided among many others, the teachers of his church; some to be severe and ever of a sad gravity, that they may win such, and check sometimes those who be of nature over-confident and jocund; others were sent more cheerful, free, and still as it were at large, in the midst of an untrespassing honesty; that they who are so tempered, may have by whom they might be drawn to salvation, and they who are too scrupulous, and dejected of spirit, might be often strengthened with wise consolations and revivings: no man being forced wholly to dissolve that groundwork of nature which God created in him, the sanguine to empty out all his sociable liveliness, the choleric to expel quite the unsinning predominance of his anger; but that each radical humor and passion, wrought upon and corrected as it ought, might be made the proper mould and foundation of every man's peculiar gifts and virtues. Some also were indued with a staid moderation and soundness of argument, to teach and convince the rational and sober-minded; yet not therefore that to be thought the only expedient course of teaching, for in times of opposition, when either against new heresies arising, or old corruptions to be reformed, this cool unpassionate mildness of positive wisdom is not enough to damp and astonish the proud resistance of carnal and false doctors, then (that I may have leave to soar awhile as the poets use) Zeal, whose substance is ethereal, arming in complete diamond, ascends his fiery chariot, drawn with two blazing meteors, figured like beasts, but of a higher breed than any the zodiac yields, resembling two of those four which Ezekiel and St. John saw; the one visaged like a lion, to express power, high authority, and indignation; the other of countenance like a man, to cast derision and scorn upon perverse and fraudulent seducers: with these the invincible warrior, Zeal, shaking loosely the slack reins, drives over the heads of scarlet prelates, and such as are insolent to maintain traditions, bruising their stiff necks under his flaming wheels.

Thus did the true prophets of old combat with the false: thus Christ himself, the fountain of meekness, found acrimony enough to be still galling and vexing the prelatical pharisees. But ye will say, these had immediate warrant from God to be thus bitter; and I say, so much the plainer is it proved that there may be a sanctified bitterness against the enemies of truth. Yet that ye may not think inspiration only the warrant thereof, but that it is as any other virtue of moral and general observation, the example of Luther may stand for all, whom God made choice of before others to be of highest eminence and power in reforming the Church; who, not of revelation, but of judgment, writ so vehemently against the chief defenders of old untruths in the Romish church, that his own friends and favorers were many times offended with the fierceness of his spirit; yet he being cited before Charles the Fifth to answer for his books, and having divided them into three sorts, whereof one was of those which he had sharply written, refused, though upon deliberation given him, to retract or unsay any word therein. . . . . Yea, he defends his eagerness, as being "of an ardent spirit, and one who could not write a dull style": and affirmed "he thought it God's will to have the invention of men thus laid open, seeing that matters quietly handled were quickly forgot.". . . . .

Now that the confutant may also know as he desires, what force of teaching there is sometimes in laughter, I shall return him in short, that laughter, being one way of answering "a fool according to his folly," teaches two sorts of persons: first, the fool himself, "not to be wise in his own conceit," as Solomon affirms; which is certainly a great document to make an unwise man know himself. Next, it teacheth the hearers, inasmuch as scorn is one of those punishments which belong to men carnally wise, which is oft in Scripture declared; for when such are punished, "the simple are thereby made wise," if Solomon's rule be true. And I would ask, to what end Eliah mocked the false prophets? was it to show his wit, or to fulfil his humor? Doubtless we cannot imagine that great servant of God had any other end, in all which he there did, but to teach and instruct the poor misled people. And we may frequently read, that many of the martyrs in the midst of their troubles were not sparing to deride and scoff their superstitious persecutors. Now may the confutant advise again with Sir Francis Bacon, whether Eliah and the martyrs did well to turn religion into a comedy or satire; "to rip up the wounds of idolatry and superstition with a laughing countenance": so that for pious gravity the author here is matched and overmatched, and for wit and morality in one that follows:

> "Laughing to teach the truth
> What hinders? as some teachers give to boys
> Junkets and knacks, that they may learn apace."

Thus Flaccus in his first satire, and his tenth:

> "Jesting decides great things
> Stronglier and better oft than earnest can."

I could urge the same out of Cicero and Seneca, but he may content him with this. And henceforward, if he can learn, may know as well what are the bounds and objects of laughter and vehement reproof, as he hath known hitherto how to deserve them both. . . . .

Now although it be a digression from the ensuing matter, yet because it shall not be said I am apter to blame others than to make trial myself, and that I may, after this harsh discord, touch upon a smoother string, awhile to entertain myself and him that list with some more pleasing fit, and not the least to testify the gratitude which I owe to those public benefactors of their country, for the share I enjoy in the common peace and good by their incessant labors; I shall be so troublesome to this disclaimer for once, as to show him what he might have better said in their praise; wherein I must mention only some few things of many, for more than that to a digression may not be granted. Although certainly their actions are worthy not thus to be spoken of by the way, yet if hereafter it befall me to attempt something more answerable to their great merits, I perceive how hopeless it will be to reach the height of their praises at the accomplishment of that expectation that waits upon their noble deeds, the unfinishing whereof already surpasses what others before them have left enacted with their utmost performance through many ages. And to the end we may be confident that what they do proceeds neither from uncertain opinion nor sudden counsels, but from mature wisdom, deliberate virtue, and dear affection to the public good, I shall begin at that which made them likeliest in the eyes of good men to effect those things for the recovery of decayed religion and the commonwealth, which they who were best minded had long wished for, but few, as the times then were desperate, had the courage to hope for.

First, therefore, the most of them being either of ancient and high nobility, or at least of known and well-reputed ancestry, which is a great advantage towards virtue one way, but in respect of wealth, ease, and flattery, which accompany a nice and tender education, is as much a hinderance another way: the good which lay before them they took, in imitating the worthiest of their progenitors: and the evil which assaulted their younger years by the temptation of riches, high birth, and that usual bringing up, perhaps too favorable and too remiss, through the strength of an inbred goodness, and with the help of divine grace, that had marked them out for no mean purposes, they nobly overcame. Yet had they a greater danger to cope with; for being trained up in the knowledge of learning, and sent to those places which were intended to be the seed-plots of piety and the liberal arts, but were become the nurseries of superstition and empty speculation, as they were prosperous against those vices which grow upon youth out of idleness and superfluity, so were they happy in working off the harms of their abused studies and labors; correcting by the clearness of their own judgment the errors of their misinstruction, and were, as David was, wiser than their teachers. And although their lot fell into such times, and to be bred in such places, where, if they chanced to be taught anything good, or of their own accord had learnt it, they might see that presently untaught them by the custom and ill-example of their elders; so far in all probability was their youth from being misled by the single power of example, as their riper years were known to be unmoved with the baits of preferment, and undaunted for any discouragement and terror which appeared often to those that loved religion and their native liberty; which two things God hath inseparably knit together, and hath disclosed to us, that they who seek to corrupt our religion are the same that would enthrall our civil liberty.

Thus in the midst of all disadvantages and disrespects, (some also at last not without imprisonment and open disgraces in the cause of their country,) having given proof of themselves to be better made and framed by nature to the love and practice of virtue, than others under the holiest precepts and best examples have been headstrong and prone to vice; and having, in all the trials of a firm ingrafted honesty, not oftener buckled in the conflict than given every opposition the foil; this moreover was added by favor from Heaven, as an ornament and happiness to their virtue, that it should be neither obscure in the opinion of men, nor eclipsed for want of matter equal to illustrate itself; God and man consenting in joint approbation to choose them out as worthiest above others to be both the great reformers of the Church, and the restorers of the commonwealth. Nor did they deceive that expectation which with the eyes and desires of their country was fixed upon them: for no sooner did the force of so much united excellence meet in one globe of brightness and efficacy, but encountering the dazzled resistance of tyranny, they gave not over, though their enemies were strong and subtle, till they had laid her grovelling upon the fatal block; with one stroke winning again our lost liberties and charters, which our forefathers, after so many battles, could scarce maintain.

And meeting next, as I may so resemble, with the second life of tyranny, (for she was grown an ambiguous monster, and to be slain in two shapes,) guarded with superstition, which hath no small power to captivate the minds of men otherwise most wise, they neither were taken with her mitred hypocrisy, nor terrified with the push of her bestial horns, but breaking them, immediately forced her to unbend the pontifical brow, and recoil; which repulse only given to the prelates (that we may imagine how happy their removal would be) was the producement of such glorious effects and consequences in the church, that if I should compare them with those exploits of highest fame in poems and panegyrics of old, I am certain it would but diminish and impair their worth, who are now my argument; for those ancient worthies delivered men from such tyrants as were content to enforce only an outward obedience, letting the mind be as free as it could; but these have freed us from a doctrine of tyranny, that offered violence and corruption even to the inward persuasion. They set at liberty nations and cities of men good and bad mixed together; but these, opening the prisons and dungeons, called out of darkness and bonds the elect martyrs and witnesses of their Redeemer. They restored the body to ease and wealth; but these, the oppressed conscience to that freedom which is the chief prerogative of the Gospel; taking off those cruel burdens, imposed not by necessity, as other tyrants are wont, for the safeguard of their lives, but laid upon our necks by the strange wilfulness and wantonness of a needless and jolly persecutor, called Indifference. Lastly, some of those ancient deliverers have had immortal praises for preserving their citizens from a famine of corn. But these, by this only repulse of an unholy hierarchy, almost in a moment, replenished with saving knowledge their country, nigh famished for want of that which should feed their souls. All this being done while two armies in the field stood gazing on: the one in reverence of such nobleness quietly gave back and dislodged; the other, spite of the unruliness and doubted fidelity in some regiments, was either persuaded or compelled to disband and retire home.

With such a majesty had their wisdom begirt itself, that whereas others had levied war to subdue a nation that sought for peace, they, sitting here in peace, could so many miles extend the force of their single words as to overawe the dissolute stoutness of an armed power, secretly stirred up and almost hired against them. And having by a solemn protestation vowed themselves and the kingdom anew to God and his service, and by a prudent foresight above what their fathers thought on, prevented the dissolution and frustrating of their designs by an untimely breaking up; notwithstanding all the treasonous plots against them, all the rumors either of rebellion or invasion, they have not been yet brought to change their constant resolution, ever to think fearlessly of their own safeties, and hopefully of the commonwealth: which hath gained them such an admiration from all good men that now they hear it as their ordinary surname, to be saluted the fathers of their country, and sit as gods among daily petitions and public thanks flowing in upon them. Which doth so little yet exalt them in their own thoughts, that, with all gentle affability and courteous acceptance, they both receive and return that tribute of thanks which is tendered them; testifying their zeal and desire to spend themselves as it were piecemeal upon the grievances and wrongs of their distressed nation; insomuch that the meanest artisans and laborers, at other times also women, and often the younger sort of servants assembling with their complaints, and that sometimes in a less humble guise than for petitioners, have gone with confidence, that neither their meanness would be rejected, nor their simplicity contemned; nor yet their urgency distasted either by the dignity, wisdom, or moderation of that supreme senate; nor did they depart unsatisfied.

And, indeed, if we consider the general concourse of suppliants, the free and ready admittance, the willing and speedy redress in what is possible, it will not seem much otherwise, than as if some divine commission from heaven were descended to take into hearing and commiseration the long and remediless afflictions of this kingdom, were it not that none more than themselves labor to remove and divert such thoughts, lest men should place too much confidence in their persons, still referring us and our prayers to Him that can grant all, and appointing the monthly return of public fasts and supplications. Therefore the more they seek to humble themselves, the more does God, by manifest signs and testimonies, visibly honor their proceedings; and sets them as the mediators of this his covenant, which he offers us to renew. Wicked men daily conspire their hurt, and it comes to nothing; rebellion rages in our Irish province, but with miraculous and lossless victories of few against many, is daily discomfited and broken; if we neglect not this early pledge of God's inclining towards us, by the slackness of our needful aids. And whereas at other times we count it ample honor when God vouchsafes to make man the instrument and subordinate worker of His gracious will, such acceptation have their prayers found with him, that to them he hath been pleased to make himself the agent and immediate performer of their desires; dissolving their difficulties when they are thought inexplicable, cutting out ways for them where no passage could be seen; as who is there so regardless of divine Providence, that from late occurrences will not confess? If, therefore, it be so high a grace when men are preferred to be but the inferior officers of good things from God, what is it when God himself condescends, and works with his own hands to fulfil the requests of men? Which I leave with them as the greatest praise that can belong to human nature: not that we should think they are at the end of their glorious progress, but that they will go on to follow his Almighty leading, who seems to have thus covenanted with them; that if the will and the endeavor shall be theirs, the performance and the perfecting shall be his. Whence only it is that I have not feared, though many wise men have miscarried in praising great designs before the utmost event, because I see who is their assistant, who is their confederate, who hath engaged his omnipotent arm to support and crown with success their faith, their fortitude, their just and magnanimous actions, till he have brought to pass all that expected good which, his servants trust, is in his thoughts to bring upon this land in the full and perfect reformation of his Church. . . . .

I shall not decline to speak my opinion in the controversy next moved, "whether the people may be allowed for competent judges of a minister's ability." For how else can be fulfilled that which God hath promised, to pour out such abundance of knowledge upon all sorts of men in the times of the Gospel? How should the people examine the doctrine which is taught them, as Christ and his apostles continually bid them do? How should they "discern and beware of false prophets, and try every spirit," if they must be thought unfit to judge of the minister's abilities? The apostles ever labored to persuade the Christian flock that they "were called in Christ to all perfectness in spiritual knowledge, and full assurance of understanding in the mystery of God."

. . . . .

We need not the authority of Pliny brought to tell us, the people cannot judge of a minister: yet that hurts not. For as none can judge of a painter or statuary but he who is an artist, that is, either in the practice or theory, which is often separated from the practice, and judges learnedly without it; so none can judge of a Christian teacher but he who hath either the practice or the knowledge of Christian religion, though not so artfully digested in him. And who almost of the meanest Christians hath not heard the Scriptures often read from his childhood, besides so many sermons and lectures, more in number than any student hath heard in philosophy, whereby he may easily attain to know when he is wisely taught, and when weakly? whereof, three ways I remember are set down in Scripture; the one is to read often that best of books written to this purpose, that not the wise only, but the simple and ignorant, may learn by them; the other way to know of a minister is, by the life he leads, whereof the meanest understanding may be apprehensive. The last way to judge aright in this point is, when he who judges, lives a Christian life himself. Which of these three will the confuter affirm to exceed the capacity of a plain artisan? And what reason then is there left, wherefore he should be denied his voice in the election of his minister, as not thought a competent discerner? . . . .

For me, readers, although I cannot say that I am utterly untrained in those rules which best rhetoricians have given, or unacquainted with those examples which the prime authors of eloquence have written in any learned tongue; yet true eloquence I find to be none, but the serious and hearty love of truth: and that whose mind soever is fully possessed with a fervent desire to know good things, and with the dearest charity to infuse the knowledge of them into others, when such a man would speak, his words, (by what I can express,) like so many nimble and airy servitors, trip about him at command, and in well-ordered files, as he would wish, fall aptly into their own places. . . . .

Therefore must the ministers of Christ not be over rich or great in the world, because their calling is spiritual, not secular; because they have a special warfare, which is not to be entangled with many impediments; because their master, Christ, gave them this precept, and set them this example, told them this was the mystery of his coming, by mean things and persons to subdue mighty ones; and lastly, because a middle estate is most proper to the office of teaching, whereas higher dignity teaches far less, and blinds the teacher.

FROM THE

TRACTATE ON EDUCATION.

AM long since persuaded, Master Hartlib, that to say or do aught worth memory and imitation, no purpose or respect should sooner move us than simply the love of God, and of mankind. . . . .

The end then of learning is to repair the ruins of our first parents by regaining to know God aright, and out of that knowledge to love him, to imitate him, to be like him, as we may the nearest by possessing our souls of true virtue, which being united to the heavenly grace of faith, makes up the highest perfection. But because our understanding cannot in this body found itself but on sensible things, nor arrive so clearly to the knowledge of God and things invisible, as by orderly conning over the visible and inferior creature, the same method is necessarily to be followed in all discreet teaching. And seeing every nation affords not experience and tradition enough for all kinds of learning, therefore we are chiefly taught the languages of those people who have at any time been most industrious after wisdom; so that language is but the instrument conveying to us things useful to be known. And though a linguist should pride himself to have all the tongues that Babel cleft the world into, yet if he have not studied the solid things in them, as well as the words and lexicons, he were nothing so much to be esteemed a learned man, as any yeoman or tradesman competently wise in his mother dialect only.

Hence appear the many mistakes which have made learning generally so unpleasing and so unsuccessful; first, we do amiss to spend seven or eight years merely in scraping together so much miserable Latin and Greek, as might be learned otherwise easily and delightfully in one year. And that which casts our proficiency therein so much behind, is our time lost partly in too oft idle vacancies given both to schools and universities; partly in a preposterous exaction, forcing the empty wits of children to compose themes, verses, and orations, which are the acts of ripest judgment, and the final work of a head filled by long reading and observing, with elegant maxims and copious invention. These are not matters to be wrung from poor striplings, like blood out of the nose, or the plucking of untimely fruit. Besides the ill habit which they get of wretched barbarizing against the Latin and Greek idiom, with their untutored Anglicisms, odious to be read, yet not to be avoided without a well-continued and judicious conversing among pure authors digested, which they scarce taste. Whereas, if after some preparatory grounds of speech by their certain forms got into memory, they were led to the praxis thereof in some chosen short book, lessoned thoroughly to them, they might then forthwith proceed to learn the substance of good things, and arts in due order, which would bring the whole language quickly into their power. This I take to be the most rational and most profitable way of learning languages, and whereby we may best hope to give account to God of our youth spent herein.

And for the usual method of teaching arts, I deem it to be an old error of universities, not yet well recovered from the scholastic grossness of barbarous ages, that instead of beginning with arts most easy, (and those be such as are most obvious to the sense,) they present their young unmatriculated novices, at first coming, with the most intellective abstractions of logic and metaphysics; so that they having but newly left those grammatic flats and shallows, where they stuck unreasonably to learn a few words with lamentable construction, and now on the sudden transported under another climate, to be tossed and turmoiled with their unballasted wits in fathomless and unquiet deeps of controversy, do for the most part grow into hatred and contempt of learning, mocked and deluded all this while with ragged notions and babblements, while they expected worthy and delightful knowledge; till poverty or youthful years call them importunately their several ways, and hasten them, with the sway of friends, either to an ambitious and mercenary, or ignorantly zealous divinity: some allured to the trade of law, grounding their purposes not on the prudent and heavenly contemplation of justice and equity, which was never taught them, but on the promising and pleasing thoughts of litigious terms, fat contentions, and flowing fees; others betake them to state affairs, with souls so unprincipled in virtue and true generous breeding, that flattery and court-shifts and tyrannous aphorisms appear to them the highest points of wisdom; instilling their barren hearts with a conscientious slavery; if, as I rather think, it be not feigned. Others, lastly, of a more delicious and airy spirit, retire themselves (knowing no better) to the enjoyments of ease and luxury, living out their days in feast and jollity; which indeed is the wisest and safest course of all these, unless they were with more integrity undertaken. And these are the errors, and these are the fruits of misspending our prime youth at the schools and universities as we do, either in learning mere words, or such things chiefly as were better unlearned.

I shall detain you now no longer in the demonstration of what we should not do, but straight conduct you to a hillside, where I will point you out the right path of a virtuous and noble education; laborious indeed at the first ascent, but else so smooth, so green, so full of goodly prospect, and melodious sounds on every side, that the harp of Orpheus was not more charming. I doubt not but ye shall have more ado to drive our dullest and laziest youth, our stocks and stubs, from the infinite desire of such a happy nurture, than we have now to hale and drag our choicest and hopefullest wits to that asinine feast of sowthistles and brambles, which is commonly set before them as all the food and entertainment of their tenderest and most docible age.

I call therefore a complete and generous education, that which fits a man to perform justly, skilfully, and magnanimously all the offices, both private and public, of peace and war. . . . .

But here the main skill and groundwork will be, to temper them such lectures and explanations, upon every opportunity, as may lead and draw them in willing obedience, inflamed with the study of learning and the admiration of virtue; stirred up with high hopes of living to be brave men, and worthy patriots, dear to God, and famous to all ages. That they may despise and scorn all their childish and ill-taught qualities, to delight in manly and liberal exercises, which he who hath the art and proper eloquence to catch them with, what with mild and effectual persuasions, and what with the intimation of some fear, if need be, but chiefly by his own example, might in a short space gain them to an incredible diligence and courage, infusing into their young breasts such an ingenuous and noble ardor, as would not fail to make many of them renowned and matchless men. . . . .

By this time, years and good general precepts will have furnished them more distinctly with that act of reason which in ethics is called Proairesis; that they may with some judgment contemplate upon moral good and evil. Then will be required a special reinforcement of constant and sound indoctrinating, to set them right and firm, instructing them more amply in the knowledge of virtue and the hatred of vice; while their young and pliant affections are led through all the moral works of Plato, Xenophon, Cicero, Plutarch, Laertius, and those Locrian remnants; but still to be reduced in their nightward studies wherewith they close the day's work, under the determinate sentence of David or Solomon, or the Evangelists and apostolic Scriptures. . . . .

The interim of unsweating themselves regularly, and convenient rest before meat, may, both with profit and delight, be taken up in recreating and composing their travailed spirits with the solemn and divine harmonies of music, heard or learned; either whilst the skilful organist plies his grave and fancied descant in lofty fugues, or the whole symphony with artful and unimaginable touches adorn and grace the well-studied chords of some choice composer; sometimes the lute or soft organ-stop waiting on elegant voices, either to religious, martial, or civil ditties; which, if wise men and prophets be not extremely out, have a great power over dispositions and manners, to smooth and make them gentle from rustic harshness and distempered passions. . . . .

Thus, Mr. Hartlib, you have a general view in writing, as your desire was, of that which at several times I have discoursed with you concerning the best and noblest way of education. . . . . Only I believe that this is not a bow for every man to shoot in, that counts himself a teacher; but will require sinews almost equal to those which Homer gave Ulysses; yet I am withal persuaded that it may prove much more easy in the assay, than it now seems at distance, and much more illustrious; howbeit, not more difficult than I imagine, and that imagination presents me with nothing but what is very happy, and very possible, according to best wishes; if God have so decreed, and this age have spirit and capacity enough to apprehend.

FROM

AREOPAGITICA.

THIS is not the liberty which we can hope, that no grievance ever should arise in the commonwealth: that let no man in this world expect; but when complaints are freely heard, deeply considered, and speedily reformed, then is the utmost bound of civil liberty obtained that wise men look for. . . . .

I deny not, but that it is of greatest concernment in the Church and commonwealth, to have a vigilant eye how books demean themselves, as well as men; and thereafter to confine, imprison, and do sharpest justice on them as malefactors; for books are not absolutely dead things, but do contain a progeny of life in them to be as active as that soul was whose progeny they are; nay, they do preserve as in a vial the purest efficacy and extraction of that living intellect that bred them. I know they are as lively, and as vigorously productive, as those fabulous dragon's teeth; and being sown up and down, may chance to spring up armed men. And yet, on the other hand, unless wariness be used, as good almost kill a man as kill a good book: who kills a man kills a reasonable creature, God's image; but he who destroys a good book, kills reason itself, kills the image of God, as it were, in the eye. Many a man lives a burden to the earth; but a good book is the precious life-blood of a master-spirit, embalmed and treasured up on purpose to a life beyond life. It is true, no age can restore a life, whereof, perhaps, there is no great loss; and revolutions of ages do not oft recover the loss of a rejected truth, for the want of which whole nations fare the worse. We should be wary, therefore, what persecution we raise against the living labors of public men, how we spill that seasoned life of man, preserved and stored up in books; since we see a kind of homicide may be thus committed, sometimes a martyrdom; and if it extend to the whole impression, a kind of massacre, whereof the execution ends not in the slaying of an elemental life, but strikes at the ethereal and fifth essence, the breath of reason itself; slays an immortality rather than a life. . . . .

Martin the Fifth, by his bull, not only prohibited, but was the first that excommunicated the reading of heretical books; for about that time Wickliffe and Husse growing terrible, were they who first drove the papal court to a stricter policy of prohibiting. Which course Leo the Tenth and his successors followed, until the Council of Trent and the Spanish Inquisition, engendering together, brought forth or perfected these catalogues and expurging indexes, that rake through the entrails of many an old good author, with a violation worse than any could be offered to his tomb.

Nor did they stay in matters heretical, but any subject that was not to their palate, they either condemned in a prohibition, or had it straight into the new purgatory of an index. To fill up the measure of encroachment, their last invention was to ordain that no book, pamphlet, or paper should be printed (as if St. Peter had bequeathed them the keys of the press also as well as of Paradise) unless it were approved and licensed under the hands of two or three gluttonous friars. . . . .

And thus ye have the inventors and the original of book licensing ripped up and drawn as lineally as any pedigree. We have it not, that can be heard of, from any ancient state, or polity, or church, nor by any statute left us by our ancestors elder or later; nor from the modern custom of any reformed city or church abroad; but from the most anti-Christian council, and the most tyrannous inquisition that ever inquired. Till then books were ever as freely admitted into the world as any other birth; the issue of the brain was no more stifled than the issue of the womb: no envious Juno sat cross-legged over the nativity of any man's intellectual offspring: but if it proved a monster, who denies but that it was justly burnt, or sunk into the sea? But that a book, in worse condition than a peccant soul, should be to stand before a jury ere it be born to the world, and undergo yet in darkness the judgment of Radamanth and his colleagues, ere it can pass the ferry backward into light, was never heard before, till that mysterious iniquity, provoked and troubled at the first entrance of reformation, sought out new limboes and new hells wherein they might include our books also within the number of their damned. . . . .

Not to insist upon the examples of Moses, Daniel, and Paul, who were skilful in all the learning of the Egyptians, Chaldeans, and Greeks, which could not probably be without reading their books of all sorts, in Paul especially, who thought it no defilement to insert into Holy Scripture the sentences of three Greek poets, and one of them a tragedian; the question was notwithstanding sometimes controverted among the primitive doctors, but with great odds on that side which affirmed it both lawful and profitable, as was then evidently perceived, when Julian the Apostate, and subtlest enemy to our faith, made a decree forbidding Christians the study of heathen learning: for, said he, they wound us with our own weapons, and with our own arts and sciences they overcome us. And indeed the Christians were put so to their shifts by this crafty means, and so much in danger to decline into all ignorance, that the two Appollinarii were fain, as a man may say, to coin all the seven liberal sciences out of the Bible, reducing it into divers forms of orations, poems, dialogues, even to the calculating of a new Christian grammar. . . . .

"To the pure, all things are pure"; not only meats and drinks, but all kind of knowledge, whether of good or evil: the knowledge cannot defile, nor consequently the books, if the will and conscience be not defiled. For books are as meats and viands are; some of good, some of evil substance; and yet God in that unapocryphal vision said without exception, "Rise, Peter, kill and eat"; leaving the choice to each man's discretion. Wholesome meats to a vitiated stomach differ little or nothing from unwholesome; and best books to a naughty mind are not unapplicable to occasions of evil. Bad meats will scarce breed good nourishment in the healthiest concoction; but herein the difference is of bad books, that they to a discreet and judicious reader serve in many respects to discover, to confute, to forewarn, and to illustrate. . . . .

Good and evil we know in the field of this world grow up together almost inseparably; and the knowledge of good is so involved and interwoven with the knowledge of evil, and in so many cunning resemblances hardly to be discerned, that those confused seeds which were imposed upon Psyche as an incessant labor to cull out, and sort asunder, were not more intermixed. It was from out the rind of one apple tasted, that the knowledge of good and evil, as two twins cleaving together, leaped forth into the world. And perhaps this is that doom which Adam fell into of knowing good and evil; that is to say, of knowing good by evil.

As therefore the state of man now is; what wisdom can there be to choose, what continence to forbear, without the knowledge of evil? He that can apprehend and consider vice with all her baits and seeming pleasures, and yet abstain, and yet distinguish, and yet prefer that which is truly better, he is the true warfaring Christian. I cannot praise a fugitive and cloistered virtue unexercised and unbreathed, that never sallies out and seeks her adversary, but slinks out of the race, where that immortal garland is to be run for, not without dust and heat. Assuredly we bring not innocence into the world, we bring impurity much rather; that which purifies us is trial, and trial is by what is contrary. That virtue therefore which is but a youngling in the contemplation of evil, and knows not the utmost that vice promises to her followers, and rejects it, is but a blank virtue, not a pure; her whiteness is but an excremental whiteness; which was the reason why our sage and serious poet Spenser, (whom I dare be known to think a better teacher than Scotus or Aquinas,) describing true temperance under the person of Guion, brings him in with his palmer through the cave of Mammon, and the bower of earthly bliss, that he might see and know, and yet abstain.

Since therefore the knowledge and survey of vice is in this world so necessary to the constituting of human virtue, and the scanning of error to the confirmation of truth, how can we more safely, and with less danger, scout into the regions of sin and falsity, than by reading all manner of tractates, and hearing all manner of reason? . . . .

If we think to regulate printing, thereby to rectify manners, we must regulate all recreations and pastimes, all that is delightful to man. No music must be heard, no song be set or sung, but what is grave and doric. There must be licensing dancers, that no gesture, motion, or deportment be taught our youth, but what by their allowance shall be thought honest; for such Plato was provided of. It will ask more than the work of twenty licensers to examine all the lutes, the violins, and the guitars in every house; they must not be suffered to prattle as they do, but must be licensed what they may say. And who shall silence all the airs and madrigals that whisper softness in chambers? The windows also, and the balconies, must be thought on; these are shrewd books, with dangerous frontispieces, set to sale: who shall prohibit them, shall twenty licensers? The villages also must have their visitors to inquire what lectures the bagpipe and the rebec reads, even to the ballatry and the gamut of every municipal fiddler; for these are the countryman's Arcadias, and his Monte Mayors.

Next, what more national corruption, for which England hears ill abroad, than household gluttony? Who shall be the rectors of our daily rioting? And what shall be done to inhibit the multitudes that frequent those houses where drunkenness is sold and harbored? Our garments also should be referred to the licensing of some more sober work-masters, to see them cut into a less wanton garb. Who shall regulate all the mixed conversation of our youth, male and female together, as is the fashion of this country? Who shall still appoint what shall be discoursed, what presumed, and no further? Lastly, who shall forbid and separate all idle resort, all evil company? These things will be, and must be; but how they shall be least hurtful, how least enticing, herein consists the grave and governing wisdom of a state. . . . .

They are not skilful considerers of human things, who imagine to remove sin, by removing the matter of sin; for, besides that it is a huge heap, increasing under the very act of diminishing, though some part of it may for a time be withdrawn from some persons, it cannot from all, in such a universal thing as books are; and when this is done, yet the sin remains entire. Though ye take from a covetous man all his treasure, he has yet one jewel left, ye cannot bereave him of his covetousness. Banish all objects of lust, shut up all youth into the severest discipline that can be exercised in any hermitage, ye cannot make them chaste, that came not thither so: such great care and wisdom is required to the right managing of this point.

Suppose we could expel sin by this means; look how much we thus expel of sin, so much we expel of virtue; for the matter of them both is the same: remove that, and ye remove them both alike. This justifies the high providence of God, who, though he commands us temperance, justice, continence, yet pours out before us even to a profuseness all desirable things, and gives us minds that can wander beyond all limit and satiety. Why should we then affect a rigor contrary to the manner of God and of nature, by abridging or scanting those means, which books, freely permitted, are, both to the trial of virtue, and the exercise of truth?

It would be better done, to learn that the law must needs be frivolous, which goes to restrain things, uncertainly and yet equally working to good and to evil. And were I the chooser, a dram of well-doing should be preferred before many times as much the forcible hinderance of evil doing. For God sure esteems the growth and completing of one virtuous person, more than the restraint of ten vicious. . . . .

If therefore ye be loath to dishearten utterly and discontent, not the mercenary crew of false pretenders to learning, but the free and ingenuous sort of such as evidently were born to study and love learning for itself, not for lucre, or any other end, but the service of God and of truth, and perhaps that lasting fame and perpetuity of praise, which God and good men have consented shall be the reward of those whose published labors advance the good of mankind: then know, that so far to distrust the judgment and the honesty of one who hath but a common repute in learning, and never yet offended, as not to count him fit to print his mind without a tutor and examiner, lest he should drop a schism, or something of corruption, is the greatest displeasure and indignity to a free and knowing spirit that can be put upon him. . . . .

How can a man teach with authority, which is the life of teaching; how can he be a doctor in his book, as he ought to be, or else had better be silent, whenas all he teaches, all he delivers, is but under the tuition, under the correction of his patriarchal licenser, to blot or alter what precisely accords not with the hide-bound humor which he calls his judgment? When every acute reader, upon the first sight of a pedantic license, will be ready with these like words to ding the book a quoit's distance from him: — "I hate a pupil teacher; I endure not an instructor that comes to me under the wardship of an overseeing fist. I know nothing of the licenser, but that I have his own hand here for his arrogance; who shall warrant me his judgment?" "The state, sir," replies the stationer; but has a quick return: — "The state shall be my governors, but not my critics; they may be mistaken in the choice of a licenser, as easily as this licenser may be mistaken in an author. This is some common stuff": and he might add from Sir Francis Bacon, that "such authorized books are but the language of the times." For though a licenser should happen to be judicious more than ordinary, which will be a great jeopardy of the next succession, yet his very office and his commission enjoins him to let pass nothing but what is vulgarly received already.

Nay, which is more lamentable, if the work of any deceased author, though never so famous in his lifetime, and even to this day, comes to their hands for license to be printed, or reprinted, if there be found in his book one sentence of a venturous edge, uttered in the height of zeal, (and who knows whether it might not be the dictate of a divine spirit?) yet, not suiting with every low decrepit humor of their own, though it were Knox himself, the reformer of a kingdom, that spake it, they will not pardon him their dash; the sense of that great man shall to all posterity be lost, for the fearfulness, or the presumptuous rashness of a perfunctory licenser. And to what an author this violence hath been lately done, and in what book, of greatest consequence to be faithfully published, I could now instance, but shall forbear till a more convenient season. Yet if these things be not resented seriously and timely by them who have the remedy in their power, but that such ironmoulds as these shall have authority to gnaw out the choicest periods of exquisitest books, and to commit such a treacherous fraud against the orphan remainders of worthiest men after death, the more sorrow will belong to that hapless race of men, whose misfortune it is to have understanding. Henceforth let no man care to learn, or care to be more than worldly wise; for certainly in higher matters to be ignorant and slothful, to be a common steadfast dunce, will be the only pleasant life, and only in request.

And as it is a particular disesteem of every knowing person alive, and most injurious to the written labors and monuments of the dead, so to me it seems an undervaluing and vilifying of the whole nation. I cannot set so light by all the invention, the art, the wit, the grave and solid judgment which is in England, as that it can be comprehended in any twenty capacities, how good soever; much less that it should not pass except their superintendence be over it, except it be sifted and strained with their strainers, that it should be uncurrent without their manual stamp. Truth and understanding are not such wares as to be monopolized and traded in by tickets, and statutes, and standards. We must not think to make a staple commodity of all the knowledge in the land, to mark and license it like our broadcloth and our woolpacks. What is it but a servitude like that imposed by the Philistines, not to be allowed the sharpening of our own axes and coulters, but we must repair from all quarters to twenty licensing forges? . . . .

Well knows he who uses to consider, that our faith and knowledge thrives by exercise, as well as our limbs and complexion. Truth is compared in Scripture to a streaming fountain; if her waters flow not in a perpetual progression, they sicken into a muddy pool of conformity and tradition. A man may be a heretic in the truth; and if he believe things only because his pastor says so, or the assembly so determines, without knowing other reason, though his belief be true, yet the very truth he holds becomes his heresy. There is not any burden that some would gladlier post off to another, than the charge and care of their religion. There be, who knows not that there be? of Protestants and professors, who live and die in as errant and implicit faith, as any lay Papist of Loretto.

A wealthy man, addicted to his pleasure and to his profits, finds religion to be a traffic so entangled, and of so many piddling accounts, that of all mysteries he cannot skill to keep a stock going upon that trade. What should he do? Fain he would have the name to be religious, fain he would bear up with his neighbors in that. What does he therefore, but resolves to give over toiling, and to find himself out some factor, to whose care and credit he may commit the whole managing of his religious affairs; some divine of note and estimation that must be. To him he adheres, resigns the whole warehouse of his religion, with all the locks and keys, into his custody; and indeed makes the very person of that man his religion; esteems his associating with him a sufficient evidence and commendatory of his own piety. So that a man may say his religion is now no more within himself, but is become a dividual movable, and goes and comes near him, according as that good man frequents the house. He entertains him, gives him gifts, feasts him, lodges him; his religion comes home at night, prays, is liberally supped, and sumptuously laid to sleep; rises, is saluted, and after the malmsey, or some well-spiced bruage, and better breakfasted than He whose morning appetite would have gladly fed on green figs between Bethany and Jerusalem, his religion walks abroad at eight, and leaves his kind entertainer in the shop trading all day without his religion.

Another sort there be, who, when they hear that all things shall be ordered, all things regulated and settled, nothing written but what passes through the custom-house of certain publicans that have the tonnaging and poundaging of all free-spoken truth, will straight give themselves up into your hands, make them and cut them out what religion ye please: there be delights, there be recreations and jolly pastimes, that will fetch the day about from sun to sun, and rock the tedious year as in a delightful dream. What need they torture their heads with that which others have taken so strictly, and so unalterably into their own purveying? These are the fruits which a dull ease and cessation of our knowledge will bring forth among the people. How goodly, and how to be wished were such an obedient unanimity as this! What a fine conformity would it starch us all into! Doubtless a stanch and solid piece of framework, as any January could freeze together. . . . .

For if we be sure we are in the right, and do not hold the truth guiltily, which becomes not, if we ourselves condemn not our own weak and frivolous teaching, and the people for an untaught and irreligious gadding rout; what can be more fair, than when a man judicious, learned, and of a conscience, for aught we know as good as theirs that taught us what we know, shall not privily from house to house, which is more dangerous, but openly by writing, publish to the world what his opinion is, what his reasons, and wherefore that which is now thought cannot be sound? Christ urged it as wherewith to justify himself, that he preached in public; yet writing is more public than preaching; and more easy to refutation if need be, there being so many whose business and profession merely it is to be the champions of truth; which if they neglect, what can be imputed but their sloth or inability? . . . .

There is yet behind of what I purposed to lay open, the incredible loss and detriment that this plot of licensing puts us to, more than if some enemy at sea should stop up all our havens, and ports, and creeks; it hinders and retards the importation of our richest merchandise, — truth: nay, it was first established and put in practice by Antichristian malice and mystery, or set purpose to extinguish, if it were possible, the light of reformation, and to settle falsehood; little differing from that policy wherewith the Turk upholds his Alcoran, by the prohibiting of printing. It is not denied, but gladly confessed, we are to send our thanks and vows to heaven, louder than most of nations, for that great measure of truth which we enjoy, especially in those main points between us and the pope, with his appurtenances the prelates: but he who thinks we are to pitch our tent here, and have attained the utmost prospect of reformation that the mortal glass wherein we contemplate can show us, till we come to beatific vision, that man by this very opinion declares that he is yet far short of truth.

Truth indeed came once into the world with her Divine Master, and was a perfect shape most glorious to look on: but when he ascended, and his Apostles after him were laid asleep, then straight arose a wicked race of deceivers, who, as that story goes of the Egyptian Typhon with his conspirators, how they dealt with the good Osiris, took the virgin Truth, hewed her lovely form into a thousand pieces, and scattered them to the four winds. From that time ever since, the sad friends of Truth, such as durst appear, imitating the careful search that Isis made for the mangled body of Osiris, went up and down gathering up limb by limb still as they could find them. We have not yet found them all, lords and commons, nor ever shall do, till her Master's second coming; he shall bring together every joint and member, and shall mould them into an immortal feature of loveliness and perfection. Suffer not these licensing prohibitions to stand at every place of opportunity forbidding and disturbing them that continue seeking, that continue to do our obsequies to the torn body of our martyred saint.

We boast our light: but if we look not wisely on the sun itself, it smites us into darkness. Who can discern those planets that are oft combust, and those stars of brightest magnitude that rise and set with the sun, until the opposite motion of their orbs bring them to such a place in the firmament where they may be seen evening or morning? The light which we have gained was given us, not to be ever staring on, but by it to discover onward things more remote from our knowledge.

. . . . .

To be still searching what we know not, by what we know, still closing up truth to truth as we find it (for all her body is homogeneal and proportional), this is the golden rule in theology as well as in arithmetic, and makes up the best harmony in a church; not the forced and outward union of cold, and neutral, and inwardly divided minds. . . . .

Now once again by all concurrence of signs, and by the general instinct of holy and devout men, as they daily and solemnly express their thoughts, God is decreeing to begin some new and great period in his Church, even to the reforming of reformation itself; what does he then but reveal himself to his servants, and, as his manner is, first to his Englishmen? I say, as his manner is, first to us, though we mark not the method of his counsels, and are unworthy. Behold now this vast city, a city of refuge, the mansion-house of liberty, encompassed and surrounded with his protection; the shop of war hath not there more anvils and hammers working, to fashion out the plates and instruments of armed justice in defence of beleaguered truth, than there be pens and heads there, sitting by their studious lamps, musing, searching, revolving new notions and ideas wherewith to present, as with their homage and their fealty, the approaching reformation: others as fast reading, trying all things, assenting to the force of reason and convincement.

What could a man require more from a nation so pliant and so prone to seek after knowledge? What wants there to such a towardly and pregnant soil, but wise and faithful laborers, to make a knowing people, a nation of prophets, of sages, and of worthies? We reckon more than five months yet to harvest; there need not be five weeks, had we but eyes to lift up, the fields are white already. Where there is much desire to learn, there of necessity will be much arguing, much writing, many opinions; for opinion in good men is but knowledge in the making. Under these fantastic terrors of sect and schism, we wrong the earnest and zealous thirst after knowledge and understanding, which God hath stirred up in this city. What some lament of, we rather should rejoice at, should rather praise this pious forwardness among men, to reassume the ill-deputed care of their religion into their own hands again. A little generous prudence, a little forbearance of one another, and some grain of charity might win all these diligencies to join and unite into one general and brotherly search after truth; could we but forego this prelatical tradition of crowding free consciences and Christian liberties into canons and precepts of men. I doubt not, if some great and worthy stranger should come among us, wise to discern the mould and temper of a people, and how to govern it, observing the high hopes and aims, the diligent alacrity of our extended thoughts and reasonings in the pursuance of truth and freedom, but that he would cry out as Pyrrhus did, admiring the Roman docility and courage, "If such were my Epirots, I would not despair the greatest design that could be attempted to make a church or kingdom happy."

Yet these are the men cried out against for schismatics and sectaries, as if, while the temple of the Lord was building, some cutting, some squaring the marble, others hewing the cedars, there should be a sort of irrational men, who could not consider there must be many schisms and many dissections made in the quarry and in the timber ere the house of God can be built. And when every stone is laid artfully together, it cannot be united into a continuity, it can but be contiguous in this world: neither can every piece of the building be of one form; nay, rather the perfection consists in this, that out of many moderate varieties and brotherly dissimilitudes that are not vastly disproportional, arises the goodly and the graceful symmetry that commends the whole pile and structure.

Let us therefore be more considerate builders, more wise in spiritual architecture, when great reformation is expected. For now the time seems come, wherein Moses, the great prophet, may sit in heaven rejoicing to see that memorable and glorious wish of his fulfilled, when not only our seventy elders, but all the Lord's people, are become prophets. No marvel then though some men, and some good men too perhaps, but young in goodness, as Joshua then was, envy them. They fret, and out of their own weakness are in agony, lest these divisions and subdivisions will undo us. The adversary again applauds, and waits the hour: when they have branched themselves out, saith he, small enough into parties and partitions, then will be our time. Fool! he sees not the firm root, out of which we all grow, though into branches; nor will beware, until he see our small divided maniples cutting through at every angle of his ill-united and unwieldy brigade. And that we are to hope better of all these supposed sects and schisms, and that we shall not need that solicitude, honest perhaps, though over-timorous, of them that vex in this behalf, but shall laugh in the end at those malicious applauders of our differences, I have these reasons to persuade me.

First, when a city shall be as it were besieged and blocked about, her navigable river infested, inroads and incursions round, defiance and battle oft rumored to be marching up, even to her walls and suburb trenches; that then the people, or the greater part, more than at other times, wholly taken up with the study of highest and most important matters to be reformed, should be disputing, reasoning, reading, inventing, discoursing, even to a rarity and admiration, things not before discoursed or written of, argues first a singular good will, contentedness, and confidence in your prudent foresight, and safe government, lords and commons; and from thence derives itself to a gallant bravery and well-grounded contempt of their enemies, as if there were no small number of as great spirits among us, as his was who, when Rome was nigh besieged by Hannibal, being in the city, bought that piece of ground, at no cheap rate, whereon Hannibal himself encamped his own regiment.

Next it is a lively and cheerful presage of our happy success and victory. For as in a body when the blood is fresh, the spirits pure and vigorous, not only to vital, but to rational faculties, and those in the acutest and the pertest operations of wit and subtlety, it argues in what good plight and constitution the body is; so when the cheerfulness of the people is so sprightly up, as that it has not only wherewith to guard well its own freedom and safety, but to spare, and to bestow upon the solidest and sublimest points of controversy and new invention, it betokens us not degenerated, nor drooping to a fatal decay, by casting off the old and wrinkled skin of corruption to outlive these pangs, and wax young again, entering the glorious ways of truth and prosperous virtue, destined to become great and honorable in these latter ages. Methinks I see in my mind a noble and puissant nation rousing herself like a strong man after sleep, and shaking her invincible locks: methinks I see her as an eagle mewing her mighty youth, and kindling her undazzled eyes at the full midday beam; purging and unscaling her long-abused sight at the fountain itself of heavenly radiance; while the whole noise of timorous and flocking birds, with those also that love the twilight, flutter about, amazed at what she means, and in their envious gabble would prognosticate a year of sects and schisms. . . . .

The temple of Janus, with his two controversial faces, might now not unsignificantly be set open. And though all the winds of doctrine were let loose to play upon the earth, so truth be in the field, we do injuriously by licensing and prohibiting to misdoubt her strength. Let her and falsehood grapple; who ever knew truth put to the worse, in a free and open encounter? Her confuting is the best and surest suppressing. . . . .

When a man hath been laboring the hardest labor in the deep mines of knowledge, hath furnished out his findings in all their equipage, drawn forth his reasons as it were a battle ranged, scattered and defeated all objections in his way, calls out his adversary into the plain, offers him the advantage of wind and sun, if he please, only that he may try the matter by dint of argument; for his opponents then to skulk, to lay ambushments, to keep a narrow bridge of licensing where the challenger should pass, though it be valor enough in soldiership, is but weakness and cowardice in the wars of truth. For who knows not that truth is strong, next to the Almighty; she needs no policies, nor stratagems, nor licensings to make her victorious; those are the shifts and the defences that error uses against her power: give her but room, and do not bind her when she sleeps, for then she speaks not true, as the old Proteus did, who spake oracles only when he was caught and bound, but then rather she turns herself into all shapes except her own, and perhaps tunes her voice according to the time, as Micaiah did before Ahab, until she be adjured into her own likeness. . . . .

In the mean while, if any one would write, and bring his helpful hand to the slow-moving reformation which we labor under, if truth have spoken to him before others, or but seemed at least to speak, who hath so bejesuited us, that we should trouble that man with asking license to do so worthy a deed; and not consider this, that if it come to prohibiting, there is not aught more likely to be prohibited than truth itself: whose first appearance to our eyes, bleared and dimmed with prejudice and custom, is more unsightly and unplausible than many errors; even as the person is of many a great man slight and contemptible to see to. . . . .

When God shakes a kingdom, with strong and healthful commotions, to a general reforming, it is not untrue that many sectaries and false teachers are then busiest in seducing.

But yet more true it is, that God then raises to his own work men of rare abilities, and more than common industry, not only to look back and revive what hath been taught heretofore, but to gain further, and to go on some new enlightened steps in the discovery of truth. For such is the order of God's enlightening his Church, to dispense and deal out by degrees his beam, so as our earthly eyes may best sustain it. Neither is God appointed and confined, where and out of what place these his chosen shall be first heard to speak; for he sees not as man sees, chooses not as man chooses, lest we should devote ourselves again to set places and assemblies, and outward callings of men.

FROM

THE DOCTRINE AND DISCIPLINE OF DIVORCE.

IF it were seriously asked, (and it would be no untimely question,) who of all teachers and masters, that have ever taught, hath drawn the most disciples after him, both in religion and in manners? it might be not untruly answered, custom. Though virtue be commended for the most persuasive in her theory, and conscience in the plain demonstration of the spirit finds most evincing; yet whether it be the secret of divine will, or the original blindness we are born in, so it happens for the most part that custom still is silently received for the best instructor. Except it be, because her method is so glib and easy, in some manner like to that vision of Ezekiel rolling up her sudden book of implicit knowledge, for him that will to take and swallow down at pleasure; which proving but of bad nourishment in the concoction, as it was heedless in the devouring, puffs up unhealthily a certain big face of pretended learning, mistaken among credulous men for the wholesome habit of soundness and good constitution, but is indeed no other than that swoln visage of counterfeit knowledge and literature, which not only in private mars our education, but also in public is the common climber into every chair, where either religion is preached, or law reported; filling each estate of life and profession with abject and servile principles, depressing the high and heaven-born spirit of man far beneath the condition wherein either God created him, or sin hath sunk him. To pursue the allegory, custom being but a mere face, as echo is a mere voice, rests not in her unaccomplishment, until by secret inclination she accorporate herself with error, who, being a blind and serpentine body without a head, willingly accepts what he wants, and supplies what her incompleteness went seeking. Hence it is, that error supports custom, custom countenances error; and these two between them would persecute and chase away all truth and solid wisdom out of human life, were it not that God, rather than man, once in many ages calls together the prudent and religious counsels of men, deputed to repress the encroachments, and to work off the inveterate blots and obscurities wrought upon our minds by the subtle insinuating of error and custom; who, with the numerous and vulgar train of their followers, make it their chief design to envy and cry down the industry of free reasoning, under the terms of humor and innovation; as if the womb of teeming truth were to be closed up, if she presume to bring forth aught that sorts not with their unchewed notions and suppositions. . . . .

He who shall endeavor the amendment of any old neglected grievance in church or state, or in the daily course of life, if he be gifted with abilities of mind that may raise him to so high an undertaking, I grant he hath already much whereof not to repent him; yet let me aread him, not to be the foreman of any misjudged opinion, unless his resolutions be firmly seated in a square and constant mind, not conscious to itself of any deserved blame, and regardless of ungrounded suspicions. For this let him be sure, he shall be boarded presently by the ruder sort, but not by discreet and well-nurtured men, with a thousand idle descants and surmises. Who, when they cannot confute the least joint or sinew of any passage in the book; yet God forbid that truth should be truth, because they have a boisterous conceit of some pretences in the writer. But were they not more busy and inquisitive than the Apostle commends, they would hear him at least, "rejoicing so the truth be preached, whether of envy or other pretence whatsoever": for truth is as impossible to be soiled by any outward touch as the sunbeam; though this ill hap wait on her nativity, that she never comes into the world but like a bastard, to the ignominy of him that brought her forth; till time, the midwife rather than the mother of truth, have washed and salted the infant, declared her legitimate, and churched the father of his young Minerva, from the needless causes of his purgation. . . . .

This question concerns not us perhaps: indeed man's disposition, though prone to search after vain curiosities, yet when points of difficulty are to be discussed, appertaining to the removal of unreasonable wrong and burden from the perplexed life of our brother, it is incredible how cold, how dull, and far from all fellow-feeling we are, without the spur of self-concernment. . . . .

He who wisely would restrain the reasonable soul of man within due bounds, must first himself know perfectly, how far the territory and dominion extends of just and honest liberty. As little must he offer to bind that which God hath loosened, as to loosen that which he hath bound. The ignorance and mistake of this high point hath heaped up one huge half of all the misery that hath been since Adam. In the Gospel we shall read a supercilious crew of masters, whose holiness, or rather whose evil eye, grieving that God should be so facile to man, was to set straiter limits to obedience than God hath set, to enslave the dignity of man, to put a garrison upon his neck of empty and over-dignified precepts: and we shall read our Saviour never more grieved and troubled than to meet with such a peevish madness among men against their own freedom. . . . .

The greatest burden in the world is superstition,

not only of ceremonies in the Church, but of imaginary and scarecrow sins at home. What greater weakening, what more subtle stratagem against our Christian warfare, when besides the gross body of real transgressions to encounter, we shall be terrified by a vain and shadowy menacing of faults that are not? When things indifferent shall be set to overfront us under the banners of sin, what wonder if we be routed, and by this art of our adversary fall into the subjection of worst and deadliest offences?

The superstition of the papist is, "Touch not, taste not," when God bids both; and ours is, "Part not, separate not," when God and charity both permits and commands. "Let all your things be done with charity," saith St. Paul; and his Master saith, "She is the fulfilling of the law." Yet now a civil, an indifferent, a sometime dissuaded law of marriage, must be forced upon us to fulfil, not only without charity but against her. No place in heaven or earth, except hell, where charity may not enter: yet marriage, the ordinance of our solace and contentment, the remedy of our loneliness, will not admit now either of charity or mercy, to come in and mediate, or pacify the fierceness of this gentle ordinance, the unremedied loneliness of this remedy. Advise ye well, supreme senate, if charity be thus excluded and expulsed, how ye will defend the untainted honor of your own actions and proceedings. He who marries, intends as little to conspire his own ruin, as he that swears allegiance: and as a whole people is in proportion to an ill government, so is one man to an ill marriage. If they, against any authority, covenant, or statute, may, by the sovereign edict of charity, save not only their lives but honest liberties from unworthy bondage, as well may he against any private covenant, which he never entered to his mischief, redeem himself from unsupportable disturbances to honest peace and just contentment. And much the rather, for that to resist the highest magistrate though tyrannizing, God never gave us express allowance, only he gave us reason, charity, nature and good example to bear us out; but in this economical misfortune thus to demean ourselves, besides the warrant of those four great directors, which doth as justly belong hither, we have an express law of God, and such a law, as whereof our Saviour with a solemn threat forbade the abrogating. For no effect of tyranny can sit more heavy on the commonwealth than this household unhappiness on the family. And farewell all hope of true reformation in the state, while such an evil as this lies undiscerned or unregarded in the house: on the redress whereof depends not only the spiritful and orderly life of our grown men, but the willing and careful education of our children. Let this therefore be new examined, this tenure and freehold of mankind, this native and domestic charter given us by a greater lord than that Saxon king the Confessor. Let the statutes of God be turned over, be scanned anew, and considered not altogether by the narrow intellectuals of quotationists and commonplaces, but (as was the ancient right of councils) by men of what liberal profession soever, of eminent spirit and breeding, joined with a diffuse and various knowledge of divine and human things; able to balance and define good and evil, right and wrong, throughout every state of life; able to show us the ways of the Lord straight and faithful as they are, not full of cranks and contradictions, and pitfalling dispenses, but with divine insight and benignity measured out to the proportion of each mind and spirit, each temper and disposition created so different each from other, and yet, by the skill of wise conducting, all to become uniform in virtue. To expedite these knots, were worthy a learned and memorable synod; while our enemies expect to see the expectation of the Church tired out with dependencies and independencies, how they will compound and in what calends. Doubt not, worthy senators! to vindicate the sacred honor and judgment of Moses your predecessor, from the shallow commenting of scholastics and canonists. Doubt not after him to reach out your steady hands to the misinformed and wearied life of man; to restore this his lost heritage, into the household state: wherewith be sure that peace and love, the best subsistence of a Christian family, will return home from whence they are now banished; places of prostitution will be less haunted, the neighbor's bed less attempted, the yoke of prudent and manly discipline will be generally submitted to; sober and well-ordered living will soon spring up in the commonwealth. Ye have an author great beyond exception, Moses; and one yet greater, he who hedged in from abolishing every smallest jot and tittle of precious equity contained in that law, with a more accurate and lasting Masoreth, than either the synagogue of Ezra or the Galilæan school at Tiberias hath left us. . . . .

Many men, whether it be their fate or fond opinion, easily persuade themselves, if God would but be pleased awhile to withdraw his just punishments from us, and to restrain what power either the Devil or any earthly enemy hath to work us woe, that then man's nature would find immediate rest and releasement from all evils. But verily they who think so, if they be such as have a mind large enough to take into their thoughts a general survey of human things, would soon prove themselves in that opinion far deceived. For though it were granted us by divine indulgence to be exempt from all that can be harmful to us from without, yet the perverseness of our folly is so bent, that we should never cease hammering out of our own hearts, as it were out of a flint, the seeds and sparkles of new misery to ourselves, till all were in a blaze again. And no marvel if out of our own hearts, for they are evil; but even out of those things which God meant us, either for a principal good, or a pure contentment, we are still hatching and contriving upon ourselves matter of continual sorrow and perplexity. . . . .

What thing more instituted to the solace and delight of man than marriage? And yet the misinterpreting of some Scripture, directed mainly against the abuses of the law for divorce given by Moses, hath changed the blessing of matrimony not seldom into a familiar and coinhabiting mischief; at least, into a drooping and disconsolate household captivity, without refuge or redemption: so ungoverned and so wild a race doth superstition run us from one extreme of abused liberty into the other of unmerciful restraint. . . . What a calamity is this? and, as the wise man, if he were alive, would sigh out in his own phrase, what a "sore evil is this under the sun!" All which we can refer justly to no other author than the canon law and her adherents, not consulting with charity, the interpreter and guide of our faith, but resting in the mere element of the text; doubtless by the policy of the Devil to make that gracious ordinance become unsupportable, that what with men not daring to venture upon wedlock, and what with men wearied out of it, all inordinate license might abound. It was for many ages that marriage lay in disgrace with most of the ancient doctors, as a work of the flesh, almost a defilement, wholly denied to priests, and the second time dissuaded to all, as he that reads Tertullian or Jerome may see at large. Afterwards it was thought so sacramental, that no adultery or desertion could dissolve it; and this is the sense of our canon courts in England to this day, but in no other Reformed Church else: yet there remains in them also a burden on it as heavy as the other two were disgraceful or superstitious, and of as much iniquity, crossing a law not only written by Moses, but charactered in us by nature, of more antiquity and deeper ground than marriage itself; which law is to force nothing against the faultless proprieties of nature, yet that this may be colorably done, our Saviour's words touching divorce are as it were congealed into a stony rigor, inconsistent both with his doctrine and his office; and that which he preached only to the conscience is by canonical tyranny snatched into the compulsive censure of a judicial court; where laws are imposed even against the venerable and secret power of nature's impression, to love, whatever cause be found to loathe: which is a heinous barbarism, both against the honor of marriage, the dignity of man and his soul, the goodness of Christianity, and all the human respects of civility.

. . . . .

This therefore shall be the task and period of this discourse to prove, first, that other reasons of divorce, besides adultery, were by the law of Moses, and are yet to be allowed by the Christian magistrate as a piece of justice, and that the words of Christ are not hereby contraried. Next, that to prohibit absolutely any divorce whatsoever, except those which Moses excepted, is against the reason of law. . . . . He therefore, who, by adventuring, shall be so happy as with success to light the way of such an expedient liberty and truth as this, shall restore the much-wronged and over-sorrowed state of matrimony, not only to those merciful and life-giving remedies of Moses, but, as much as may be, to that serene and blissful condition it was in at the beginning, and shall deserve of all apprehensive men, (considering the troubles and distempers, which, for want of this insight have been so oft in kingdoms, in states, and families,) shall deserve to be reckoned among the public benefactors of civil and human life, above the inventors of wine and oil ; for this is a far dearer, far nobler, and more desirable cherishing to man's life, unworthily exposed to sadness and mistake, which he shall vindicate. Not that license, and levity, and unconsented breach of faith should herein be countenanced, but that some conscionable and tender pity might be had of those who have unwarily, in a thing they never practised before, made themselves the bondmen of a luckless and helpless matrimony. In which argument, he whose courage can serve him to give the first onset, must look for two several oppositions: the one from those who, having sworn themselves to long custom, and the letter of the text, will not out of the road; the other from those whose gross and vulgar apprehensions conceit but low of matrimonial purposes, and in the work of male and female think they have all. Nevertheless, it shall be here sought by due ways to be made appear, that those words of God in the institution, promising a meet help against loneliness, and those words of Christ, that "his yoke is easy and his burden light," were not spoken in vain: for if the knot of marriage may in no case be dissolved but for adultery, all the burdens and services of the law are not so intolerable. This only is desired of them who are minded to judge hardly of thus maintaining, that they would be still, and hear all out, nor think it equal to answer deliberate reason with sudden heat and noise; remembering this, that many truths now of reverend esteem and credit, had their birth and beginning once from singular and private thoughts, while the most of men were otherwise possessed; and had the fate at first to be generally exploded and exclaimed on by many violent opposers: yet I may err perhaps in soothing myself, that this present truth revived will deserve on all hands to be not sinisterly received, in that it undertakes the cure of an inveterate disease crept into the best part of human society; and to do this with no smarting corrosive, but a smooth and pleasing lesson, which received both the virtue to soften and dispel rooted and knotty sorrows, and without enchantment, if that be feared, or spell used, hath regard at once both to serious pity and upright honesty; that tends to the redeeming and restoring of none but such as are the object of compassion, having in an ill hour hampered themselves, to the utter despatch of all their most beloved comforts and repose for this life's term. But if we shall obstinately dislike this new overture of unexpected ease and recovery, what remains but to deplore the frowardness of our hopeless condition, which neither can endure the estate we are in, nor admit of remedy either sharp or sweet? Sharp we ourselves distaste; and sweet, under whose hands we are, is scrupled and suspected as too luscious. In such a posture Christ found the Jews, who were neither won with the austerity of John the Baptist, and thought it too much license to follow freely the charming pipe of him who sounded and proclaimed liberty and relief to all distresses; yet truth in some age or other will find her witness, and shall be justified at last by her own children. . . . .

Lest therefore so noble a creature as man should be shut up incurably under a worse evil by an easy mistake in that ordinance which God gave him to remedy a less evil, reaping to himself sorrow while he went to rid away solitariness, it cannot avoid to be concluded, that if the woman be naturally so of disposition, as will not help to remove, but help to increase that same God-forbidden loneliness, which in time draws on with it a general discomfort and dejection of mind, not beseeming either Christian profession or moral conversation, unprofitable and dangerous to the commonwealth, when the household estate, out of which must flourish forth the vigor and spirit of all public enterprises, is so ill-contented and procured at home, and cannot be supported; such a marriage can be no marriage, whereto the most honest end is wanting; and the aggrieved person shall do more manly, to be extraordinary and singular in claiming the due right whereof he is frustrated, than to piece up his lost contentment by visiting the stews, or stepping to his neighbor's bed, which is the common shift in this misfortune; or else by suffering his useful life to waste away, and be lost under a secret affliction of an unconscionable size to human strength. Against all which evils the mercy of this Mosaic law was graciously exhibited. . . . .

St. Paul saith, "It is better to marry than to burn." Marriage, therefore, was given as a remedy of that trouble: but what might this burning mean? Certainly not the mere motion of carnal lust, not the mere goad of a sensitive desire: God does not principally take care for such cattle. What is it then but that desire which God put into Adam in Paradise, before he knew the sin of incontinence; that desire which God saw it was not good that man should be left alone to burn in; the desire and longing to put off an unkindly solitariness by uniting another body, but not without a fit soul to his, in the cheerful society of wedlock? Which, if it were so needful before the fall, when man was much more perfect in himself, how much more is it needful now against all the sorrows and casualties of this life, to have an intimate and speaking help, a ready and reviving associate in marriage? . . . . As for that other burning, which is but as it were the venom of a lusty and over-abounding concoction, strict life and labor, with the abatement of a full diet, may keep that low and obedient enough; but this pure and more inbred desire of joining to itself in conjugal fellowship a fit conversing soul (which desire is properly called love) "is stronger than death," as the spouse of Christ thought; "many waters cannot quench it, neither can the floods drown it." . . . .

But all ingenuous men will see that the dignity and blessing of marriage is placed rather in the mutual enjoyment of that which the wanting soul needfully seeks, than of that which the plenteous body would joyfully give away. Hence it is that Plato in his festival discourse brings in Socrates relating what he feigned to have learned from the prophetess Diotima, how Love was the son of Penury, begot of Plenty in the garden of Jupiter. Which divinely sorts with that which in effect Moses tells us, that Love was the son of Loneliness, begot in Paradise by that sociable and helpful aptitude which God implanted between man and woman toward each other. The same, also, is that burning mentioned by St. Paul, whereof marriage ought to be the remedy: the flesh hath other mutual and easy curbs which are in the power of any temperate man. When, therefore, this original and sinless penury, or loneliness of the soul, cannot lay itself down by the side of such a meet and acceptable union as God ordained in marriage, at least in some proportion, it cannot conceive and bring forth love, but remains utterly unmarried under a former wedlock, and still burns, in the proper meaning of St. Paul. Then enters Hate; not that hate that sins, but that which only is natural dissatisfaction, and the turning aside from a mistaken object: if that mistake have done injury, it fails not to dismiss with recompense; for to retain still, and not be able to love, is to heap up more injury. Thence this wise and pious law of dismission now defended took beginning: he, therefore, who, lacking of his due in the most native and humane end of marriage, thinks it better to part than to live sadly and injuriously to that cheerful covenant, (for not to be beloved, and yet retained, is the greatest injury to a gentle spirit,) he, I say, who therefore seeks to part, is one who highly honors the married life and would not stain it: and the reasons which now move him to divorce are equal to the best of those that could first warrant him to marry; for, as was plainly shown, both the hate which now diverts him, and the loneliness which leads him still powerfully to seek a fit help, hath not the least grain of a sin in it, if he be worthy to understand himself. . . . .

Marriage is a covenant, the very being whereof consists not in a forced cohabitation, and counterfeit performance of duties, but in unfeigned love and peace: and of matrimonial love, no doubt but that was chiefly meant, which by the ancient sages was thus parabled; that Love, if he be not twin born, yet hath a brother wondrous like him, called Anteros; whom, while he seeks all about, his chance is to meet with many false and feigning desires, that wander singly up and down in his likeness: by them in their borrowed garb, Love, though not wholly blind, as poets wrong him, yet having but one eye, as being born an archer aiming, and that eye not the quickest in this dark region here below, which is not Love's proper sphere, partly out of the simplicity and credulity which is native to him, often deceived, embraces and consorts him with these obvious and suborned striplings, as if they were his mother's own sons; for so he thinks them, while they subtilely keep themselves most on his blind side. But after a while, as his manner is, when soaring up into the high tower of his Apogæum, above the shadow of the earth, he darts out the direct rays of his then most piercing eyesight upon the impostures and trim disguises that were used with him, and discerns that this is not his genuine brother, as he imagined; he has no longer the power to hold fellowship with such a personated mate: for straight his arrows lose their golden heads, and shed their purple feathers, his silken braids untwine, and slip their knots, and that original and fiery virtue given him by fate all on a sudden goes out, and leaves him undeified and despoiled of all his force; till finding Anteros at last, he kindles and repairs the almost-faded ammunition of his deity by the reflection of a coequal and homogeneal fire. Thus mine author sung it to me: and by the leave of those who would be counted the only grave ones, this is no mere amatorious novel; (though to be wise and skilful in these matters, men heretofore of greatest name in virtue have esteemed it one of the highest arcs, that human contemplation circling upwards can make from the globy sea whereon she stands;) but this is a deep and serious verity, showing us that love in marriage cannot live nor subsist unless it be mutual; and where love cannot be, there can be left of wedlock nothing but the empty husk of an outside matrimony, as undelightful and unpleasing to God as any other kind of hypocrisy. . . . .

As those priests of old were not to be long in sorrow, or if they were, they could not rightly execute their function; so every true Christian, in a higher order of priesthood, is a person dedicate to joy and peace, offering himself a lively sacrifice of praise and thanksgiving, and there is no Christian duty that is not to be seasoned and set off with cheerishness. . . . .

That there is a hidden efficacy of love and hatred in man as well as in other kinds, not moral but natural, which, though not always in the choice, yet in the success of marriage will ever be most predominant: besides daily experience, the author of Ecclesiasticus, whose wisdom hath set him next the Bible, acknowledges, xiii. 16, "A man," saith he, "will cleave to his like." But what might be the cause, whether each one's allotted genius or proper star, or whether the supernal influence of schemes and angular aspects, or this elemental crasis here below; whether all these jointly or singly meeting friendly, or unfriendly in either party, I dare not, with the men I am like to clash, appear so much a philosopher as to conjecture. The ancient proverb in Homer, less abstruse, entitles this work of leading each like person to his like, peculiarly to God himself: which is plain enough also by his naming of a meet or like help in the first espousal instituted; and that every woman is meet for every man, none so absurd as to affirm. Seeing then there is a twofold seminary, or stock in nature, from whence are derived the issues of love and hatred, distinctly flowing through the whole mass of created things, and that God's doing ever is to bring the due likenesses and harmonies of his works together, except, when out of two contraries met to their own destruction, he moulds a third existence; and that it is error, or some evil angel which either blindly or maliciously hath drawn together, in two persons ill embarked in wedlock, the sleeping discords and enmities of nature, lulled on purpose with some false bait, that they may wake to agony and strife, later than prevention could have wished, if from the bent of just and honest intentions beginning what was begun and so continuing, all that is equal, all that is fair and possible hath been tried, and no accommodation likely to succeed; what folly is it still to stand combating and battering against invincible causes and effects, with evil upon evil, till either the best of our days be lingered out, or ended with some speeding sorrow! . . . .

If the law allow sin, it enters into a kind of covenant with sin; and if it do, there is not a greater sinner in the world than the law itself. The law, to use an allegory something different from that in Philo Judæus concerning Amalek, though haply more significant, the law is the Israelite, and hath this absolute charge given it, Deut. xxv. "To blot out memory of sin, the Amalekite, from under heaven, not to forget it." Again, the law is the Israelite, and hath this express repeated command, "to make no covenant with sin, the Canaanite," but to expel him, lest he prove a snare. And to say truth, it were too rigid and reasonless to proclaim such an enmity between man and man, were it not the type of a greater enmity between law and sin. I speak even now, as if sin were condemned in a perpetual villanage never to be free by law, never to be manumitted: but sure sin can have no tenure by law, at all, but is rather an eternal outlaw, and in hostility with law past all atonement; both diagonal contraries, as much allowing one another, as day and night together in one hemisphere. Or if it be possible, that sin with his darkness may come to composition, it cannot be without a foul eclipse and twilight to the law, whose brightness ought to surpass the noon. . . . .

If it were such a cursed act of Pilate, a subordinate judge to Cæsar, overswayed by those hard hearts, with much ado to suffer one transgression of law but once; what is it then with less ado to publish a law of transgression for many ages? Did God for this come down and cover the mount of Sinai with his glory, uttering in thunder those his sacred ordinances out of the bottomless treasures of his wisdom and infinite pureness, to patch up an ulcerous and rotten commonwealth with strict and stern injunctions, to wash the skin and garments for every unclean touch; and such easy permission given to pollute the soul with adulteries by public authority, without disgrace or question? . . . .

The hidden ways of his providence we adore and search not, but the law is his revealed will, his complete, his evident and certain will: herein he appears to us, as it were, in human shape, enters into covenant with us, swears to keep it, binds himself like a just lawgiver to his own prescriptions, gives himself to be understood by men, judges and is judged, measures and is commensurate to right reason ; cannot require less of us in one cantle of his law than in another; his legal justice cannot be so fickle and variable, sometimes like a devouring fire, and by and by connivent in the embers, or if I may so say, oscitant and supine. The vigor of his law could no more remit, than the hallowed fire upon his altar could be let go out. The lamps that burned before him might need snuffing, but the light of his law never. . . . .

Whenas the doctrine of Plato and Chrysippus, with their followers, the academics and the stoics, who knew not what a consummate and most adorned Pandora was bestowed upon Adam, to be the nurse and guide of his arbitrary happiness and perseverance, I mean, his native innocence and perfection, which might have kept him from being our true Epimetheus: and though they taught of virtue and vice to be both the gift of divine destiny, they could yet give reasons, not invalid, to justify the councils of God and fate from the insulsity of mortal tongues: that man's own free will self-corrupted, is the adequate and sufficient cause of his disobedience besides fate ; as Homer also wanted not to express, both in his Iliad and Odyssee. And Manilius the poet, although in his fourth book he tells of some "created both to sin and punishment"; yet without murmuring, and with an industrious cheerfulness, he acquits the Deity. They were not ignorant, in their heathen lore, that it is most godlike to punish those who of his creatures became his enemies with the greatest punishment; and they could attain also to think, that the greatest, when God himself throws a man furthest from him; which then they held he did, when he blinded, hardened, and stirred up his offenders, to finish and pile up their desperate work since they had undertaken it. To banish forever into a local hell, whether in the air or in the centre, or in that uttermost and bottomless gulf of chaos, deeper from holy bliss than the world's diameter multiplied; they thought not a punishing so proper and proportionate for God to inflict, as to punish sin with sin. Thus were the common sort of Gentiles wont to think, without any wry thoughts cast upon divine governance. And therefore Cicero, not in his Tusculan or Campanian retirements among the learned wits of that age, but even in the senate to a mixed auditory, (though he were sparing otherwise to broach his philosophy among statists and lawyers,) yet as to this point, both in his Oration against Piso, and in that which is about the answers of the soothsayers against Clodius, he declares it publicly, as no paradox to common ears, that God cannot punish man more, nor make him more miserable, than still by making him more sinful. Thus we see how in this controversy the justice of God stood upright even among heathen disputers. . . . .

But it was not approved. So much the worse that it was allowed; as if sin had overmastered the word of God, to conform her steady and straight rule to sin's crookedness, which is impossible. Besides, what needed a positive grant of that which was not approved? It restrained no liberty to him that could but use a little fraud; it had been better silenced, unless it were approved in some case or other. But still it was not approved. Miserable excusers! he who doth evil, that good may come thereby, approves not what he doth; and yet the grand rule forbids him, and counts his damnation just if he do it. The sorceress Medea did not approve her own evil doings, yet looked not to be excused for that: and it is the constant opinion of Plato in Protagoras, and other of his dialogues, agreeing with that proverbial sentence among the Greeks, that "no man is wicked willingly." Which also the Peripatetics do rather distinguish than deny. What great thank then if any man, reputed wise and constant, will neither do, nor permit others under his charge to do, that which he approves not, especially in matter of sin? but for a judge, but for a magistrate, the shepherd of his people, to surrender up his approbation against law, and his own judgment, to the obstinacy of his herd, what more unjudgelike, unmagistratelike, and in war more uncommanderlike? Twice in a short time it was the undoing of the Roman state, first when Pompey, next when Marcus Brutus, had not magnanimity enough but to make so poor a resignation of what they approved, to what the boisterous tribunes and soldiers bawled for. Twice it was the saving of two of the greatest commonwealths in the world, of Athens by Themistocles at the seafight of Salamis, of Rome by Fabius Maximus in the Punic war; for that these two matchless generals had the fortitude at home, against the rashness and the clamors of their own captains and confederates, to withstand the doing or permitting of what they could not approve in their duty of their great command. Thus far of civil prudence. But when we speak of sin, let us look again upon the old reverend Eli, who in his heavy punishment found no difference between the doing and permitting of what he did not approve. If hardness of heart in the people may be an excuse, why then is Pilate branded through all memory? He approved not what he did, he openly protested, he washed his hands, and labored not a little ere he would yield to the hard hearts of a whole people, both princes and plebeians, importuning and tumulting even to the fear of a revolt.....

The political law, since it cannot regulate vice, is to restrain it by using all means to root it out. But if it suffer the weed to grow up to any pleasurable or contented height upon what pretext soever, it fastens the root, it prunes and dresses vice, as if it were a good plant. Let no man doubt therefore to affirm, that it is not so hurtful or dishonorable to a commonwealth, nor so much to the hardening of hearts, when those worse faults pretended to be feared are committed, by who so dares under strict and executed penalty, as when those less faults tolerated for fear of greater, harden their faces, not their hearts only, under the protection of public authority. For what less indignity were this, than as if justice herself, the queen of virtues, descending from her sceptred royalty, instead of conquering, should compound and treat with sin, her eternal adversary and rebel, upon ignoble terms? or as if the judicial law were like that untrusty steward in the Gospel, and instead of calling in the debts of his moral master, should give out subtile and sly acquittances to keep himself from begging? or let us person him like some wretched itinerary judge, who, to gratify his delinquents before him, would let them basely break his head, lest they should pull him from the bench, and throw him over the bar. Unless we had rather think both moral and judicial, full of malice and deadly purpose, conspired to let the debtor Israelite, the seed of Abraham, run on about a bankrupt score, flattered with insufficient and ensnaring discharges, that so he might be haled to a more cruel forfeit for all the indulgent arrears which those judicial acquittances had engaged him in. No, no, this cannot be, that the law, whose integrity and faithfulness is next to God, should be either the shameless broker of our impunities, or the intended instrument of our destruction. The method of holy correction, such as became the commonwealth of Israel, is not to bribe sin with sin, to capitulate and hire out one crime with another; but with more noble and graceful severity than Popilius the Roman legate used with Antiochus, to limit and level out the direct way from vice to virtue, with straightest and exactest lines on either side, not winding or indenting so much as to the right hand of fair pretences. Violence indeed and insurrection may force the law to suffer what it cannot mend; but to write a decree in allowance of sin, as soon can the hand of justice rot off. Let this be ever concluded as a truth that will outlive the faith of those that seek to bear it down. . . . .

God loves not to plough out the heart of our endeavors with over-hard and sad tasks. God delights not to make a drudge of virtue, whose actions must be all elective and unconstrained. Forced virtue is as a bolt overshot, it goes neither forward nor backward, and does no good as it stands. . . . .

If any, therefore, hath been through misadventure ill engaged in this contracted evil, and finds the fits and workings of a high impatience frequently upon him; of all those wild words which men in misery think to ease themselves by uttering, let him not open his lips against the providence of Heaven, or tax the ways of God and his divine truth; for they are equal, easy and not burdensome; nor do they ever cross the just and reasonable desires of men, nor involve this our portion of mortal life into a necessity of sadness and malcontent, by laws commanding over the unreducible antipathies of nature, sooner or later found, but allow us to remedy and shake off those evils into which human error hath led us through the midst of our best intentions, and to support our incident extremities by that authentic precept of sovereign charity, whose grand commission is to do and to dispose over all the ordinances of God to man, that love and truth may advance each other to everlasting. While we, literally superstitious, through customary faintness of heart, not venturing to pierce with our free thoughts into the full latitude of nature and religion, abandon ourselves to serve under the tyranny of usurped opinions; suffering those ordinances which were allotted to our solace and reviving, to trample over us, and hale us into a multitude of sorrows, which God never meant us. And where he sets us in a fair allowance of way, with honest liberty and prudence to our guard, we never leave subtilizing and casuisting till we have straitened and pared that liberal path into a razor's edge to walk on; between a precipice of unnecessary mischief on either side, and starting at every false alarm, we do not know which way to set a foot forward with manly confidence and Christian resolution, through the confused ringing in our ears of panic scruples and amazements.....

Hate is of all things the mightiest divider; nay, is

division itself. To couple hatred therefore, though wedlock try all her golden links, and borrow to her aid all the iron manacles and fetters of law, it does but seek to twist a rope of sand, which was a task they say that posed the Devil; and that sluggish fiend in hell, Ocnus, whom the poems tell of, brought his idle cordage to as good effect, which never served to bind with, but to feed the ass that stood at his elbow.

FROM

TETRACHORDON.

MEN of most renowned virtue have sometimes by transgressing most truly kept the law; and wisest magistrates have permitted and dispensed it; while they looked not peevishly at the letter, but with a greater spirit at the good of mankind, if always not written in the characters of law, yet engraven in the heart of man by a divine impression. This heathens could see, as the well-read in story can recount of Solon and Epaminondas, whom Cicero, in his first book of "Invention," nobly defends. "All law," saith he, "we ought to refer to the common good, and interpret by that, not by the scroll of letters. No man observes law for law's sake, but for the good of them for whom it was made." The rest might serve well to lecture these times, deluded through belly doctrines into a devout slavery. The Scripture also affords us David in the showbread, Hezekiah in the passover, sound and safe transgressors of the literal command, which also dispensed not seldom with itself; and taught us on what just occasions to do so: until our Saviour, for whom that great and godlike work was reserved, redeemed us to a state above prescriptions, by dissolving the whole law into charity. . . . .

No mortal nature can endure, either in the actions of religion, or study of wisdom, without sometime slackening the cords of intense thought and labor, which, lest we should think faulty, God himself conceals us not his own recreations before the world was built: "I was," saith the Eternal Wisdom, "daily his delight, playing always before him." And to him, indeed, wisdom is as a high tower of pleasure, but to us a steep hill, and we toiling ever about the bottom. He executes with ease the exploits of his omnipotence, as easy as with us it is to will; but no worthy enterprise can be done by us without continual plodding and wearisomeness to our faint and sensitive abilities. We cannot, therefore, always be contemplative, or pragmatical abroad, but have need of some delightful intermissions, wherein the enlarged soul may leave off a while her severe schooling, and, like a glad youth in wandering vacancy, may keep her holidays to joy and harmless pastime; which, as she cannot well do without company, so in no company so well as where the different sex, in most resembling unlikeness, and most unlike resemblance, cannot but please best, and be pleased in the aptitude of that variety. Whereof, lest we should be too timorous, in the awe that our flat sages would form us and dress us, wisest Solomon among his gravest proverbs countenances a kind of ravishment and erring fondness in the entertainment of wedded leisures; and in the Song of Songs, which is generally believed, even in the jolliest expressions, to figure the spousals of the Church with Christ, sings of a thousand raptures between those two lovely ones far on the hither side of carnal enjoyment. By these instances, and more which might be brought, we may imagine how indulgently God provided against man's loneliness; that he approved it not, as by himself declared not good; that he approved the remedy thereof, as of his own ordaining, consequently good; and as he ordained it, so doubtless proportionably to our fallen estate he gives it; else were his ordinance at least in vain, and we for all his gifts still empty handed. . . . .

This I amaze me at, that though all the superior and nobler ends both of marriage and of the married persons be absolutely frustrate, the matrimony stirs not, loses no hold, remains as rooted as the centre: but if the body bring but in a complaint of frigidity, by that cold application only this adamantine Alp of wedlock has leave to dissolve; which else all the machinations of religious or civil reason at the suit of a distressed mind, either for divine worship or human conversation violated, cannot unfasten. What courts of concupiscence are these, wherein fleshly appetite is heard before right reason, lust before love or devotion? They may be pious Christians together, they may be loving and friendly, they may be helpful to each other in the family, but they cannot couple; that shall divorce them, though either party would not. They can neither serve God together, nor one be at peace with the other, nor be good in the family one to other; but live as they were dead, or live as they were deadly enemies in a cage together: it is all one, they can couple, they shall not divorce till death, no, though this sentence be their death. What is this besides tyranny, but to turn nature upside down, to make both religion and the mind of man wait upon the slavish errands of the body, and not the body to follow either the sanctity or the sovereignty of the mind, unspeakably wronged, and with all equity complaining? what is this but to abuse the sacred and mysterious bed of marriage to be the compulsive sty of an ingrateful and malignant lust, stirred up only from a carnal acrimony, without either love or peace, or regard to any other thing holy or human? This I admire, how possibly it should inhabit thus long in the sense of so many disputing theologians, unless it be the lowest lees of a canonical infection liver-grown to their sides, which, perhaps, will never uncling, without the strong abstersive of some heroic magistrate, whose mind, equal to his high office, dares lead him both to know and to do without their frivolous case-putting. . . . .

All arts acknowledge, that then only we know certainly, when we can define; for definition is that which refines the pure essence of things from the circumstance. . . . .

For no other cause did Christ assure us that whatsoever things we bind or slacken on earth, are so in heaven, but to signify that the Christian arbitrement of charity is supreme decider of all controversy, and supreme resolver of all Scripture, not as the pope determines for his own tyranny, but as the Church ought to determine for its own true liberty. . . . . I omit many instances, many proofs and arguments of this kind, which alone would compile a just volume, and shall content me here to have shown briefly, that the great and almost only commandment of the Gospel is, to command nothing against the good of man, and much more no civil command against his civil good. If we understand not this, we are but cracked cymbals, we do but tinkle, we know nothing, we do nothing, all the sweat of our toilsomest obedience will but mock us. And what we suffer superstitiously returns us no thanks. . . . .

In every commonwealth, when it decays, corruption makes two main steps: first, when men cease to do according to the inward and uncompelled actions of virtue, caring only to live by the outward constraint of law, and turn the simplicity of real good into the craft of seeming so by law. To this hypocritical honesty was Rome declined in that age wherein Horace lived, and discovered it to Quintius.

> "Whom do we count a good man, whom but he
> Who keeps the laws and statutes of the Senate?
> Who judges in great suits and controversies?
> Whose witness and opinion wins the cause?
> But his own house, and the whole neighborhood
> Sees his foul inside through his whited skin."

The next declining is, when law becomes now too strait for the secular manners, and those too loose for the cincture of law. This brings in false and crooked interpretations to eke out law, and invents the subtle encroachments of obscure traditions hard to be disproved. . . . .

If these be the limits of law to restrain sin, who so lame a sinner but may hop over them more easily than over those Romulean circumscriptions, not as Remus did, with hard success, but with all indemnity? Such a limiting as this were not worth the mischief that accompanies it. This law therefore, not bounding the supposed sin, by permitting enlarges it, gives it enfranchisement. And never greater confusion, than when law and sin move their landmarks, mix their territories, and correspond, have intercourse, and traffic together. When law contracts a kindred and hospitality with transgression, becomes the godfather of sin, and names it lawful; when sin revels and gossips within the arsenal of law, plays and dandles the artillery of justice that should be bent against her, this is a fair limitation indeed. Besides, it is an absurdity to say that law can measure sin, or moderate sin: sin is not in a predicament to be measured and modified, but is always an excess. The least sin that is exceeds the measure of the largest law that can be good; and is as boundless as that vacuity beyond the world. If once it square to the measure of law, it ceases to be an excess, and consequently ceases to be a sin; or else law, conforming itself to the obliquity of sin, betrays itself to be not straight, but crooked, and so immediately no law. And the improper conceit of moderating sin by law will appear, if we can imagine any lawgiver so senseless as to decree, that so far a man may steal, and thus far be drunk, that moderately he may cozen, and moderately commit adultery. To the same extent it would be as pithily absurd to publish, that a man may moderately divorce, if to do that be entirely naught. But to end this moot: the law of Moses is manifest to fix no limit therein at all, or such at least as impeaches the fraudulent abuser no more than if it were not set; only requires the dismissive writing without other caution, leaves that to the inner man, and the bar of conscience. But it stopped other sins. This is as vain as the rest, and dangerously uncertain: the contrary to be feared rather, that one sin, admitted courteously by law, opened the gate to another. However, evil must not be done for good. And it were a fall to be lamented, and indignity unspeakable, if law should become tributary to sin, her slave, and forced to yield up into his hands her awful minister, punishment; should buy out our peace with sin for sin, paying, as it were, her so many Philistian foreskins to the proud demand of transgression. But suppose it any way possible to limit sin, to put a girdle about that chaos, suppose it also good; yet if to permit sin by law be an abomination in the eyes of God, as Cameron acknowledges, the evil of permitting will eat out the good of limiting. For though sin be not limited, there can but evil come out of evil; but if it be permitted and decreed lawful by divine law, of force then sin must proceed from the Infinite Good, which is a dreadful thought. But if the restraining of sin by this permission being good, as this author testifies, be more good than the permission of more sin by the restraint of divorce, and that God, weighing both these like two ingots, in the perfect scales of his justice and providence, found them so, and others, coming without authority from God, shall change this counterpoise, and judge it better to let sin multiply by setting a judicial restraint upon divorce which Christ never set; then to limit sin by this permission, as God himself thought best to permit it, it will behove them to consult betimes whether these their balances be not false and abominable, and this their limiting that which God loosened, and their loosening the sins that he limited, which they confess was good to do: and were it possible to do by law, doubtless it would be most morally good; and they so believing, as we hear they do, and yet abolishing a law so good and moral, the limiter of sin, what are they else but contrary to themselves? For they can never bring us to that time wherein it will not be good to limit sin, and they can never limit it better than so as God prescribed in his law. . . . .

The New Testament, though it be said originally writ in Greek, yet hath nothing near so many Atticisms as Hebraisms, and Syriacisms, which was the majesty of God, not filing the tongue of Scripture to a Gentilish idiom, but in a princely manner offering to them as to Gentiles and foreigners grace and mercy, though not in foreign words, yet in a foreign style that might induce them to the fountains; and though their calling were high and happy, yet still to acknowledge God's ancient people their betters, and that language the metropolitan language. . . . .

For nature hath her zodiac also, keeps her great annual circuit over human things, as truly as the sun and planets in the firmament; hath her anomalies, hath her obliquities in ascensions and declinations, accesses and recesses, as blamelessly as they in heaven. And sitting in her planetary orb with two reins in each hand, one strait, the other loose, tempers the course of minds as well as bodies to several conjunctions and oppositions, friendly or unfriendly aspects, consenting oftest with reason, but never contrary.

FROM THE

TENURE OF KINGS AND MAGISTRATES.

BAD MEN FAVORABLE TO TYRANTS.

IF men within themselves would be governed by reason, and not generally give up their understanding to a double tyranny, of custom from without, and blind affections within, they would discern better what it is to favor and uphold the tyrant of a nation. But, being slaves within doors, no wonder that they strive so much to have the public state conformably governed to the inward vicious rule by which they govern themselves. For, indeed, none can love freedom heartily but good men; the rest love not freedom but license, which never hath more scope, or more indulgence than under tyrants. Hence is it that tyrants are not oft offended, nor stand much in doubt of bad men, as being all naturally servile; but in whom virtue and true worth most is eminent, them they fear in earnest, as by right their masters; against them lies all their hatred and suspicion. Consequently, neither do bad men hate tyrants, but have been always readiest, with the falsified names of loyalty and obedience, to color over their base compliances.

. . . . .

It is true, that most men are apt enough to civil wars and commotions as a novelty, and for a flash hot and active; but through sloth or inconstancy, and weakness of spirit, either fainting ere their own pretences, though never so just, be half attained, or through an inbred falsehood and wickedness, betray, ofttimes to destruction with themselves, men of noblest temper joined with them for causes whereof they in their rash undertakings were not capable. If God and a good cause give them victory, the prosecution whereof for the most part inevitably draws after it the alteration of laws, change of government, downfall of princes with their families; then comes the task to those worthies which are the soul of that enterprise, to be sweat and labored out amidst the throng and noses of vulgar and irrational men. Some contesting for privileges, customs, forms, and that old entanglement of iniquity, their gibberish laws, though the badge of their ancient slavery. Others, who have been fiercest against their prince, under the notion of a tyrant, and no mean incendiaries of the war against them, when God, out of his providence and high disposal hath delivered him into the hand of their brethren, on a sudden and in a new garb of allegiance, which their doings have long since cancelled, they plead for him, pity him, extol him, protest against those that talk of bringing him to the trial of justice, which is the sword of God, superior to all mortal things, in whose hand soever by apparent signs his testified will is to put it. . . . .

JUSTICE AGAINST THE TYRANT.

But who in particular is a tyrant, cannot be determined in a general discourse, otherwise than by supposition; his particular charge, and the sufficient proof of it, must determine that: which I leave to magistrates, at least to the uprighter sort of them, and of the people, though in number less by many, in whom faction least hath prevailed above the law of nature and right reason, to judge as they find cause. But this I dare own as part of my faith, that if such a one there be, by whose commission whole massacres have been committed on his faithful subjects, his provinces offered to pawn or alienation, as the hire of those whom he had solicited to come in and destroy whole cities and countries; be he king, or tyrant, or emperor, the sword of justice is above him; in whose hand soever is found sufficient power to avenge the effusion, and so great a deluge of innocent blood. For if all human power to execute, not accidentally but intendedly, the wrath of God upon evildoers without exception, be of God: then that power, whether ordinary, or if that fail, extraordinary, so executing that intent of God, is lawful, and not to be resisted. . . . .

THE ORIGIN OF KINGLY GOVERNMENT.

No man, who knows aught, can be so stupid to deny, that all men naturally were born free, being the image and resemblance of God himself, and were, by privilege above all the creatures, born to command, and not to obey: and that they lived so, till from the root of Adam's transgression falling among themselves to do wrong and violence, and foreseeing that such courses must needs tend to the destruction of them all, they agreed by common league to bind each other from mutual injury, and jointly to defend themselves against any that gave disturbance or opposition to such agreement. Hence came cities, towns, and commonwealths. And because no faith in all was found sufficiently binding, they saw it needful to ordain some authority that might restrain by force and punishment what was violated against peace and common right.

This authority and power of self-defence and preservation being originally and naturally in every one of them, and unitedly in them all; for ease, for order, and lest each man should be his own partial judge, they communicated and derived either to one, whom for the eminence of his wisdom and integrity they chose above the rest, or to more than one, whom they thought of equal deserving: the first was called a king; the other, magistrates: not to be their lords and masters, (though afterward those names in some places were given voluntarily to such as had been authors of inestimable good to the people,) but to be their deputies and commissioners, to execute, by virtue of their intrusted power, that justice, which else every man by the bond of nature and of covenant must have executed for himself, and for one another. And to him that shall consider well, why among free persons one man by civil right should bear authority and jurisdiction over another, no other end or reason can be imaginable.

POPULAR CHECKS ON KINGLY POWER.

THESE for a while governed well, and with much equity decided all things at their own arbitrament; till the temptation of such a power, left absolute in their hands, perverted them at length to injustice and partiality. Then did they, who now by trial had found the danger and inconveniences of committing arbitrary power to any, invent laws, either framed or consented to by all, that should confine and limit the authority of whom they chose to govern them: that so man, of whose failing they had proof, might no more rule over them, but law and reason, abstracted as much as might be from personal errors and frailties. "While, as the magistrate was set above the people, so the law was set above the magistrate." When this would not serve, but that the law was either not executed, or misapplied, they were constrained from that time, the only remedy left them, to put conditions and take oaths from all kings and magistrates at their first instalment, to do impartial justice by law: who, upon those terms and no other received allegiance from the people, that is to say, bond or covenant to obey them in execution of those laws, which they, the people, had themselves made or assented to. And this ofttimes with express warning, that if the king or magistrate proved unfaithful to his trust, the people would be disengaged. They added also counsellors and parliaments, not to be only at his beck, but, with him or without him, at set times, or at all times, when any danger threatened, to have care of the public safety. . . . .

KINGS ACCOUNTABLE TO LAW.

To say kings are accountable to none but God, is the overturning of all law and government. For if they may refuse to give account, then all covenants made with them at coronation, all oaths are in vain, and mere mockeries; all laws which they swear to keep, made to no purpose: for if the king fear not God, (as how many of them do not,) we hold then our lives and estates by the tenure of his mere grace and mercy, as from a god, not a mortal magistrate: a position that none but court-parasites or men besotted would maintain! Aristotle, therefore, whom we commonly allow for one of the best interpreters of nature and morality, writes in the fourth of his Politics, chap. x. that "monarchy unaccountable is the worst sort of tyranny, and least of all to be endured by free-born men."

And surely no Christian prince, not drunk with high mind, and prouder than those pagan Cæsars that deified themselves, would arrogate so unreasonably above human condition, or derogate so basely from a whole nation of men, his brethren, as if for him only subsisting, and to serve his glory, valuing them in comparison of his own brute will and pleasure no more than so many beasts, or vermin under his feet, not to be reasoned with, but to be trod on; among whom there might be found so many thousand men for wisdom, virtue, nobleness of mind, and all other respects but the fortune of his dignity, far above him. Yet some would persuade us that this absurd opinion was King David's, because in the 51st Psalm he cries out to God, "Against thee only have I sinned"; as if David had imagined, that to murder Uriah and adulterate his wife had been no sin against his neighbor, whenas that law of Moses was to the king expressly, (Deut. xvii.,) not to think so highly of himself above his brethren. David, therefore, by those words, could mean no other, than either that the depth of his guiltiness was known to God only, or to so few as had not the will or power to question him, or that the sin against God was greater beyond compare than against Uriah. Whatever his meaning were, any wise man will see, that the pathetical words of a psalm can be no certain decision to a point that hath abundantly more certain rules to go by.

How much more rationally spoke the heathen king Demophoön, in a tragedy of Euripides, than these interpreters would put upon King David! "I rule not my people by tyranny, as if they were barbarians; but am myself liable, if I do unjustly, to suffer justly." Not unlike was the speech of Trajan, the worthy emperor, to one whom he made general of his prætorian forces: "Take this drawn sword," saith he, "to use for me if I reign well; if not, to use against me." Thus Dion relates. And not Trajan only, but Theodosius, the younger, a Christian emperor, and one of the best, caused it to be enacted, as a rule undeniable and fit to be acknowledged by all kings and emperors, that a prince is bound to the laws; that on the authority of law the authority of a prince depends, and to the laws ought to submit. Which edict of his remains yet unrepealed in the Code of Justinian, (l. I. tit. 24,) as a sacred constitution to all the succeeding emperors. How can any king in

Europe maintain and write himself accountable to none but God, when emperors in their own imperial statutes have written and decreed themselves accountable to law? And indeed, where such account is not feared, he that bids a man reign over him above law, may bid as well a savage beast.

POWER OF CHANGE RESIDES WITH THE PEOPLE.

SINCE the king or magistrate holds his authority of the people, both originally and naturally for their good, in the first place, and not his own, then may the people, as oft as they shall judge it for the best, either choose him or reject him, retain him or depose him, though no tyrant, merely by the liberty and right of freeborn men to be governed as seems to them best. This, though it cannot but stand with plain reason, shall be made good also by Scripture: (Deut. xvii. 14:) "When thou art come into the land which the Lord thy God giveth thee, and shalt say, I will set a king over me, like as all the nations about me." These words confirm us that the right of choosing, yea of changing their own government, is by the grant of God himself in the people. And therefore when they desired a king, though then under another form of government, and though their changing displeased him, yet he that was himself their king, and rejected by them, would not be a hinderance to what they intended, further than by persuasion, but that they might do therein as they saw good, (1 Sam. viii.,) only he reserved to himself the nomination of who should reign over them. Neither did that exempt the king, as if he were to God only accountable, though by his especial command anointed. Therefore "David first made a covenant with the elders of Israel, and so was by them anointed king." (2 Sam. v. 3; 1 Chron. xi.) And Jehoiada the priest, making Jehoash king, made a covenant between him and the people. (2 Kings, xi. 17.) Therefore when Roboam, at his coming to the crown, rejected those conditions which the Israelites brought him, hear what they answer him: "What portion have we in David, or inheritance in the son of Jesse? See to thine own house, David." And for the like conditions not performed, all Israel before that time deposed Samuel; not for his own default, but for the misgovernment of his sons.

RIGHT OF TYRANNICIDE.

We may from hence with more ease and force of argument determine what a tyrant is, and what the people may do against him. A tyrant, whether by wrong or by right coming to the crown, is he who, regarding neither law nor the common good, reigns only for himself and his faction: thus St. Basil, among others, defines him. And because his power is great, his will boundless and exorbitant, the fulfilling whereof is for the most part accompanied with innumerable wrongs and oppressions of the people, murders, massacres, rapes, adulteries, desolation, and subversion of cities and whole provinces; look how great a good and happiness a just king is, so great a mischief is a tyrant; as he the public father of his country, so this the common enemy. Against whom what the people lawfully may do, as against a common pest and destroyer of mankind, I suppose no man of clear judgment need go further to be guided than by the very principles of nature in him.

But because it is the vulgar folly of men to desert their own reason, and, shutting their eyes, to think they see best with other men's, I shall show, by such examples as ought to have most weight with us, what hath been done in this case heretofore. The Greeks and Romans, as their prime authors witness, held it not only lawful, but a glorious and heroic deed, rewarded publicly with statues and garlands, to kill an infamous tyrant at any time without trial; and but reason, that he who trod down all law should not be vouchsafed the benefit of law. Insomuch that Seneca, the tragedian, brings in Hercules, the grand suppressor of tyrants, thus speaking: —

> "Victima haud ulla amplior
> Potest, magisque opima mactari Jovi
> Quam rex iniquus."

> "There can be slain
> No sacrifice to God more acceptable
> Than an unjust and wicked king."

But of these I name no more, lest it be objected they were heathen; and come to produce another sort of men, that had the knowledge of true religion. Among the Jews this custom of tyrant-killing was not unusual. First, Ehud, a man whom God had raised to deliver Israel from Eglon, king of Moab, who had conquered and ruled over them eighteen years, being sent to him as an ambassador with a present, slew him in his own house. But he was a foreign prince, an enemy, and Ehud besides had special warrant from God. To the first I answer, it imports not whether foreign or native: for no prince so native but professes to hold by law; which, when he himself overturns, breaking all the covenants and oaths that gave title to his dignity, and were the bond and alliance between him and his people, what differs he from an outlandish king, or from an enemy? . . . .

There is nothing that so actually makes a king of England, as rightful possession and supremacy in all causes both civil and ecclesiastical: and nothing that so actually makes a subject of England, as those two oaths of allegiance and supremacy, observed without equivocating, or any mental reservation. Out of doubt then, when the king shall command things already constituted in church or state, obedience is the true essence of a subject, either to do, if it be lawful, or if he hold the thing unlawful, to submit to that penalty which the law imposes, so long as he intends to remain a subject.

Therefore when the people, or any part of them, shall rise against the king and his authority, executing the law in anything established, civil or ecclesiastical, I do not say it is rebellion, if the thing commanded though established be unlawful, and that they sought first all due means of redress; (and no man is further bound to law;) but I say it is an absolute renouncing both of supremacy and allegiance, which, in one word, is an actual and total deposing of the king, and the setting up of another supreme authority over them. . . . .

If then, their oaths of subjection broken, new supremacy obeyed, new oaths and covenant taken, notwithstanding frivolous evasions, have in plain terms unkinged the king, much more than hath their seven years' war, not deposed him only, but outlawed him, and defied him as an alien, a rebel to law, and enemy to the state, it must needs be clear to any man, not averse from reason, that hostility and subjection are two direct and positive contraries, and can no more in one subject stand together in respect of the same king, than one person at the same time can be in two remote places. Against whom therefore the subject is in act of hostility, we may be confident, that to him he is in no subjection: and in whom hostility takes place of subjection, for they can by no means consist together, to him the king can be not only no king, but an enemy.

So that from hence we shall not need dispute,

whether they have deposed him, or what they have defaulted towards him as no king, but show manifestly how much they have done towards the killing him. Have they not levied all these wars against him, whether offensive or defensive, (for defence in war equally offends, and most prudently beforehand,) and given commission to slay, where they knew his person could not be exempt from danger? And if chance or flight had not saved him, how often had they killed him, directing their artillery, without blame or prohibition, to the very place where they saw him stand? Have they not sequestered him, judged or unjudged, and converted his revenue to other uses, detaining from him, as a grand delinquent, all means of livelihood, so that for them long since he might have perished, or have starved? Have they not hunted and pursued him round about the kingdom with sword and fire? Have they not formerly denied to treat with him, and their now recanting ministers preached against him, as a reprobate incurable, an enemy to God and his Church, marked for destruction, and therefore not to be treated with? Have they not besieged him, and to their power forbid him water and fire, save what they shot against him to the hazard of his life?

RIGHTS AND POWERS OF A FREE NATION.

But God, as we have cause to trust, will put other thoughts into the people, and turn them from giving ear or heed to these mercenary noisemakers, of whose fury and false prophecies we have enough experience; and from the murmurs of new discord will incline them to hearken rather with erected minds to the voice of our supreme magistracy, calling us to liberty, and the flourishing deeds of a reformed commonwealth; with this hope, that as God was heretofore angry with the Jews who rejected him and his form of government to choose a king, so that he will bless us, and be propitious to us, who reject a king to make him only our leader, and supreme governor, in the conformity, as near as may be, of his own ancient government; if we have at least but so much worth in us to entertain the sense of our future happiness, and the courage to receive what God vouchsafes us; wherein we have the honor to precede other nations, who are now laboring to be our followers.

For as to this question in hand, what the people by their just right may do in change of government, or of governor, we see it cleared sufficiently besides other ample authority even from the mouths of princes themselves. And surely they that shall boast, as we do, to be a free nation, and not have in themselves the power to remove or abolish any governor supreme, or subordinate, with the government itself upon urgent causes, may please their fancy with a ridiculous and painted freedom, fit to cozen babies; but we are indeed under tyranny and servitude, as wanting that power, which is the root and source of all liberty, to dispose and economize in the land which God hath given them, as masters of family in their own house and free inheritance. Without which natural and essential power of a free nation, though bearing high their heads, they can in due esteem be thought no better than slaves and vassals born, in the tenure and occupation of another inheriting lord; whose government, though not illegal, or intolerable, hangs over them as a lordly scourge, not as a free government; and therefore to be abrogated.

How much more justly then may they fling off tyranny, or tyrants; who being once deposed can be no more than private men, as subject to the reach of justice and arraignment as any other transgressors? And certainly if men, not to speak of heathen, both wise and religious, have done justice upon tyrants what way they could soonest, how much more mild and humane then is it, to give them fair and open trial; to teach lawless kings, and all who so much adore them, that not mortal man, or his imperious will, but justice, is the only true sovereign and supreme majesty upon earth? Let men cease therefore, out of faction and hypocrisy, to make outcries and horrid things of things so just and honorable. Though perhaps till now, no Protestant state or kingdom can be alleged to have openly put to death their king, which lately some have written, and imputed to their great glory; much mistaking the matter. It is not, neither ought to be, the glory of a Protestant state never to have put their king to death; it is the glory of a Protestant king never to have deserved death. And if the Parliament and military council do what they do without precedent, if it appear their duty, it argues the more wisdom, virtue, and magnanimity, that they know themselves able to be a precedent to others; who perhaps, in future ages, if they prove not too degenerate, will look up with honor, and aspire towards these exemplary and matchless deeds of their ancestors, as to the highest top of their civil glory and emulation; which heretofore, in the pursuance of fame and foreign dominion, spent itself vaingloriously abroad; but henceforth may learn a better fortitude, to dare execute highest justice on them that shall by force of arms endeavor the oppressing and bereaving of religion and their liberty at home. That no unbridled potentate or tyrant, but to his sorrow, for the future may presume such high and irresponsible license over mankind, to havoc and turn upside down whole kingdoms of men, as though they were no more in respect of his perverse will than a nation of pismires. . . . .

For divines if we observe them have their postures, and their motions no less expertly, and with no less variety, than they that practice feats in the Artillery-ground. Sometimes they seem furiously to march on, and presently march counter; by and by they stand, and then retreat; or, if need be, can face about, or wheel in a whole body, with that cunning and dexterity as is almost unperceivable, to wind themselves by shifting ground into places of more advantage. And providence only must be the drum, providence the word of command, that calls them from above, but always to some larger benefice, or acts them into such or such figures and promotions. At their turns and doublings no men readier, to the right, or to the left; for it is their turns which they serve chiefly; herein only singular, that with them there is no certain hand, right or left, but as their own commodity thinks best to call it. But if there come a truth to be defended, which to them and their interest of this world seems not so profitable, straight these nimble motionists can find not even legs to stand upon; and are no more of use to reformation thoroughly performed, and not superficially, or to the advancement of truth, (which among mortal men is always in her progress,) than if on a sudden they were struck maim and crippled. Which the better to conceal, or the more to countenance by a general conformity to their own limping, they would have Scripture, they would have reason also, made to halt with them for company; and would put us off with impotent conclusions, lame and shorter than the premises.

In this posture they seem to stand with great zeal and confidence on the wall of Sion; but like Jebusites, not like Israelites, or Levites: blind also as well as lame, they discern not David from Adonibezec: but cry him up for the lord's anointed, whose thumbs and great toes not long before they had cut off upon their pulpit cushions. Therefore he who is our only King, the Root of David, and whose kingdom is eternal righteousness, with all those that war under him, whose happiness and final hopes are laid up in that only just and rightful kingdom, (which we pray incessantly may come soon, and in so praying wish hasty ruin and destruction to all tyrants,) even he our immortal King, and all that love him, must of necessity have in abomination these blind and lame defenders of Jerusalem, as the soul of David hated them, and forbid them entrance into God's house, and his own. But as to those before them, ... being the best and chief of Protestant divines, we may follow them for faithful guides, and without doubting may receive them, as witnesses abundant of what we here affirm concerning tyrants. And indeed I find it generally the clear and positive determination of them all, (not prelatical, or of this late faction sub-prelatical,) who have written on this argument, that to do justice on a lawless king is to a private man unlawful; to an inferior magistrate, lawful.

FROM

OBSERVATIONS ON THE ARTICLES OF PEACE, &c.

HE accuses first, "That we are the subverters of religion, the protectors and inviters not only of all false ones, but of irreligion and atheism"; an accusation that no man living could more unjustly use than our accuser himself; and which, without a strange besottedness, he could not expect but to be retorted upon his own head; all men who are true Protestants, of which number he gives out to be one, know not a more immediate and killing subverter of all true religion than Antichrist, whom they generally believe to be the pope and Church of Rome; he therefore, who makes peace with this grand enemy and persecutor of the true Church, he who joins with him, strengthens him, gives him root to grow up and spread his poison, removing all opposition against him, granting him schools, abbeys, and revenues, garrisons, towns, fortresses, as in so many of those articles may be seen, he of

* James, Earl of Ormond, Lord Lieutenant of Ireland.

all Protestants may be called most justly the subverter of true religion, the protector and inviter of irreligion and atheism, whether it be Ormond or his master. And if it can be no way proved that the Parliament hath countenanced Popery or Papists, but have everywhere broken their temporal power, thrown down their public superstitions, and confined them to the bare enjoyment of that which is not in our reach, their consciences; if they have encouraged all true ministers of the Gospel, that is to say, afforded them favor and protection in all places where they preached, and although they think not money or stipend to be the best encouragement of a true pastor, yet therein also have not been wanting nor intend to be, they doubt not then to affirm themselves, not the subverters, but the maintainers and defenders, of true religion; which of itself and by consequence is the surest and the strongest subversion, not only of all false ones, but of irreligion and atheism. For "the weapons of that warfare," as the apostle testifies, who best knew, "are not carnal, but mighty through God to the pulling down of strongholds, and all reasonings, and every high thing exalted against the knowledge of God, surprising every thought unto the obedience of Christ, and easily revenging all disobedience." 2 Cor. x. What minister or clergyman, that either understood his high calling, or sought not to erect a secular and carnal tyranny over spiritual things, would neglect this ample and sublime power conferred upon him, and come a-begging to the weak hand of magistracy for that kind of aid which the magistrate hath no commission to afford him, and in the way he seeks it hath been always found helpless and unprofitable. Neither is it unknown, or by wisest men unobserved, that the Church began then most apparently, to degenerate, and go to ruin, when she borrowed of the civil power more than fair encouragement and protection, more than which Christ himself and his apostles never required. To say, therefore, that we protect and invite all false religions, with irreligion also and atheism, because we lend not, or rather misapply not, the temporal power to help out, though in vain, the sloth, the spleen, the insufficiency of churchmen, in the execution of spiritual discipline over those within their charge, or those without, is an imputation that may be laid as well upon the best regulated states and governments through the world; who have been so prudent as never to employ the civil sword further than the edge of it could reach, that is, to civil offences only; proving always against objects that were spiritual a ridiculous weapon. Our protection therefore to men in civil matters unoffensive we cannot deny; their consciences we leave, as not within our cognizance, to the proper cure of instruction, praying for them. Nevertheless, if any be found among us declared atheists, malicious enemies of God, and of Christ; the Parliament, I think, professes not to tolerate such, but with all befitting endeavors to suppress them. Otherways to protect none that in a larger sense may be taxed of irreligion and atheism, may perhaps be the ready way to exclude none sooner out of protection, than those themselves that most accuse it to be so general to others. Lastly, that we invite such as these, or encourage them, is a mere slander without proof.

FROM

EIKONOKLASTES.

BUT the people, exorbitant and excessive in all their motions, are prone ofttimes not to a religious only, but to a civil kind of idolatry, in idolizing their kings: though never more mistaken in the object of their worship; heretofore being wont to repute for saints those faithful and courageous barons, who lost their lives in the field, making glorious war against tyrants for the common liberty; as Simon de Montfort, Earl of Leicester, against Henry III.; Thomas Plantagenet, Earl of Lancaster, against Edward II. But now, with a besotted and degenerate baseness of spirit, except some few who yet retain in them the old English fortitude and love of freedom, and have testified it by their matchless deeds, the rest, imbastardized from the ancient nobleness of their ancestors, are ready to fall flat, and give adoration to the image and memory of this man, who hath offered at more cunning fetches to undermine our liberties, and put tyranny into an art, than any British king before him. Which low dejection and debasement of mind in the people, I must confess, I cannot willingly ascribe to the natural disposition of an Englishman, but rather to two other causes; first, to the prelates and their fellow-teachers, though of another name and sect, whose pulpit-stuff, both first and last, hath been the doctrine and perpetual infusion of servility and wretchedness to all their hearers, and whose lives, the type of worldliness and hypocrisy, without the least true pattern of virtue, righteousness, or self-denial in their whole practice. I attribute it, next, to the factious inclination of most men, divided from the public by several ends and humors of their own. . . . .

I NEVER knew that time in England, when men of truest religion were not counted sectaries: but wisdom now, valor, justice, constancy, prudence united and embodied to defend religion and our liberties, both by word and deed, against tyranny, is counted schism and faction.

Thus in a graceless age things of highest praise and imitation under a right name, to make them infamous and hateful to the people, are miscalled. Certainly, if ignorance and perverseness will needs be national and universal, then they who adhere to wisdom and to truth, are not therefore to be blamed, for being so few as to seem a sect or faction. But in my opinion it goes not ill with that people where these virtues grow so numerous and well joined together, as to resist and make head against the rage and torrent of that boisterous folly and superstition, that possesses and hurries on the vulgar sort. This therefore we may conclude to be a high honor done us from God, and a special mark of his favor, whom he hath selected as the sole remainder, after all these changes and commotions, to stand upright and steadfast in his cause; dignified with the defence of truth and public liberty; while others, who aspired to be the top of zealots, and had almost brought religion to a kind of trading monopoly, have not only by their late silence and neutrality belied their profession, but foundered themselves and their consciences, to comply with enemies in that wicked cause and interest, which they have too often cursed in others, to prosper now in the same themselves. . . . .

"He hoped by his freedom and their moderation to prevent misunderstandings." * And wherefore not by their freedom and his moderation? But freedom he thought too high a word for them, and moderation too mean a word for himself: this was not the way to prevent misunderstandings. He still "feared passion and prejudice in other men"; not in himself: "and doubted not by the weight of his" own "reason, to counterpoise any faction";

* This and quotations following are from the Eikon Basilikè, which claimed to have been written by Charles I.

it being so easy for him, and so frequent, to call his obstinacy reason, and other men's reason, faction. We in the mean while must believe that wisdom and all reason came to him by title with his crown; passion, prejudice, and faction came to others by being subjects.

"He was sorry to hear, with what popular heat elections were carried in many places." Sorry rather, that court-letters and intimations prevailed no more, to divert or to deter the people from their free election of those men whom they thought best affected to religion and their country's liberty, both at that time in danger to be lost. And such men they were, as by the kingdom were sent to advise him, not sent to be cavilled at, because elected, or to be entertained by him with an undervalue and misprision of their temper, judgment, or affection. In vain was a Parliament thought fittest by the known laws of our nation, to advise and regulate unruly kings, if they, instead of hearkening to advice, should be permitted to turn it off, and refuse it by vilifying and traducing their advisers, or by accusing of a popular heat those that lawfully elected them. . . . .

AND this is the substance of his first section, till we come to the devout of it, modelled into the form of a private psalter. Which they who so much admire, either for the matter or the manner, may as well admire the archbishop's late breviary, and many other as good manuals and handmaids of devotion, the lip-work of every prelatical liturgist, clapped together and quilted out of Scripture phrase, with as much ease and as little need of Christian diligence or judgment, as belongs to the compiling of any ordinary and salable piece of English divinity, that the shops value. But he who, from such a kind of psalmistry, or any other verbal devotion, without the pledge and earnest of suitable deeds, can be persuaded of a zeal and true righteousness in the person, hath much yet to learn; and knows not that the deepest policy of a tyrant hath been ever to counterfeit religious. And Aristotle, in his Politics, hath mentioned that special craft among twelve other tyrannical sophisms. Neither want we examples: Andronicus Comnenus, the Byzantine emperor, though a most cruel tyrant, is reported by Nicetas to have been a constant reader of Saint Paul's Epistles; and by continual study had so incorporated the phrase and style of that transcendent apostle into all his familiar letters, that the imitation seemed to vie with the original. Yet this availed not to deceive the people of that empire, who, notwithstanding his saint's vizard, tore him to pieces for his tyranny.

From stories of this nature both ancient and modern which abound, the poets also, and some English, have been in this point so mindful of decorum, as to put never more pious words in the mouth of any person, than of a tyrant. I shall not instance an abstruse author, wherein the king might be less conversant, but one whom we well know was the closest companion of these his solitudes, William Shakespeare; who introduces the person of Richard the Third, speaking in as high a strain of piety and mortification as is uttered in any passage of this book, and sometimes to the same sense and purpose with some words in this place: "I intended," saith he, "not only to oblige my friends, but my enemies." The like saith Richard, act ii. scene 1:

> "I do not know that Englishman alive,
> With whom my soul is any jot at odds,
> More than the infant that is born to-night;
> I thank my God for my humility."

Other stuff of this sort may be read throughout the whole tragedy, wherein the poet used not much license in departing from the truth of history, which delivers him a deep dissembler, not of his affections only, but of religion.

In praying, therefore, and in the outward work of devotion, this king we see hath not at all exceeded the worst of kings before him. But herein the worst of kings, professing Christianism, have by far exceeded him. They, for aught we know, have still prayed their own, or at least borrowed from fit authors. But this king, not content with that which, although in a thing holy, is no holy theft, to attribute to his own making other men's whole prayers, hath as it were unhallowed and unchristened the very duty of prayer itself, by borrowing to a Christian use prayers offered to a heathen god. Who would have imagined so little fear in him of the true all-seeing Deity, so little reverence of the Holy Ghost, whose office is to dictate and present our Christian prayers, so little care of truth in his last words, or honor to himself, or to his friends, or sense of his afflictions, or of that sad hour which was upon him, as immediately before his death to pop into the hand of that grave bishop who attended him, for a special relique of his saintly exercises, a prayer stolen word for word from the mouth of a heathen woman praying to a heathen god; and that in no serious book, but the vain amatorious poem of Sir Philip Sidney's Arcadia; a book in that kind full of worth and wit, but among religious thoughts and duties not worthy to be named; nor to be read at any time without good caution, much less in time of trouble and affliction to be a Christian's prayer-book? . . . .

However, to the benefit of others much more worth the gaining, I shall proceed in my assertion; that if only but to taste wittingly of meat or drink offered to an idol be in the doctrine of St. Paul judged a pollution, much more must be his sin who takes a prayer so dedicated into his mouth and offers it to God. Yet hardly can it be thought upon (though how sad a thing!) without some kind of laughter at the manner and solemn transaction of so gross a cozenage, that he, who had trampled over us so stately and so tragically, should leave the world at last so ridiculously in his exit, as to bequeath among his deifying friends that stood about him such a precious piece of mockery to be published by them, as must needs cover both his and their heads with shame, if they have any left. Certainly, they that will may now see at length how much they were deceived in him, and were ever like to be hereafter, who cared not, so near the minute of his death, to deceive his best and dearest friends with the trumpery of such a prayer, not more secretly than shamefully purloined; yet given them as the royal issue of his own proper zeal. And sure it was the hand of God to let them fall, and be taken in such a foolish trap, as hath exposed them to all derision; if for nothing else, to throw contempt and disgrace in the sight of all men upon this his idolized book, and the whole rosary of his prayers; thereby testifying how little he accepted them from those who thought no better of the living God than of a buzzard idol, fit to be so served and worshipped in reversion, with the polluted orts and refuse of Arcadias and romances, without being able to discern the affront rather than the worship of such an ethnic prayer.

But leaving what might justly be offensive to God, it was a trespass also more than usual against human right, which commands, that every author should have the property of his own work reserved to him after death, as well as living. Many princes have been rigorous in laying taxes on their subjects by the head; but of any king heretofore that made a levy upon their wit, and seized it as his own legitimate, I have not whom besides to instance. True it is, I looked rather to have found him gleaning out of books written purposely to help devotion. And if, in likelihood, he had borrowed much more out of prayer-books than out of pastorals, then are these painted feathers, that set him off so gay among the people, to be thought few or none of them his own. But if from his divines he have borrowed nothing, nothing out of all the magazine, and the rheum of their mellifluous prayers and meditations, let them who now mourn for him as for Thammuz, them who howl in their pulpits, and by their howling declare themselves right wolves, remember and consider, in the midst of their hideous faces, when they do only not cut their flesh for him like those rueful priests whom Elijah mocked, that he who was once their Ahab, now their Josiah, though feigning outwardly to reverence churchmen, yet here hath so extremely set at naught both them and their praying faculty, that, being at a loss himself what to pray in captivity, he consulted neither with the liturgy, nor with the directory, but, neglecting the huge fardell of all their honeycomb devotions, went directly where he doubted not to find better praying to his mind with Pamela, in the Countess's Arcadia.

What greater argument of disgrace and ignominy could have been thrown with cunning upon the whole clergy, than that the king, among all his priestery, and all those numberless volumes of their theological distillations, not meeting with one man or book of that coat that could befriend him with a prayer in captivity, was forced to rob Sir Philip and his captive shepherdess of their heathen orisons, to supply in any fashion his miserable indigence, not of bread, but of a single prayer to God? I say therefore not of bread, for that want may befall a good man, and yet not make him totally miserable: but he who wants a prayer to beseech God in his necessity, it is inexpressible how poor he is; far poorer within himself than all his enemies can make him. And the unfitness, the indecency of that pitiful supply which he sought, expresses yet further the deepness of his poverty.

Thus much be said in general to his prayers, and in special to that Arcadian prayer used in his captivity; enough to undeceive us what esteem we are to set upon the rest. For he certainly, whose mind could serve him to seek a Christian prayer out of a pagan legend, and assume it for his own, might gather up the rest God knows from whence; one perhaps out of the French Astræa, another out of the Spanish Diana; Amadis and Palmerin could hardly scape him. Such a person we may be sure had it not in him to make a prayer of his own, or at least would excuse himself the pains and cost of his invention, so long as such sweet rhapsodies of heathenism and knight-errantry could yield him prayers. How dishonorable then, and how unworthy of a Christian king, were these ignoble shifts to seem holy, and to get a saintship among the ignorant and wretched people; to draw them by this deception, worse than all his former injuries, to go a whoring after him! And how unhappy, how forsook of grace, and unbeloved of God that people who resolve to know no more of piety or of goodness, than to account him their chief saint and martyr, whose bankrupt devotion came not honestly by his very prayers; but having sharked them from the mouth of a heathen worshipper, (detestable to teach him prayers!) sold them to those that stood and honored him next to the Messiah, as his own heavenly compositions in adversity; for hopes no less vain and presumptuous (and death at that time so imminent upon him) than by these goodly reliques to be held a saint and martyr in opinion with the cheated people!

And thus far in the whole chapter we have seen and considered, and it cannot but be clear to all men, how, and for what ends, what concernments and necessities, the late king was no way induced, but every way constrained, to call this last Parliament; yet here in his first prayer he trembles not to avouch, as in the ears of God, "That he did it with an upright intention to his glory, and his people's good": of which dreadful attestation, how sincerely meant, God, to whom it was avowed, can only judge; and he hath judged already, and hath written his impartial sentence in characters legible to all Christendom; and besides hath taught us, that there be some, whom he hath given over to delusion, whose very mind and conscience is defiled; of whom St. Paul to Titus makes mention. . . . .

But let us hear what that sin was that lay so sore upon him, and, as one of his prayers given to Dr. Juxon testifies, to the very day of his death; it was his signing the bill of Strafford's execution; a man whom all men looked upon as one of the boldest and most impetuous instruments that the King had to advance any violent or illegal design. . . . .

No marvel, then, if being as deeply criminous as the Earl himself, it stung his conscience to adjudge to death those misdeeds, whereof himself had been the chief author: no marvel though, instead of blaming and detesting his ambition, his evil counsel, his violence, and oppression of the people, he fall to praise his great abilities; and with scholastic flourishes, beneath the decency of a king, compares him to the sun, which in all figurative use and significance bears allusion to a king, not to a subject: no marvel though he knit contradictions as close as words can lie together, "not approving in his judgment," and yet approving in his subsequent reason, all that Strafford did, as "driven by the necessity of times, and the temper of that people"; for this excuses all his misdemeanors. Lastly, no marvel that he goes on building many fair and pious conclusions upon false and wicked premises, which deceive the common reader, not well discerning the antipathy of such connections: but this is the marvel, and may be the astonishment, of all that have a conscience, how he durst in the sight of God (and with the same words of contrition wherewith David repents the murdering of Uriah) repent his lawful compliance to that just act of not saving him, whom he ought to have delivered up to speedy punishment, though himself the guiltier of the two.

If the deed were so sinful, to have put to death so great a malefactor, it would have taken much doubtless from the heaviness of his sin, to have told God in his confession how he labored, what dark plots he had contrived, into what a league entered, and with what conspirators, against his Parliament and kingdoms, to have rescued from the claim of justice so notable and so dear an instrument of tyranny; which would have been a story, no doubt, as pleasing in the ears of heaven, as all these equivocal repentances. For it was fear, and nothing else, which made him feign before both the scruple and the satisfaction of his conscience, that is to say, of his mind: his first fear pretended conscience, that he might be borne with to refuse signing; his latter fear, being more urgent, made him find a conscience both to sign and to be satisfied. As for repentance, it came not on him till a long time after; when he saw "he could have suffered nothing more, though he had denied that bill." For how could he understandingly repent of letting that be treason, which the Parliament and whole nation so judged? This was that which repented him, to have given up to just punishment so stout a champion of his designs, who might have been so useful to him in his following civil broils. It was a worldly repentance, not a conscientious; or else it was a strange tyranny, which his conscience had got over him, to vex him like an evil spirit for doing one act of justice, and by that means to "fortify his resolution" from ever doing so any more. That mind must needs be irrecoverably depraved, which, either by chance or importunity, tasting but once of one just deed, spatters at it, and abhors the relish ever after.

To the Scribes and Pharisees woe was denounced by our Saviour, for straining at a gnat and swallowing a camel, though a gnat were to be strained at: but to a conscience with whom one good is so hard to pass down as to endanger almost a choking, and bad deeds without number, though as big and bulky as the ruin of three kingdoms, go down currently without straining, certainly a far greater woe appertains. If his conscience were come to that unnatural dyscrasy, as to digest poison and to keck at wholesome food, it was not for the Parliament or any of his kingdoms to feed with him any longer. Which to conceal he would persuade us, that the Parliament also in their conscience escaped not "some touches of remorse" for putting Strafford to death, in forbidding it by an after-act to be a precedent for the future. But, in a fairer construction, that act implied rather a desire in them to pacify the king's mind, whom they perceived by this means quite alienated: in the mean while not imagining that this after-act should be retorted on them to tie up justice for the time to come upon like occasion, whether this were made a precedent or not, no more than the want of such a precedent, if it had been wanting, had been available to hinder this.

But how likely is it, that this after-act argued in the Parliament their least repenting for the death of Strafford, when it argued so little in the king himself; who, notwithstanding this after-act, which had his own hand and concurrence, if not his own instigation, within the same year accused of high-treason no less than six members at once for the same pretended crimes, which his conscience would not yield to think treasonable in the earl? So that this his subtle argument to fasten a repenting, and, by that means, a guiltiness of Strafford's death upon the Parliament, concludes upon his own head; and shows us plainly, that either nothing in his judgment was treason against the commonwealth, but only against the king's person, (a tyrannical principle!) or that his conscience was a perverse and prevaricating conscience, to scruple that the commonwealth should punish for treasonous in one eminent offender that which he himself sought so vehemently to have punished in six guiltless persons. If this were "that touch of conscience, which he bore with greater regret" than for any sin committed in his life, whether it were that proditory aid sent to Rochelle and religion abroad, or that prodigality of shedding blood at home, to a million of his subjects' lives not valued in comparison to one Strafford; we may consider yet at last, what true sense and feeling could be in that conscience, and what fitness to be the master-conscience of three kingdoms.

But the reason why he labors, that we should take notice of so much "tenderness and regret in his soul for having any hand in Strafford's death," is worth the marking ere we conclude: "he hoped it would be some evidence before God and man to all posterity, that he was far from bearing that vast load and guilt of blood" laid upon him by others: which hath the likeness of a subtle dissimulation; bewailing the blood of one man, his commodious instrument, put to death, most justly, though by him unwillingly, that we might think him too tender to shed willingly the blood of those thousands whom he counted rebels. And thus by dipping voluntarily his finger's end, yet with show of great remorse, in the blood of Strafford, whereof all men clear him, he thinks to scape that sea of innocent blood, wherein his own guilt inevitably hath plunged him all over. And we may well perceive to what easy satisfactions and purgations he had inured his secret conscience, who thought by such weak policies and ostentations as these to gain belief and absolution from understanding men. . . . .

That the king was so emphatical and elaborate on this theme against tumults, and expressed with such a vehemence his hatred of them, will redound less perhaps than he was aware to the commendation of his government. For, besides that in good governments they happen seldomest, and rise not without cause, if they prove extreme and pernicious, they were never counted so to monarchy, but to monarchical tyranny; and extremes one with another are at most antipathy. If then the king so extremely stood in fear of tumults, the inference will endanger him to be the other extreme. . . . .

The bill for a triennial Parliament was but the third part of one good step toward that which in times past was our annual right. The other bill for settling this Parliament was new indeed, but at that time very necessary; and, in the king's own words, no more than what the world "was fully confirmed he might in justice, reason, honor, and conscience grant them"; for to that end he affirms to have done it.

But whereas he attributes the passing of them to his own act of grace and willingness, (as his manner is to make virtues of his necessities,) and giving to himself all the praise, heaps ingratitude upon the Parliament, a little memory will set the clean contrary before us; that for those beneficial acts we owe what we owe to the Parliament, but to his granting them neither praise nor thanks. The first bill granted much less than two former statutes yet in force by Edward the Third; that a Parliament should be called every year, or oftener, if need were; nay, from a far ancienter law-book, called the "Mirror," it is affirmed in a late treatise called "Rights of the Kingdom," that Parliaments by our old laws ought twice a year to be at London. From twice in one year to once in three years, it may be soon cast up how great a loss we fell into of our ancient liberty by that act, which in the ignorant and slavish minds we then were, was thought a great purchase.

Wisest men perhaps were contented (for the present, at least) by this act to have recovered Parliaments, which were then upon the brink of danger to be forever lost. And this is that which the king preaches here for a special token of his princely favor, to have abridged and overreached the people five parts in six what their due was, both by ancient statute and originally. And thus the taking from us all but a triennial remnant of that English freedom which our fathers left us double, in a fair annuity enrolled, is set out, and sold to us here for the gracious and over-liberal giving of a new enfranchisement. How little, may we think, did he ever give us, who in the bill of his pretended givings writes down imprimis that benefit or privilege once in three years given us, which by so giving he more than twice every year illegally took from us: such givers as give single to take away sixfold, be to our enemies! for certainly this commonwealth, if the statutes of our ancestors be worth aught, would have found it hard and hazardous to thrive under the damage of such a guileful liberality. . . . .

Our forefathers were of that courage and severity of zeal to justice and their native liberty, against the proud contempt and misrule of their kings, that when Richard the Second departed but from a committee of lords, who sat preparing matter for the Parliament not yet assembled, to the removal of his evil counsellors, they first vanquished and put to flight Robert de Vere, his chief favorite; and then, coming up to London with a huge army, required the king, then withdrawn for fear, but no further off than the Tower, to come to Westminster. Which he refusing, they told him flatly, that unless he came they would choose another. So high a crime it was accounted then for kings to absent themselves, not from a Parliament, which none ever durst, but from any meeting of his peers and counsellors, which did but tend towards a Parliament. Much less would they have suffered, that a king, for such trivial and various pretences, one while for fear of tumults, another while "for shame to see them," should leave his regal station, and the whole kingdom bleeding to death of those wounds, which his own unskilful and perverse government had inflicted. . . . .

It being therefore most unlike a law, to ordain a remedy so slender and unlawlike, to be the utmost means of all public safety or prevention, as advice is, which may at any time be rejected by the sole judgment of one man, the king, and so unlike the law of England, which lawyers say is the quintessence of reason and mature wisdom; we may conclude, that the king's negative voice was never any law, but an absurd and reasonless custom, begotten and grown up either from the flattery of basest times or the usurpation of immoderate princes. Thus much to the law of it, by a better evidence than rolls and records,—reason. But is it possible he should pretend also to reason, that the judgment of one man, not as a wise or good man, but as a king, and ofttimes a wilful, proud, and wicked king, should outweigh the prudence and all the virtue of an elected Parliament? What an abusive thing were it then to summon Parliaments, that by the major part of voices greatest matters may be there debated and resolved, whenas one single voice after that shall dash all their resolutions?

He attempts to give a reason why it should: "Because the whole Parliaments represent not him in any kind." But mark how little he advances; for if the Parliament represent the whole kingdom, as is sure enough they do, then doth the king represent only himself; and if a king without his kingdom be in a civil sense nothing, then without or against the representative of his whole kingdom, he himself represents nothing; and by consequence his judgment and his negative is as good as nothing. And though we should allow him to be something, yet not equal or comparable to the whole kingdom, and so neither to them who represent it; much less that one syllable of his breath put into the scales should be more ponderous than the joint voice and efficacy of a whole Parliament, assembled by election, and endued with the plenipotence of a free nation, to make laws, not to be denied laws; and with no more but "no!" a sleeveless reason, in the most pressing times of danger and disturbance to be sent home frustrate and remediless.

Yet here he maintains, "to be no further bound to agree with the votes of both houses, than he sees them to agree with the will of God, with his just rights as a king, and the general good of his people." As to the freedom of his agreeing or not agreeing, limited with due bounds, no man reprehends it; this is the question here, or the miracle rather, why his only not agreeing should lay a negative bar and inhibition upon that which is agreed to by a whole Parliament, though never so conducing to the public good or safety? To know the will of God better than his whole kingdom, whence should he have it? Certainly his court-breeding and his perpetual conversation with flatterers was but a bad school. To judge of his own rights could not belong to him, who had no right by law in any court to judge of so much as felony or treason, being held a party in both these cases, much more in this; and his rights however should give place to the general good, for which end all his rights were given him.

Lastly, to suppose a clearer insight and discerning of the general good, allotted to his own singular judgment, than to the Parliament and all the people, and from that self-opinion of discerning, to deny them that good which they, being all freemen, seek earnestly and call for, is an arrogance, and iniquity beyond imagination rude and unreasonable; they undoubtedly having most authority to judge of the public good, who for that purpose are chosen out and sent by the people to advise him. And if it may be in him to see oft "the major part of them not in the right," had it not been more his modesty, to have doubted their seeing him more often in the wrong? . . . . In all wise nations the legislative power, and the judicial execution of that power, have been most commonly distinct, and in several hands; but yet the former supreme, the other subordinate. If then the king be only set up to execute the law, which is indeed the highest of his office, he ought no more to make or forbid the making of any law, agreed upon in Parliament, than other inferior judges, who are his deputies. Neither can he more reject a law offered him by the Commons, than he can new make a law, which they reject. And yet the more to credit and uphold his cause, he would seem to have philosophy on his side; straining her wise dictates to unphilosophical purposes. But when kings come so low, as to fawn upon philosophy, which before they neither valued nor understood, it is a sign that fails not, they are then put to their last trump. And philosophy as well requites them, by not suffering her golden sayings either to become their lips, or to be used as masks and colors of injurious and violent deeds. So that what they presume to borrow from her sage and virtuous rules, like the riddle of the Sphinx not understood, breaks the neck of their own cause.

But now again to politics: "He cannot think the majesty of the crown of England to be bound by any coronation oath in a blind and brutish formality, to consent to whatever its subjects in Parliament shall require." What tyrant could presume to say more, when he meant to kick down all law, government, and bond of oath? But why he so desires to absolve himself the oath of his coronation would be worth the knowing. It cannot but be yielded, that the oath, which binds him to the performance of his trust, ought in reason to contain the sum of what his chief trust and office is. But if it neither do enjoin, nor mention to him, as a part of his duty, the making nor the marring of any law, or scrap of law, but requires only his assent to those laws which the people have already chosen, or shall choose; (for so both the Latin of that oath, and the old English; and all reason admits, that the people should not lose under a new king what freedom they had before;) then that negative voice so contended for, to deny the passing of any law which the Commons choose, is both against the oath of his coronation, and his kingly office.

And if the king may deny to pass what the Parliament hath chosen to be a law, then doth the king make himself superior to his whole kingdom; which not only the general maxims of policy gainsay, but even our own standing laws, as hath been cited to him in remonstrances heretofore, that "the king hath two superiors, the law, and his court of Parliament." But this he counts to be a blind and brutish formality, whether it be law, or oath, or his duty, and thinks to turn it off with wholesome words and phrases, which he then first learnt of the honest people, when they were so often compelled to use them against those more truly blind and brutish formalities thrust upon us by his own command, not in civil matters only, but in spiritual. And if his oath to perform what the people require, when they crown him, be in his esteem a brutish formality, then doubtless those other oaths of allegiance and supremacy, taken absolute on our part, may most justly appear to us in all respects as brutish and as formal; and so by his own sentence no more binding to us, than his oath to him. . . . .

Thus much of what he suffered by Hotham, and with what patience; now of what Hotham suffered, as he judges, for opposing him: "he could not but observe how God, not long after, pleaded and avenged his cause." Most men are too apt, and commonly the worst of men, so to interpret, and expound the judgments of God, and all other events of Providence or chance, as makes most to the justifying of their own cause, though never so evil; and attribute all to the particular favor of God towards them. Thus when Saul heard that David was in Keilah, "God," saith he, "hath delivered him into my hands, for he is shut in." But how far that king was deceived in his thought that God was favoring to his cause, that story unfolds; and how little reason this king had to impute the death of Hotham to God's avengement of his repulse at Hull, may easily be seen.

For while Hotham continued faithful to his trust, no man more safe, more successful, more in reputation than he; but from the time he first sought to make his peace with the king, and to betray into his hands that town, into which before he had denied him entrance, nothing prospered with him. Certainly had God purposed him such an end for his opposition to the king, he would not have deferred to punish him till then, when of an enemy he was changed to be the king's friend, nor have made his repentance and amendment the occasion of his ruin. How much more likely is it, since he fell into the act of disloyalty to his charge, that the judgment of God concurred with the punishment of man, and justly cut him off for revolting to the king; to give the world an example, that glorious deeds done to ambitious ends find reward answerable, not to their outward seeming, but to their inward ambition! In the mean while, what thanks he had from the king for revolting to his cause, and what good opinion for dying in his service, they who have ventured like him, or intend, may here take notice.

He proceeds to declare, not only in general wherefore God's judgment was upon Hotham, but undertakes by fancies and allusions to give a criticism upon every particular, "that his head was divided from his body, because his heart was divided from the king; two heads cut off in one family for affronting the head of the commonwealth; the eldest son being infected with the sin of his father, against the father of his country." These petty glosses and conceits on the high and secret judgments of God, besides the boldness of unwarrantable commenting, are so weak and shallow, and so like the quibbles of a court sermon, that we may safely reckon them either fetched from such a pattern, or that the hand of some household priest foisted them in; lest the world should forget how much he was a disciple of those cymbal doctors. But that argument, by which the author would commend them to us, discredits them the more; for if they be so "obvious to every fancy," the more likely to be erroneous, and to misconceive the mind of those high secrecies, whereof they presume to determine. For God judges not by human fancy. . . . .

"He is sorry that Hotham felt the justice of others, and fell not rather into the hands of his mercy." But to clear that, he should have shown us what mercy he had ever used to such as fell into his hands before, rather than what mercy he intended to such as never could come to ask it. Whatever mercy one man might have expected, it is too well known the whole nation found none; though they besought it often, and so humbly; but had been swallowed up in blood and ruin, to set his private will above the Parliament, had not his strength failed him. "Yet clemency he counts a debt, which he ought to pay to those that crave it; since we pay not anything to God for his mercy but prayers and praises." By this reason we ought as freely to pay all things to all men; for all that we receive from God, what do we pay for, more than prayers and praises? We looked for the discharge of his office, the payment of his duty to the kingdom, and are paid court-payment, with empty sentences that have the sound of gravity, but the significance of nothing pertinent. . . . .

"But he had a soul invincible." What praise is that? The stomach of a child is ofttimes invincible to all correction. The unteachable man hath a soul to all reason and good advice invincible; and he who is intractable, he whom nothing can persuade, may boast himself invincible; whenas in some things to be overcome, is more honest and laudable than to conquer.

He labors to have it thought, "that his fearing God more than man" was the ground of his sufferings; but he should have known that a good principle not rightly understood may prove as hurtful as a bad; and his fear of God may be as faulty as a blind zeal. He pretended to fear God more than the Parliament, who never urged him to do otherwise; he should also have feared God more than he did his courtiers, and the bishops, who drew him as they pleased to things inconsistent with the fear of God. Thus boasted Saul to have "performed the commandment of God," and stood in it against Samuel; but it was found at length, that he had feared the people more than God, in saving those fat oxen for the worship of God, which were appointed for destruction. Not much unlike, if not much worse, was that fact of his, who, for fear to displease his court and mongrel clergy, with the dissolutest of the people, upheld in the Church of God, while his power lasted, those beasts of Amalec, the prelates, against the advice of his Parliament and the example of all Reformation; in this more inexcusable than Saul, that Saul was at length convinced, he to the hour of death fixed in his false persuasion; and soothes himself in the flattering peace of an erroneous and obdurate conscience; singing to his soul vain psalms of exultation, as if the Parliament had assailed his reason with the force of arms, and not he on the contrary their reason with his arms; which hath been proved already, and shall be more hereafter. . . . .

He complains "that civil war must be the fruits of his seventeen years' reigning with such a measure of justice, peace, plenty, and religion, as all nations either admired or envied." For the justice we had, let the council-table, star-chamber, high-commission speak the praise of it; not forgetting the unprincely usage, and, as far as might be, the abolishing of Parliaments, the displacing of honest judges, the sale of offices, bribery, and exaction, not found out to be punished, but to be shared in with impunity for the time to come. Who can number the extortions, the oppressions, the public robberies and rapines committed on the subject both by sea and land, under various pretences? their possessions also taken from them, one while as forest-land, another while as crown-land; nor were their goods exempted, no, not the bullion in the mint; piracy was become a project owned and authorized against the subject. For the peace we had, what peace was that which drew out the English to a needless and dishonorable voyage against the Spaniard at Cales? Or that which lent our shipping to a treacherous and antichristian war against the poor Protestants of Rochelle, our suppliants? What peace was that which fell to rob the French by sea, to the embarring of all our merchants in that kingdom? which brought forth that unblest expedition to the Isle of Rhé, doubtful whether more calamitous in the success, or in the design, betraying all the flower of our military youth and best commanders to a shameful surprisal and execution. This was the peace we had, and the peace we gave, whether to friends or to foes abroad. And if at home any peace were intended us, what meant those Irish billeted soldiers in all parts of the kingdom, and the design of German horse to subdue us in our peaceful houses?

For our religion, where was there a more ignorant, profane, and vicious clergy, learned in nothing but the antiquity of their pride, their covetousness, and superstition? whose unsincere and leavenous doctrine, corrupting the people, first taught them looseness, then bondage; loosening them from all sound knowledge and strictness of life, the more to fit them for the bondage of tyranny and superstition. So that what was left us for other nations not to pity, rather than admire or envy, all those seventeen years, no wise man could see. For wealth and plenty in a land where justice reigns not is no argument of a flourishing state, but of a nearness rather to ruin or commotion.

These were not "some miscarriages" only of government, "which might escape," but a universal distemper, and reducement of law to arbitrary power; not through the evil counsels of "some men," but through the constant course and practice of all that were in highest favor: whose worst actions frequently avowing he took upon himself; and what faults did not yet seem in public to be originally his, such care he took by professing and proclaiming openly, as made them all at length his own adopted sins. The persons also, when he could no longer protect, he esteemed and favored to the end; but never otherwise than by constraint yielded any of them to due punishment; thereby manifesting that what they did was by his own authority and approbation.

Yet here he asks, "whose innocent blood he hath shed, what widows' or orphans' tears can witness against him?" After the suspected poisoning of his father, not inquired into but smothered up, and him protected and advanced to the very half of his kingdom, who was accused in Parliament to be the author of the fact; (with much more evidence than Duke Dudley, that false protector, is accused upon record to have poisoned Edward the Sixth;) after all his rage and persecution, after so many years of cruel war on his people in three kingdoms! Whence the author of "Truths Manifest," a Scotsman, not unacquainted with affairs, positively affirms, "that there hath been more Christian blood shed by the commission, approbation, and connivance of King Charles, and his father James, in the latter end of their reign, than in the ten Roman persecutions." Not to speak of those many whippings, pillories, and other corporal inflictions, wherewith his reign also, before this war, was not unbloody; some have died in prison under cruel restraint, others in banishment, whose lives were shortened through the rigor of that persecution wherewith so many years he infested the true Church.

And those six members all men judged to have escaped no less than capital danger, whom he, so greedily pursuing into the House of Commons, had not there the forbearance to conceal how much it troubled him, "that the birds were flown." If some vulture in the mountains could have opened his beak intelligibly and spoke, what fitter words could he have uttered at the loss of his prey? The tyrant Nero, though not yet deserving that name, set his hand so unwillingly to the execution of a condemned person, as to wish "he had not known letters." Certainly for a king himself to charge his subjects with high-treason, and so vehemently to prosecute them in his own cause, as to do the office of a searcher, argued in him no great aversation from shedding blood, were it but to "satisfy his anger," and that revenge was no unpleasing morsel to him, whereof he himself thought not much to be so diligently his own caterer. But we insist rather upon what was actual than what was probable. . . . .

It were a folly beyond ridiculous, to count ourselves a free nation, if the king, not in Parliament, but in his own person, and against them, might appropriate to himself the strength of a whole nation as his proper goods. What the laws of the land are, a Parliament should know best, having both the life and death of laws in their law-giving power: and the law of England is, at best, but the reason of Parliament. . . . .

But what needed that? "They knew his chiefest arms left him were those only which the ancient Christians were wont to use against their persecutors, — prayers and tears." O sacred reverence of God! respect and shame of men! whither were ye fled when these hypocrisies were uttered? Was the kingdom then at all that cost of blood to remove from him none but prayers and tears? What were those thousands of blaspheming cavaliers about him, whose mouths let fly oaths and curses by the volley: were those the prayers; and those carouses drunk to the confusion of all things good or holy, did those minister the tears? Were they prayers and tears that were listed at York, mustered on Heworth Moor, and laid siege to Hull for the guard of his person? Were prayers and tears at so high a rate in Holland, that nothing could purchase them but the crown jewels? Yet they in Holland (such word was sent us) sold them for guns, carabines, mortar-pieces, cannons, and other deadly instruments of war; which, when they came to York, were all, no doubt by the merit of some great saint, suddenly transformed into prayers and tears: and, being divided into regiments and brigades, were the only arms that mischieved us in all those battles and encounters.

These were his chief arms, whatever we must call them, and yet such arms as they who fought for the commonwealth have, by the help of better prayers, vanquished and brought to nothing. . . . .

As for sole power of the militia, which he claims as a right no less undoubted than the crown, it hath been oft enough told him that he hath no more authority over the sword than over the law: over the law he hath none, either to establish or to abrogate, to interpret or to execute, but only by his courts and in his courts, whereof the Parliament is highest; no more, therefore, hath he power of the militia, which is the sword, either to use or to dispose, but with consent of Parliament: give him but that, and as good give him in a lump all our laws and liberties. For if the power of the sword were anywhere separate and undepending from the power of the law, which is originally seated in the highest court, then would that power of the sword be soon master of the law: and being at one man's disposal might, when he pleased, control the law; and in derision of our Magna Charta, which were but weak resistance against an armed tyrant, might absolutely enslave us. And not to have in ourselves, though vaunting to be freeborn, the power of our own freedom, and the public safety, is a degree lower than not to have the property of our own goods. For liberty of person, and the right of self-preservation, is much nearer, much more natural, and more worth to all men, than the property of their goods and wealth. Yet such power as all this did the king in open terms challenge to have over us, and brought thousands to help him win it; so much more good at fighting than at understanding, as to persuade themselves, that they fought then for the subject's liberty. . . . .

"This honor," he saith, "they did him, to put him on the giving part." And spake truer than he intended, it being merely for honor's sake that they did so; not that it belonged to him of right: for what can he give to a Parliament, who receives all he hath from the people, and for the people's good? Yet now he brings his own conditional rights to contest and be preferred before the people's good; and yet, unless it be in order to their good, he hath no rights at all; reigning by the laws of the land, not by his own; which laws are in the hands of Parliament to change or abrogate as they see best for the commonwealth, even to the taking away of kingship itself, when it grows too masterful and burdensome.

For every commonwealth is in general defined, a society sufficient of itself, in all things conducible to well-being and commodious life. Any of which requisite things, if it cannot have without the gift and favor of a single person, or without leave of his private reason or his conscience, it cannot be thought sufficient of itself, and by consequence no commonwealth, nor free; but a multitude of vassals in the possession and domain of one absolute lord, and wholly obnoxious to his will. If the king have power to give or deny anything to his Parliament, he must do it either as a person several from them, or as one greater: neither of which will be allowed him: not to be considered severally from them; for as the king of England can do no wrong, so neither can he do right but in his courts and by his courts; and what is legally done in them, shall be deemed the king's assent, though he as a several person shall judge or endeavor the contrary; so that indeed without his courts, or against them, he is no king. If therefore he obtrude upon us any public mischief, or withhold from us any general good, which is wrong in the highest degree, he must do it as a tyrant, not as a king of England, by the known maxims of our law. Neither can he, as one greater, give aught to the Parliament which is not in their own power, but he must be greater also than the kingdom which they represent: so that to honor him with the giving part was a mere civility, and may be well termed the courtesy of England, not the king's due. . . . .

But the "incommunicable jewel of his conscience" he will not give, "but reserve to himself." It seems that his conscience was none of the crown jewels; for those we know were in Holland, not incommunicable, to buy arms against his subjects. Being therefore but a private jewel, he could not have done a greater pleasure to the kingdom, than by reserving it to himself. But he, contrary to what is here professed, would have his conscience not an incommunicable, but a universal conscience, the whole kingdom's conscience. Thus what he seems to fear lest we should ravish from him, is our chief complaint that he obtruded upon us; we never forced him to part with his conscience, but it was he that would have forced us to part with ours.

. . . . .

Some things they proposed "which would have wounded the inward peace of his conscience." The more our evil hap, that three kingdoms should be thus pestered with one conscience; who chiefly scrupled to grant us that, which the Parliament advised him to, as the chief means of our public welfare and reformation. These scruples to many perhaps will seem pretended; to others, upon as good grounds, may seem real; and that it was the just judgment of God, that he who was so cruel and so remorseless to other men's consciences, should have a conscience within him as cruel to himself; constraining him as he constrained others, and ensnaring him in such ways and counsels as were certain to be his destruction. . . . .

But "to exclude him from all power of denial seems an arrogance"; in the Parliament, he means: what in him then to deny against the Parliament? None at all, by what he argues: for, "by petitioning they confess their inferiority, and that obliges them to rest, if not satisfied, yet quieted, with such an answer as the will and reason of their superior thinks fit to give." First, petitioning, in better English, is no more than requesting or requiring; and men require not favors only, but their due; and that not only from superiors, but from equals, and inferiors also. The noblest Romans, when they stood for that which was a kind of regal honor, the consulship, were wont in a submissive manner to go about, and beg that highest dignity of the meanest plebeians, naming them man by man; which in their tongue was called *petitio consulatus*. And the Parliament of England petitioned the king, not because all of them were inferior to him, but because he was inferior to any one of them, which they did of civil custom, and for fashion's sake, more than of duty; for by plain law cited before, the Parliament is his superior.

But what law in any trial or dispute enjoins a freeman to rest quieted, though not satisfied, with the will and reason of his superior? It were a mad law that would subject reason to superiority of place. And if our highest consultations and purposed laws must be terminated by the king's will, then is the will of one man our law, and no subtlety of dispute can redeem the Parliament and nation from being slaves: neither can any tyrant require more than that his will or reason, though not satisfying, should yet be rested in, and determine all things. We may conclude, therefore, that when the Parliament petitioned the king, it was but merely form, let it be as "foolish and absurd" as he pleases. It cannot certainly be so absurd as what he requires, that the Parliament should confine their own and all the kingdom's reason to the will of one man, because it was his hap to succeed his father. For neither God nor the laws have subjected us to his will, nor set his reason to be our sovereign above law, (which must needs be, if he can strangle it in the birth,) but set his person over us in the sovereign execution of such laws as the Parliament establish. The Parliament, therefore, without any usurpation, hath had it always in their power to limit and confine the exorbitancy of kings, whether they call it their will, their reason, or their conscience. . . . .

He falls next to flashes, and a multitude of words, in all which is contained no more than what might be the plea of any guiltiest offender: — he was not the author, because "he hath the greatest share of loss and dishonor by what is committed." Who is there that offends God, or his neighbor, on whom the greatest share of loss and dishonor lights not in the end? But in act of doing evil, men use not to consider the event of these evil doings; or if they do, have then no power to curb the sway of their own wickedness; so that the greatest share of loss and dishonor to happen upon themselves, is no argument that they were not guilty. . . . .

It must needs seem strange, where men accustom themselves to ponder and contemplate things in their first original and institution, that kings, who, as all other officers of the public, were at first chosen and installed only by consent and suffrage of the people, to govern them as freemen by laws of their own making, and to be, in consideration of that dignity and riches bestowed upon them, the intrusted servants of the commonwealth, should, notwithstanding, grow up to that dishonest encroachment, as to esteem themselves masters, both of that great trust which they serve, and of the people that betrusted them; counting what they ought to do, both in discharge of their public duty, and for the great reward of honor and revenue which they receive, as done all of mere grace and favor; as if their power over us were by nature, and from themselves, or that God had sold us into their hands.

Indeed, if the race of kings were eminently the best of men, as the breed at Tutbury is of horses, it would in reason then be their part only to command, ours always to obey. But kings, by generation no way excelling others, and most commonly not being the wisest or the worthiest by far of whom they claim to have the governing; that we should yield them subjection to our own ruin, or hold of them the right of our common safety, and our natural freedom by mere gift, from the superfluity of their royal grace and beneficence, we may be sure was never the intent of God, whose ways are just and equal; never the intent of nature, whose works are also regular; never of any people not wholly barbarous, whom prudence, or no more but human sense, would have better guided when they first created kings, than so to nullify and tread to dirt the rest of mankind, by exalting one person and his lineage without other merit looked after, but the mere contingency of a begetting, into an absolute and unaccountable dominion over them and their posterity. . . . .

He imagines his "own judicious zeal to be most concerned in his tuition of the Church." So thought Saul when he presumed to offer sacrifice, for which he lost his kingdom; so thought Uzziah when he went into the temple, but was thrust out with a leprosy for his opinioned zeal, which he thought judicious. It is not the part of a king, because he ought to defend the Church, therefore to set himself supreme head over the Church, or to meddle with ecclesial government, or to defend the Church otherwise than the Church would be defended; for such defence is bondage; not to defend abuses, and stop all reformation, under the name of "new moulds fancied and fashioned to private designs."

The holy things of Church are in the power of other keys than were delivered to his keeping. Christian liberty, purchased with the death of our Redeemer, and established by the sending of his free Spirit to inhabit in us, is not now to depend upon the doubtful consent of any earthly monarch; nor to be again fettered with a presumptuous negative voice, tyrannical to the Parliament, but much more tyrannical to the Church of God; which was compelled to implore the aid of Parliament, to remove his force and heavy hands from off our consciences, who therefore complains now of that most just defensive force, because only it removed his violence and persecution. If this be a violation to his conscience, that it was hindered by the Parliament from violating the more tender consciences of so many thousand good Christians, let the usurping conscience of all tyrants be ever so violated! . . . .

This is evident, that they "who use no set forms of prayer," have words from their affections; while others are to seek affections fit and proportionable to a certain dose of prepared words; which, as they are not rigorously forbid to any man's private infirmity, so to imprison and confine by force, into a pinfold of set words, those two most unimprisonable things, our prayers, and that divine spirit of utterance that moves them, is a tyranny that would have longer hands than those giants who threatened bondage to heaven. What we may do in the same form of words is not so much the question, as whether liturgy may be forced as he forced it. It is true that we "pray to the same God"; must we, therefore, always use the same words? Let us then use but one word, because we pray to one God. "We profess the same truths": but the liturgy comprehends not all truths: "we read the same Scriptures," but never read that all those sacred expressions, all benefit and use of Scripture, as to public prayer, should be denied us, except what was barrelled up in a common-prayer book with many mixtures of their own, and, which is worse, without salt.

But suppose them savory words and unmixed, suppose them manna itself, yet, if they shall be hoarded up and enjoined us, while God every morning rains down new expressions into our hearts; instead of being fit to use, they will be found, like reserved manna, rather to breed worms and stink. "We have the same duties upon us, and feel the same wants"; yet not always the same, nor at all times alike; but with variety of circumstances, which ask variety of words, whereof God hath given us plenty; not to use so copiously upon all other occasions, and so niggardly to him alone in our devotions. As if Christians were now in a worse famine of words fit for prayer, than was of food at the siege of Jerusalem, when perhaps the priests being to remove the show-bread, as was accustomed, were compelled every Sabbath-day, for want of other loaves, to bring again still the same. If the "Lord's Prayer" had been the "warrant, or the pattern of set liturgies," as is here affirmed, why was neither that prayer, nor any other set form, ever after used, or so much as mentioned by the apostles, much less commended to our use? Why was their care wanting in a thing so useful to the Church? so full of danger and contention to be left undone by them to other men's penning, of whose authority we could not be so certain? Why was this forgotten by them, who declare that they have revealed to us the whole counsel of God? who, as he left our affections to be guided by his sanctifying Spirit, so did he likewise our words to be put into us without our premeditation; not only those cautious words to be used before Gentiles and tyrants, but much more those filial words, of which we have so frequent use in our access with freedom of speech to the throne of grace. Which to lay aside for other outward dictates of men, were to injure him and his perfect gift, who is the spirit, and giver of our ability to pray: as if his ministration were incomplete, and that to whom he gave affections, he did not also afford utterance to make his gift of prayer a perfect gift; to them especially, whose office in the Church is to pray publicly.

And although the gift were only natural, yet

voluntary prayers are less subject to formal and superficial tempers than set forms. For in those, at least for words and matter, he who prays must consult first with his heart, which in likelihood may stir up his affections; in these, having both words and matter ready made to his lips, which is enough to make up the outward act of prayer, his affections grow lazy, and come not up easily at the call of words not their own. The prayer also having less intercourse and sympathy with a heart wherein it was not conceived, saves itself the labor of so long a journey downward, and flying up in haste on the specious wings of formality, if it fall not back again headlong, instead of a prayer which was expected, presents God with a set of stale and empty words. . . . .

We may have learnt, both from sacred history and times of reformation, that the kings of this world have both ever hated and instinctively feared the Church of God. Whether it be for that their doctrine seems much to favor two things to them so dreadful, liberty and equality; or because they are the children of that kingdom, which, as ancient prophecies have foretold, shall in the end break to pieces and dissolve all their great power and dominion. And those kings and potentates who have strove most to rid themselves of this fear, by cutting off or suppressing the true Church, have drawn upon themselves the occasion of their own ruin, while they thought with most policy to prevent it. Thus Pharaoh, when once he began to fear and wax jealous of the Israelites, lest they should multiply and fight against him, and that fear stirred him up to afflict and keep them under, as the only remedy of what he feared, soon found that the evil which before slept, came suddenly upon him, by the preposterous way he took to prevent it.

Passing by examples between, and not shutting wilfully our eyes, we may see the like story brought to pass in our own land. This king, more than any before him, except perhaps his father, from his first entrance to the crown, harboring in his mind a strange fear and suspicion of men most religious, and their doctrine, which in his own language he here acknowledges, terming it "the seditious ex orbitancy" of ministers' tongues, and doubting "lest they," as he not Christianly express it, "should with the keys of heaven let out peace and loyalty from the people's hearts." Though they never preached or attempted aught that might justly raise in him such thoughts, he could not rest, or think himself secure, so long as they remained in any of his three kingdoms unrooted out.

But outwardly professing the same religion with them, he could not presently use violence as Pharaoh did; and that course had with others before but ill succeeded. He chooses therefore a more mystical way, a newer method of antichristian fraud, to the Church more dangerous; and, like to Balak the son of Zippor, against a nation of prophets thinks it best to hire other esteemed prophets, and to undermine and wear out the true Church by a false ecclesiastical policy. To this drift he found the government of bishops most serviceable; an order in the Church, as by men first corrupted, so mutually corrupting them who receive it, both in judgment and manners. He, by conferring bishoprics and great livings on whom he thought most pliant to his will, against the known canons and universal practice of the ancient Church, whereby those elections were the people's right, sought, as he confesses to have "greatest influence upon churchmen." They on the other side finding themselves in a high dignity, neither founded by Scripture, nor allowed by reformation, nor supported by any spiritual gift or grace of their own, knew it their best course to have dependence only upon him; and wrought his fancy by degrees to that degenerate and unkingly persuasion of "No bishop, no king." Whenas on the contrary all prelates in their own subtle sense are of another mind; according to that of Pius IV., remembered in the history of Trent, that bishops then grow to be most vigorous and potent, when princes happen to be most weak and impotent.

Thus when both interest of tyranny and episcopacy were incorporate into each other, the king, whose principal safety and establishment consisted in the righteous execution of his civil power, and not in bishops and their wicked counsels, fatally driven on, set himself to the extirpating of those men whose doctrine and desire of Church-discipline he so feared would be the undoing of his monarchy. And because no temporal law could touch the innocence of their lives, he begins with the persecution of their consciences, laying scandals before them; and makes that the argument to inflict his unjust penalties both on their bodies and estates. In this war against the Church, if he had sped so, as other haughty monarchs whom God heretofore hath hardened to the like enterprise, we ought to look up with praise and thanksgiving to the Author of our deliverance, to whom victory and power, majesty, honor, and dominion belong forever.

In the mean while, from his own words we may perceive easily that the special motives which he had to endear and deprave his judgment to the favoring and utmost defending of episcopacy, are such as here we represent them; and how unwillingly, and with what mental reservation, he condescended, against his interest, to remove it out of the Peers' House, hath been shown already. The reasons, which, he affirms, wrought so much upon his judgment, shall be so far answered as they be urged. . . . .

"If the way of treaties be looked upon," in general, "as retiring" from bestial force to human reason, his first aphorism here is in part deceived.

For men may treat like beasts as well as fight. If some fighting were not manlike, then either fortitude were no virtue, or no fortitude in fighting. And as politicians ofttimes through dilatory purposes and emulations handle the matter, there hath been nowhere found more bestiality than in treating; which hath no more commendations in it, than from fighting to come to undermining, from violence to craft; and when they can no longer do as lions, to do as foxes. . . . .

For if neither God nor nature put civil power in the hands of any whomsoever, but to a lawful end, and commands our obedience to the authority of law only, not to the tyrannical force of any person; and if the laws of our land have placed the sword in no man's single hand, so much as to unsheath against a foreign enemy, much less upon the native people; but have placed it in that elective body of the Parliament, to whom the making, repealing, judging, and interpreting of law itself was also committed, as was fittest, so long as we intended to be a free nation, and not the slaves of one man's will; then was the king himself disobedient and rebellious to that law by which he reigned: and by authority of Parliament to raise arms against him in defence of law and liberty, we do not only think, but believe and know, was justifiable both "by the word of God, the laws of the land, and all lawful oaths"; and they who sided with him fought against all these.

The same allegations which he uses for himself and his party, may as well fit any tyrant in the world; for let the Parliament be called a faction when the king pleases, and that no law must be made or changed, either civil or religious, because no law will content all sides, then must be made or changed no law at all, but what a tyrant, be he Protestant or Papist, thinks fit. Which tyrannous assertion forced upon us by the sword, he who fights against, and dies fighting, if his other sins outweigh not, dies a martyr undoubtedly both of the faith and of the commonwealth; and I hold it not as the opinion, but as the full belief and persuasion, of far holier and wiser men than parasitic preachers; who, without their dinner-doctrine, know that neither king, law, civil oaths, nor religion, was ever established without the Parliament. And their power is the same to abrogate as to establish; neither is anything to be thought established, which that House declares to be abolished. Where the Parliament sits, there inseparably sits the king, there the laws, there our oaths, and whatsoever can be civil in religion. They who fought for the Parliament, in the truest sense, fought for all these; who fought for the king divided from his Parliament, fought for the shadow of a king against all these; and for things that were not, as if they were established. It were a thing monstrously absurd and contradictory, to give the Parliament a legislative power, and then to upbraid them for transgressing old establishments. . . . .

He would work the people to a persuasion, that "if he be miserable, they cannot be happy." What should hinder them? Were they all born twins of Hippocrates with him and his fortune, one birth, one burial? It were a nation miserable indeed, not worth the name of a nation, but a race of idiots, whose happiness and welfare depended upon one man. The happiness of a nation consists in true religion, piety, justice, prudence, temperance, fortitude, and the contempt of avarice and ambition. They in whomsoever these virtues dwell eminently, need not kings to make them happy, but are the architects of their own happiness; and, whether to themselves or others, are not less than kings. . . . .

Hitherto his meditations, now his vows; which, as the vows of hypocrites used to be, are most commonly absurd, and some wicked. Jacob vowed that God should be his God, if he granted him but what was necessary to perform that vow, life and subsistence: but the obedience proffered here is nothing so cheap. He, who took so heinously to be offered nineteen propositions from the Parliament, capitulates here with God almost in as many articles.

"If he will continue that light," or rather that darkness of the Gospel, which is among his prelates, settle their luxuries, and make them gorgeous bishops;

If he will "restore" the grievances and mischiefs of those obsolete and Popish laws, which the Parliament without his consent had abrogated, and will suffer justice to be executed according to his sense;

"If he will suppress the many schisms in Church," to contradict himself in that which he had foretold must and shall come to pass, and will remove reformation as the greatest schism of all, and factions in state, by which he means in every leaf, the Parliament;

If he will "restore him" to his negative voice and the militia, as much as to say, to arbitrary power, which he wrongfully avers to be the "right of his predecessors";

"If he will turn the hearts of his people" to their old cathedral and parochial service in the liturgy, and their passive obedience to the king;

"If he will quench" the army, and withdraw our forces from withstanding the piracy of Rupert, and the plotted Irish invasion;

"If he will bless him with the freedom" of bishops again in the House of Peers, and of fugitive delinquents in the House of Commons, and deliver the honor of Parliament into his hands, from the most natural and due protection of the people that intrusted them with the dangerous enterprise of being faithful to their country against the rage and malice of his tyrannous opposition;

"If he will keep him from that great offence," of following the counsel of his Parliament, and enacting what they advise him to: which in all reason, and by the known law, and oath of his coronation, he ought to do, and not to call that sacrilege, which necessity, through the continuance of his own civil war, hath compelled him to; necessity, which made David eat the showbread, made Ezekiah take all the silver which was found in God's house, and cut off the gold which overlaid those doors and pillars, and gave it to Sennacherib; necessity which ofttimes made the primitive Church to sell her sacred utensils, even to the communion-chalice;

"If he will restore him to a capacity of glorifying him by doing" that both in Church and State, which must needs dishonor and pollute his name;

"If he will bring him again with peace, honor, and safety to his chief city," without repenting, without satisfying for the blood spilt, only for a few politic concessions, which are as good as nothing;

"If he will put again the sword into his hand, to punish" those that have delivered us, and to protect delinquents against the justice of Parliament";

Then, if it be possible to reconcile contradictions, he will praise him by displeasing him, and serve him by disserving him.

"His glory," in the gaudy copes and painted windows, mitres, rochets, altars, and the chanted service-book, "shall be dearer to him," than the establishing his crown in righteousness, and the spiritual power of religion. "He will pardon those that have offended him in particular"; but there shall want no subtle ways to be even with them upon another score of their supposed offences against the commonwealth; whereby he may at once affect the glory of a seeming justice, and destroy them pleasantly, while he feigns to forgive them as to his own particular, and outwardly bewails them.

These are the conditions of his treating with God, to whom he bates nothing of what he stood upon with the Parliament: as if commissions of array could deal with him also. But of all these conditions, as it is now evident in our eyes, God accepted none, but that final petition, which he so oft, no doubt but by the secret judgment of God, importunes against his own head; praying God, "That his mercies might be so toward him, as his resolutions of truth and peace were toward his people." It follows then, God having cut him off without granting any of these mercies, that his resolutions were as feigned as his vows were frustrate. . . . .

It being now no more in his hand to be revenged on his opposers, he seeks to satiate his fancy with the imagination of some revenge upon them from above; and, like one who in a drouth observes the sky, he sits and watches when anything will drop, that might solace him with the likeness of a punishment from heaven upon us; which he straight expounds how he pleases. No evil can befall the Parliament or city but he positively interprets it a judgment upon them for his sake; as if the very manuscript of God's judgments had been delivered to his custody and exposition. But his reading declares it well to be a false copy which he uses; dispensing often to his own bad deeds and successes the testimony of divine favor, and to the good deeds and successes of other men divine wrath and vengeance.

But to counterfeit the hand of God is the boldest of all forgery. And he who without warrant but his own fantastic surmise, takes upon him perpetually to unfold the secret and unsearchable mysteries of high providence, is likely for the most part to mistake and slander them; and approaches to the madness of those reprobate thoughts that would wrest the sword of justice out of God's hand, and employ it more justly in their own conceit. It was a small thing to contend with the Parliament about the sole power of the militia, when we see him doing little less than laying hands on the weapons of God himself, which are his judgments, to wield and manage them by the sway and bent of his own frail cogitations. Therefore "they that by tumults first occasioned the raising of armies" in his doom must needs "be chastened by their own army for new tumults."

. . . . .

"He cannot but observe this divine justice, yet with sorrow and pity." But sorrow and pity in a weak and over-mastered enemy is looked upon no otherwise than as the ashes of his revenge burnt out upon himself, or as the damp of a cooled fury, when we say, it gives. But in this manner to sit spelling and observing divine justice upon every accident and slight disturbance that may happen humanly to the affairs of men, is but another fragment of his broken revenge; and yet the shrewdest and the cunningest obloquy that can be thrown upon their actions. For if he can persuade men that the Parliament and their cause is pursued with divine vengeance, he hath attained his end, to make all men forsake them, and think the worst that can be thought of them.

Nor is he only content to suborn divine justice in his censure of what is past, but he assumes the person of Christ himself, to prognosticate over us what he wishes would come. So little is anything or person sacred from him, no not in heaven, which he will not use, and put on, if it may serve him plausibly to wreak his spleen, or ease his mind upon the Parliament. Although, if ever fatal blindness did both attend and punish wilfulness, if ever any enjoyed not comforts for neglecting counsel belonging to their peace, it was in none more conspicuously brought to pass than in himself; and his predictions against the Parliament and their adherents have for the most part been verified upon his own head, and upon his chief counsellors. . . . .

It is a rule and principle worthy to be known by Christians, that no Scripture, no, nor so much as any ancient creed, binds our faith, or our obedience to any church whatsoever, denominated by a particular name; far less, if it be distinguished by a several government from that which is indeed catholic. No man was ever bid be subject to the church of Corinth, Rome, or Asia, but to the Church without addition, as it held faithful to the rules of Scripture, and the government established in all places by the Apostles; which at first was universally the same in all churches and congregations; not differing or distinguished by the diversity of countries, territories, or civil bounds. That church, that from the name of a distinct place takes authority to set up a distinct faith or government, is a schism and faction, not a church. It were an injury to condemn the Papist of absurdity and contradiction, for adhering to his Catholic Romish religion, if we, for the pleasure of a king and his politic considerations, shall adhere to a Catholic English. . . . .

It happened once, as we find in Esdras and Josephus, authors not less believed than any under sacred, to be a great and solemn debate in the court of Darius, what thing was to be counted strongest of all other. He that could resolve this, in reward of his excellent wisdom, should be clad in purple, drink in gold, sleep on a bed of gold, and sit next Darius. None but they, doubtless, who were reputed wise, had the question propounded to them; who, after some respite given them by the king to consider, in full assembly of all his lords and gravest counsellors, returned severally what they thought. The first held that wine was strongest; another, that the king was strongest; but Zorobabel, prince of the captive Jews, and heir to the crown of Judah, being one of them, proved women to be stronger than the king, for that he himself had seen a concubine take his crown from off his head to set it upon her own; and others beside him have likewise seen the like feat done, and not in jest. Yet he proved on, and it was so yielded by the king himself, and all his sages, that neither wine, nor women, nor the king, but truth of all other things was the strongest.

For me, though neither asked, nor in a nation that gives such rewards to wisdom, I shall pronounce my sentence somewhat different from Zorobabel; and shall defend that either truth and justice are all one, (for truth is but justice in our knowledge, and justice is but truth in our practice;) and he indeed so explains himself, in saying that with truth is no accepting of persons, which is the property of justice, or else if there be any odds, that justice, though not stronger than truth, yet by her office, is to put forth and exhibit more strength in the affairs of mankind. For truth is properly no more than contemplation; and her utmost efficiency is but teaching: but justice in her very essence is all strength and activity; and hath a sword put into her hand, to use against all violence and oppression on the earth. She it is most truly, who accepts no person, and exempts none from the severity of her stroke. She never suffers injury to prevail, but when falsehood first prevails over truth; and that also is a kind of justice done on them who are so deluded. Though wicked kings and tyrants counterfeit her sword, as some did that buckler fabled to fall from heaven into the capitol, yet she communicates her power to none but such as, like herself, are just, or at least will do justice. For it were extreme partiality and injustice, the flat denial and overthrow of herself, to put her own authentic sword into the hand of an unjust and wicked man, or so far to accept and exalt one mortal person above his equals, that he alone shall have the punishing of all other men transgressing, and not receive like punishment from men, when he himself shall be found the highest transgressor.

We may conclude, therefore, that justice, above all other things, is and ought to be the strongest; she is the strength, the kingdom, the power, and majesty of all ages. Truth herself would subscribe to this, though Darius and all the monarchs of the world should deny. And if by sentence thus written it were my happiness to set free the minds of Englishmen from longing to return poorly under that captivity of kings from which the strength and supreme sword of justice hath delivered them, I shall have done a work not much inferior to that of Zorobabel; who, by well-praising and extolling the force of truth, in that contemplative strength conquered Darius, and freed his country and the people of God from the captivity of Babylon. Which I shall yet not despair to do, if they in this land, whose minds are yet captive, be but as ingenuous to acknowledge the strength and supremacy of justice, as that heathen king was to confess the strength of truth: or let them but, as he did, grant that, and they will soon perceive that truth resigns all her outward strength to justice: justice therefore must needs be strongest, both in her own, and in the strength of truth. But if a king may do among men whatsoever is his will and pleasure, and notwithstanding be unaccountable to men, then, contrary to his magnified wisdom of Zorobabel, neither truth nor justice, but the king, is strongest of all other things, which that Persian monarch himself, in the midst of all his pride and glory, durst not assume. . . . .

So much he thinks to abound in his own defence, that he undertakes an unmeasurable task, to bespeak "the singular care and protection of God over all kings," as being the greatest patrons of law, justice, order, and religion on earth. But what patrons they be, God in the Scripture oft enough hath expressed; and the earth itself hath too long groaned under the burden of their injustice, disorder, and irreligion. Therefore "to bind their kings in chains, and their nobles with links of iron," is an honor belonging to his saints; not to build Babel, (which was Nimrod's work, the first king, and the beginning of his kingdom was Babel,) but to destroy it, especially that spiritual Babel: and first to overcome those European kings, which receive their power, not from God, but from the beast; and are counted no better than his ten horns. "These shall hate the great whore," and yet "shall give their kingdoms to the beast that carries her; they shall commit fornication with her," and yet "shall burn her with fire," and yet "shall lament the fall of Babylon," where they fornicated with her. Rev. xvii. xviii.

Thus shall they be to and fro, doubtful and ambiguous in all their doings, until at last, "joining their armies with the beast," whose power first raised them, they shall perish with him by the "King of kings," against whom they have rebelled; and "the fowls shall eat their flesh." This is their doom written, Rev. xix., and the utmost that we find concerning them in these latter days; which we have much more cause to believe, than his unwarranted revelation here, prophesying what shall follow after his death, with the spirit of enmity, not of St. John.

He would fain bring us out of conceit with the good success, which God vouchsafed us. We measure not our cause by our success, but our success by our cause. Yet certainly in a good cause success is a good confirmation; for God hath promised it to good men almost in every leaf of Scripture. If it argue not for us, we are sure it argues not against us; but as much or more for us, than ill success argues for them; for to the wicked God hath denounced ill success in all they take in hand.

FROM

A DEFENCE OF THE PEOPLE OF ENGLAND,

IN ANSWER TO

SALMASIUS'S DEFENCE OF THE KING.

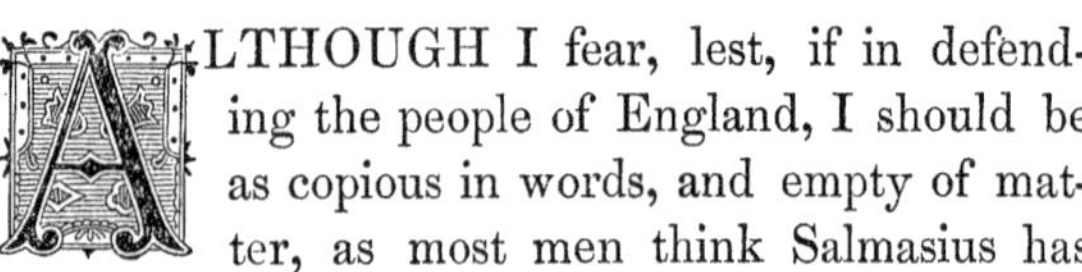

ALTHOUGH I fear, lest, if in defending the people of England, I should be as copious in words, and empty of matter, as most men think Salmasius has been in his defence of the king, I might seem to deserve justly to be accounted a verbose and silly defender; yet since no man thinks himself obliged to make so much haste, though in the handling but of any ordinary subject, as not to premise some introduction at least, according as the weight of the subject requires; if I take the same course in handling almost the greatest subject that ever was (without being too tedious in it) I am in hopes of attaining two things, which indeed I earnestly desire: the one, not to be at all wanting, as far as in me lies, to this most noble cause and most worthy to be recorded to all future ages; the other, that I may appear to have myself avoided that frivolousness of matter, and redundancy of words, which I blame in my antagonist. For I am about to discourse of matters neither inconsiderable nor common, but how a most potent king, after he had trampled upon the laws of the nation, and given a shock to its religion, and began to rule at his own will and pleasure, was at last subdued in the field by his own subjects, who had undergone a long slavery under him; how afterwards he was cast into prison, and when he gave no ground, either by words or actions, to hope better things of him, was finally by the supreme council of the kingdom condemned to die, and beheaded before the very gates of the royal palace. I shall likewise relate (which will much conduce to the easing men's minds of a great superstition) by what right, especially according to our law, this judgment was given, and all these matters transacted; and shall easily defend my valiant and worthy countrymen (who have extremely well deserved of all subjects and nations in the world) from the most wicked calumnies both of domestic and foreign railers, and especially from the reproaches of this most vain and empty sophist, who sets up for a captain and ringleader to all the rest. For what king's majesty, sitting upon an exalted throne, ever shone so brightly, as that of the people of England then did, when, shaking off that old superstition, which had prevailed a long time, they gave judgment upon the king himself, or rather upon an enemy who had been their king, caught as it were in a net by his own laws, (who alone of all mortals challenged to himself impunity by a divine right,) and scrupled not to inflict the same punishment upon him, being guilty, which he would have inflicted upon any other? But why do I mention these things as performed by the people, which almost open their voice themselves, and testify the presence of God throughout? who, as often as it seems good to his infinite wisdom, uses to throw down proud and unruly kings, exalting themselves above the condition of human nature, and utterly to extirpate them and all their family. By his manifest impulse being set at work to recover our almost lost liberty, following him as our guide, and adoring the impresses of his divine power manifested upon all occasions, we went on in no obscure, but an illustrious passage, pointed out and made plain to us by God himself. Which things, if I should so much as hope by any diligence or ability of mine, such as it is, to discourse of as I ought to do, and to commit them so to writing, as that perhaps all nations and all ages may read them, it would be a very vain thing in me. For what style can be august and magnificent enough, what man has ability sufficient, to undertake so great a task? Since we find by experience, that in so many ages as are gone over the world, there has been but here and there a man found, who has been able worthily to recount the actions of great heroes, and potent states; can any man have so good an opinion of his own talents, as to think himself capable of reaching these glorious and wonderful works of Almighty God, by any language, by any style of his? Which enterprise, though some of the most eminent persons in our commonwealth have prevailed upon me by their authority to undertake, and would have it be my business to vindicate with my pen against envy and calumny (which are proof against arms) those glorious performances of theirs, (whose opinion of me I take as a very great honor, that they should pitch upon me before others to be serviceable in this kind of those most valiant deliverers of my native country; and true it is, that from my very youth, I have been bent extremely upon such sort of studies, as inclined me, if not to do great things myself, at least to celebrate those that did,) yet as having no confidence in any such advantages, I have recourse to the divine assistance; and invoke the great and holy God, the giver of all good gifts, that I may as substantially, and as truly, discourse and refute the sauciness and lies of this foreign declaimer, as our noble generals piously and successfully by force of arms broke the king's pride, and his unruly domineering, and afterwards put an end to both by inflicting a memorable punishment upon himself, and as thoroughly as a single person did with ease but of late confute and confound the king himself, rising as it were from the grave, and recommending himself to the people in a book published after his death, with new artifices and allurements of words and expressions. . . . .

"A horrible message had lately struck our ears, but our minds more, with a heinous wound concerning a parricide committed in England in the person of a king, by a wicked conspiracy of sacrilegious men." Indeed that horrible message must either have had a much longer sword than that which Peter drew, or those ears must have been of a wonderful length, that it could wound at such a distance; for it could not so much as in the least offend any ears but those of an ass. For what harm is it to you, that are foreigners? are any of you hurt by it, if we amongst ourselves put our own enemies, our own traitors to death, be they commoners, noblemen, or kings? Do you, Salmasius, let alone what does not concern you: for I have a horrible message to bring of you too; which I am mistaken if it strike not a more heinous wound into the ears of all grammarians and critics, provided they have any learning and delicacy in them, to wit, your crowding so many barbarous expressions together in one period in the person of (Aristarchus) a grammarian; and that so great a critic as you, hired at the king's charge to write a defence of the king his father, should not only set so fulsome a preface before it, much like those lamentable ditties that used to be sung at funerals, and which can move compassion in none but a coxcomb; but in the very first sentence should provoke your readers to laughter with so many barbarisms all at once. "Persona regis," you cry. Where do you find any such Latin? or are you telling us some tale or other of a Perkin Warbec, who, taking upon him the person of a king, has, forsooth, committed some horrible parricide in England? which expression, though dropping carelessly from your pen, has more truth in it than you are aware of. For a tyrant is but like a king upon a stage, a man in a visor, and acting the part of a king in a play; he is not really a king. But as for these Gallicisms, that are so frequent in your book, I won't lash you for them myself, for I am not at leisure; but shall deliver you over to your fellow-grammarians, to be laughed to scorn and whipped by them. . . . .

Men at first united into civil societies, that they might live safely, and enjoy their liberty, without being wronged or oppressed; and that they might live religiously, and according to the doctrine of Christianity, they united themselves into churches. Civil societies have laws, and churches have a discipline peculiar to themselves, and far differing from each other. And this has been the occasion of so many wars in Christendom; to wit, because the civil magistrate and the Church confounded their jurisdictions. . . . .

You are in perfect darkness, that make no difference betwixt a paternal power, and a regal; and that when you had called kings fathers of their country, could fancy that with that metaphor you had persuaded us, that whatever is applicable to a father, is so to a king. Alas! there is a great difference betwixt them. Our fathers begot us. Our king made not us, but we him. Nature has given fathers to us all, but we ourselves appointed our own king. So that the people is not for the king, but the king for them. "We bear with a father, though he be harsh and severe"; and so we do with a king. But we do not bear with a father, if he be a tyrant. If a father murder his son, he himself must die for it; and why should not a king be subject to the same law, which certainly is a most just one? especially considering that a father cannot by any possibility divest himself of that relation, but a king may easily make himself neither king nor father of his people. If this action of ours be considered according to its quality, as you call it, I, who am both an Englishman born, and was an eye-witness of the transactions of these times, tell you, who are both a foreigner and an utter stranger to our affairs, that we have put to death neither a good, nor a just, nor a merciful, nor a devout, nor a godly, nor a peaceable king, as you style him; but an enemy, that has been so to us almost ten years to an end; nor one that was a father, but a destroyer to his country. . . . .

That it is lawful to depose a tyrant, and to punish him according to his deserts; nay, that this is the opinion of very eminent divines, and of such as have been most instrumental in the late reformation, do you deny it if you dare. You confess, that many kings have come to an unnatural death; some by the sword, some poisoned, some strangled, and some in a dungeon; but for a king to be arraigned in a court of judicature, to be put to plead for his life, to have sentence of death pronounced against him, and that sentence executed; this you think a more lamentable instance than all the rest, and make it a prodigious piece of impiety. Tell me, thou superlative fool, whether it be not more just, more agreeable to the rules of humanity, and the laws of all human societies, to bring a criminal, be his offence what it will, before a court of justice, to give him leave to speak for himself; and, if the law condemn him, then to put him to death as he has deserved, so as he may have time to repent or to recollect himself; than presently, as soon as ever he is taken, to butcher him without more ado? Do you think there is a malefactor in the world, that if he might have his choice, would not choose to be thus dealt withal? And if this sort of proceeding against a private person be accounted the fairer of the two, why should it not be counted so against a prince? Nay, why should we not think, that himself liked it better? You would have had him killed privately, and none to have seen it, either that future ages might have lost the advantage of so good an example; or that they that did this glorious action, might seem to have avoided the light, and to have acted contrary to law and justice. You aggravate the matter by telling us, that it was not done in an uproar, or brought about by any faction amongst great men, or in the heat of a rebellion, either of the people or the soldiers: that there was no hatred, no fear, no ambition, no blind precipitate rashness in the case; but that it was long consulted on, and done with deliberation. You did well in leaving off being an Advocate, and turn grammarian, who, from the accidents and circumstances of a thing, which in themselves considered sway neither one way nor other, argue in dispraise of it, before you have proved the thing itself to be either good or bad. See how open you lie: if the action you are discoursing of be commendable and praiseworthy, they that did it deserve the greater honor, in that they were prepossessed with no passions, but did what they did for virtue's sake. If there were great difficulty in the enterprise, they did well in not going about it rashly, but upon advice and consideration. Though for my own part, when I call to mind with how unexpected an importunity and fervency of mind, and with how unanimous a consent, the whole army, and a great part of the people from almost every county in the kingdom, cried out with one voice for justice against the king, as being the sole author of all their calamities, I cannot but think, that these things were brought about by a divine impulse. Whatever the matter was, whether we consider the magistrates, or the body of the people, no men ever undertook with more courage, and, which our adversaries themselves confess, in a more sedate temper of mind, so brave an action; an action that might have become those famous heroes, of whom we read in former ages; an action, by which they ennobled not only laws, and their execution, which seem for the future equally restored to high and low against one another; but even justice, and to have rendered it, after so signal a judgment, more illustrious and greater than in its own self. . . . .

If whatever a king has a mind to do, the right of kings will bear him out in, (which was a lesson that the bloody tyrant, Antoninus Caracalla, though his step-mother Julia preached it to him, and endeavored to inure him to the practice of it, by making him commit incest with herself, yet could hardly suck in,) then there neither is, nor ever was, that king, that deserved the name of a tyrant. They may safely violate all the laws of God and man: their very being kings keeps them innocent. What crime was ever any of them guilty of? They did but make use of their own right upon their own vassals. No king can commit such horrible cruelties and outrages, as will not be within this right of kings. So that there is no pretence left for any complaints or expostulations with any of them. And dare you assert, that "this right of kings," as you call it, "is grounded upon the law of nations, or rather upon that of nature," you brute beast? for you deserve not the name of a man, that are so cruel and unjust towards all those of your own kind; that endeavor, as much as in you lies, so to bear down and vilify the whole race of mankind, that were made after the image of God, as to assert and maintain, those cruel and unmerciful taskmasters, that through the superstitious whimsies, or sloth, or treachery of some persons, get into the chair, are provided and appointed by nature herself, that mild and gentle mother of us all, to be the governors of those nations they enslave. By which pestilent doctrine of yours, having rendered them more fierce and untractable, you not only enable them to make havoc of, and trample under foot, their miserable subjects; but endeavor to arm them for that very purpose with the law of nature, the right of kings, and the very constitutions of government, than which nothing can be more impious or ridiculous. . . . .

I confess there are but few, and those men of great wisdom and courage, that are either desirous of liberty, or capable of using it. The greatest part of the world choose to live under masters; but yet they would have them just ones. As for such as are unjust and tyrannical, neither was God ever so much an enemy to mankind, as to enjoin a necessity of submitting to them; nor was there ever any people so destitute of all sense, and sunk into such a depth of despair, as to impose so cruel a law upon themselves and their posterity. . . . .

If one should consider attentively the countenance of a man, and inquire after whose image so noble a creature were framed, would not any one that heard him presently make answer, that he was made after the image of God himself? Being therefore peculiarly God's own, and consequently things that are to be given to him, we are entirely free by nature, and cannot without the greatest sacrilege imaginable be reduced into a condition of slavery to any man, especially to a wicked, unjust, cruel tyrant. . . . .

Every good emperor acknowledged that the laws of the empire, and the authority of the senate, was above himself; and the same principle and notion of government has obtained all along in civilized nations. Pindar, as he is cited by Herodotus, calls the law *πάντων βασιλέα*, king over all. Orpheus in his hymns calls it the king both of gods and men: and he gives the reason why it is so; because, says he, it is that that sits at the helm of all human affairs. Plato in his book De Legibus calls it *τὸ κρατοῦν ἐν τῇ πόλει*: that that ought to have the greatest sway in the commonwealth. In his epistles he commends that form of government in which the law is made lord and master, and no scope given to any man to tyrannize over the laws. Aristotle is of the same opinion in his

Politics; and so is Cicero in his book De Legibus, that the laws ought to govern the magistrates, as they do the people. The law therefore having always been accounted the highest power on earth, by the judgment of the most learned and wise men that ever were, and by the constitutions of the best-ordered states; and it being very certain that the doctrine of the Gospel is neither contrary to reason, nor the law of nations, that man is truly and properly subject to the higher powers, who obeys the law and the magistrates, so far as they govern according to law. So that St. Paul does not only command the people, but princes themselves, to be in subjection; who are not above the laws, but bound by them: "for there is no power but of God": that is, no form, no lawful constitution of any government. The most ancient laws that are known to us were formerly ascribed to God as their author. For the law, says Cicero in his Philippics, is no other than a rule of well-grounded reason, derived from God himself, enjoining whatever is just and right, and forbidding the contrary. So that the institution of magistracy is jure Divino, and the end of it is, that mankind might live under certain laws, and be governed by them. But what particular form of government each nation would live under, and what persons should be intrusted with the magistracy, without doubt, was left to the choice of each nation. . . . .

Do you pretend that kings are infallible? If

you do not, why do you make them omnipotent? And how comes it to pass, that an unlimited power in one man should be accounted less destructive to temporal things than it is to ecclesiastical? Or do you think that God takes no care at all of civil affairs? If he takes none himself, I am sure he does not forbid us to take care which way they go; if he does take any care about them, certainly he would have the same reformation made in the commonwealth, that he would have made in the Church, especially it being obvious to every man's experience, that infallibility and omnipotency being arrogated to one man, are equally mischievous in both. God has not so modelled the government of the world as to make it the duty of any civil community to submit to the cruelties of tyrants, and yet to leave the Church at liberty to free themselves from slavery and tyranny; nay, rather quite contrary, he has put no arms into the Church's hand but those of patience and innocence, prayer and ecclesiastical discipline; but in the commonwealth, all the magistracy are by him entrusted with the preservation and execution of the laws, with the power of punishing and revenging: he has put the sword into their hands. . . . .

Though I am of opinion, Salmasius, and always was, that the law of God does exactly agree with the law of nature; so that, having shown what the law of God is, with respect to princes, and what the practice has been of the people of God, both

Jews and Christians, I have at the same time, and by the same discourse, made appear what is most agreeable to the law of nature; yet because you pretend "to confute us most powerfully by the law of nature," I will be content to admit that to be necessary, which before I had thought would be superfluous, that in this chapter I may demonstrate, that nothing is more suitable to the law of nature, than that punishment be inflicted upon tyrants. Which if I do not evince, I will then agree with you, that likewise by the law of God they are exempt. I do not purpose to frame a long discourse of nature in general, and the original of civil societies; that argument has been largely handled by many learned men, both Greek and Latin. But I shall endeavor to be as short as may be; and my design is not so much to confute you, (who would willingly have spared this pains,) as to show that you confute yourself, and destroy your own positions. I will begin with that first position, which you lay down as a fundamental, and that shall be the groundwork of my ensuing discourse. "The law of nature," say you, "is a principle imprinted on all men's minds, to regard the good of all mankind, considering men as united together in societies. But this innate principle cannot procure that common good, unless, as there are people that must be governed, so that very principle ascertain who shall govern them." To wit, lest the stronger oppress the weaker, and those persons, who, for their mutual safety and protection have united themselves together, should be disunited and divided by injury and violence, and reduced to a bestial savage life again. This I suppose is what you mean. "Out of the number of those that united into one body," you say, "there must needs have been some chosen, who excelled the rest in wisdom and valor; that they, either by force or by persuasion, might restrain those that were refractory, and keep them within due bounds. Sometimes it would so fall out, that one single person, whose conduct and valor was extraordinary, might be able to do this, and sometimes more assisted one another with their advice and counsel. But since it is impossible that any one man should order all things himself, there was a necessity of his consulting with others, and taking some into part of the government with himself; so that whether a single person reign, or whether the supreme power reside in the body of the people, since it is impossible that all should administer the affairs of the commonwealth, or that any one man should do all, the government does always lie upon the shoulders of many." And afterwards you say, "both forms of government, whether by many or a few, or by a single person, are equally according to the law of nature, viz., That it is impossible for any single person so to govern alone, as not to admit others into a share of the government with himself." Though I might have taken all this out of the third book of Aristotle's Politics, I chose rather to transcribe it out of your own book; for you stole it from him as Prometheus did fire from Jupiter, to the ruin of monarchy, and overthrow of yourself and your own opinion. For inquire as diligently as you can for your life into the law of nature, as you have described it, you will not find the least footstep in it of kingly power, as you explain it. "The law of nature," say you, "in ordering who should govern others, respected the universal good of all mankind." It did not then regard the private good of any particular person, not of a prince; so that the king is for the people, and consequently the people superior to him: which being allowed, it is impossible that princes should have any right to oppress or enslave the people; that the inferior should have right to tyrannize over the superior. So that since kings cannot pretend to any right to do mischief, the right of the people must be acknowledged, according to the law of nature, to be superior to that of princes; and therefore, by the same right, that before kingship was known, men united their strength and counsels for their mutual safety and defence; by the same right, that for the preservation of all men's liberty, peace, and safety, they appointed one or more to govern the rest; by the same right they may depose those very persons whom for their valor or wisdom they advanced to the government, or any others that rule disorderly, if they find them, by reason of their slothfulness, folly, or impiety, unfit for government: since nature does not regard the good of one, or of a few, but of all in general. For what sort of persons were they whom you suppose to have been chosen? You say, "They were such as excelled in courage and conduct," to wit, such as by nature seemed fittest for government; who by reason of their excellent wisdom and valor were enabled to undertake so great a charge. The consequence of this I take to be, that right of succession is not by the law of nature; that no man by the law of nature has right to be king, unless he excel all others in wisdom and courage; that all such as reign and want these qualifications, are advanced to the government by force or faction, have no right by the law of nature to be what they are, but ought rather to be slaves than princes. For nature appoints that wise men should govern fools, not that wicked men should rule over good men, fools over wise men; and consequently they that take the government out of such men's hands, act according to the law of nature. To what end nature directs wise men should bear the rule, you shall hear in your own words: viz. "That by force or by persuasion, they may keep such as are unruly within due bounds." But how should he keep others within the bounds of their duty, that neglects, or is ignorant of, or wilfully acts contrary to his own? Allege now, if you can, any dictate of nature by which we are enjoined to neglect the wise institutions of this law of nature, and have no regard to them in civil and public concerns, when we see what great and admirable things nature herself effects in things that are inanimate and void of sense, rather than lose her end. Produce any rule of nature, or natural justice, by which inferior criminals ought to be punished, but kings and princes to go unpunished; and not only so, but though guilty of the greatest crimes imaginable, be had in reverence and almost adored. You agree, that "all forms of government, whether by many, or few, or by a single person, are equally agreeable to the law of nature." So that the person of a king is not by the law of nature more sacred than a senate of nobles, or magistrates, chosen from amongst the common people, who you grant may be punished, and ought to be if they offend; and consequently, kings ought to be so too, who are appointed to rule for the very same end and purpose that other magistrates are. "For," say you, "nature does not allow any single person to rule so entirely, as not to have partners in the government." It does not therefore allow of a monarch; it does not allow one single person to rule so, as that all others should be in a slavish subjection to his commands only. . . . .

It is not to the purpose for us here to dispute which form of government is best, by one single person, or by many. I confess many eminent and famous men have extolled monarchy; but it has always been upon this supposition, that the prince was a very excellent person, and one that of all others deserved best to reign; without which supposition, no form of government can be so prone to tyranny as monarchy is. And whereas you resemble a monarchy to the government of the world by one Divine Being, I pray answer me, whether you think that any other can deserve to be invested with a power here on earth, that shall resemble his power that governs the world, except such a person as does infinitely excel all other men, and both for wisdom and goodness in some measure resemble the Deity? and such a person, in my opinion, none can be but the Son of God himself. . . . .

What principles, what law, what religion ever taught men rather to consult their ease, to save their money, their blood, nay, their lives themselves, than to oppose an enemy with force? for I make no difference between a foreign enemy and another, since both are equally dangerous and destructive to the good of the whole nation. The people of Israel saw very well, that they could not possibly punish the Benjamites for murdering the Levite's wife, without the loss of many men's lives: and did that induce them to sit still? Was that accounted a sufficient argument why they should abstain from war, from a very bloody civil war? Did they therefore suffer the death of one poor woman to be unrevenged? Certainly if nature teaches us rather to endure the government of a king, though he be never so bad, than to endanger the lives of a great many men in the recovery of our liberty; it must teach us likewise not only to endure a kingly government, which is the only one that you argue ought to be submitted to, but even an aristocracy and a democracy: nay, and sometimes it will persuade us, to submit to a multitude of highwaymen, and to slaves that mutiny. Fulvius and Rupilius, if your principles had been received in their days, must not have engaged in the servile war (as their writers call it) after the Prætorian armies were slain; Crassus must not have marched against Spartacus, after the rebels had destroyed one Roman army, and spoiled their tents; nor must Pompey have undertaken the Piratic war. But the state of Rome must have pursued the dictates of nature, and must have submitted to their own slaves, or to the pirates, rather than run the hazard of losing some men's lives. You do not prove at all, that nature has imprinted any such notion as this of yours on the minds of men: and yet you cannot forbear boding us ill luck, and denouncing the wrath of God against us, (which may heaven divert, and inflict it upon yourself, and all such prognosticators as you!) who have punished as he deserved, one that had the name of our king, but was in fact our implacable enemy; and we have made atonement for the death of so many of our countrymen, as our civil wars have occasioned, by shedding his blood, that was the author and cause of them. . . . .

After having discoursed upon the law of God and of nature, and handled both so untowardly, that you have got nothing by the bargain but a deserved reproach of ignorance and knavery, I cannot apprehend what you can have further to allege in defence of your royal cause, but mere trifles. I for my part hope I have given satisfaction already to all good and learned men, and done this noble cause right, should I break off here; yet lest I should seem to any to decline your variety of arguing and ingenuity, rather than your immoderate impertinence and tittle-tattle, I will follow you wherever you have a mind to go; but with such brevity as shall make it appear, that after having performed whatever the necessary defence of the cause required, if not what the dignity of it merited, I now do but comply with some men's expectation, if not their curiosity. "Now," say you, "I shall allege other and greater arguments." What! greater arguments than what the law of God and nature afforded? Help, Lucina! the mountain Salmasius is in labor! It is not for nothing that he has got a she-husband. Mortals, expect some extraordinary birth. "If he that is, and is called a king, might be accused before any other power, that power must of necessity be greater than that of the king; and if so, then must that power be indeed the kingly power, and ought to have the name of it: for a kingly power is thus defined; to wit, the supreme power in the state residing in a single person, and which has no superior." O ridiculous birth! a mouse crept out of the mountain! help, grammarians! one of your number is in danger of perishing! the law of God and of nature are safe; but Salmasius's dictionary is undone. What if I should answer you thus? That words ought to give place to things; that we, having taken away kingly government itself, do not think ourselves concerned about its name and definition; let others look to that, who are in love with kings: we are contented with the enjoyment of our liberty; such an answer would be good enough for you. But to let you see that I deal fairly with you throughout, I will answer you, not only from my own, but from the opinion of very wise and good men, who have thought that the name and power of a king are very consistent with a power in the people and the law superior to that of the king himself. In the first place, Lycurgus, a man very eminent for wisdom, designing, as Plato says, to secure a kingly government as well as it was possible, could find no better expedient to preserve it, than by making the power of the senate, and of the Ephori, that is, the power of the people, superior to it. Theseus, in Euripides, king of Athens, was of the same opinion; for he to his great honor restored the people to their liberty, and advanced the power of the people above that of the king, and yet left the regal power in that city to his posterity. Whence Euripides, in his play called "The Suppliants," introduces him speaking on this manner: "I have advanced the people themselves into the throne, having freed the city from slavery, and admitted the people to a share in the government, by giving them an equal right of suffrage." And in another place to the herald of Thebes: "In the first place," says he, "you begin your speech, friend, with a thing that is not true, in styling me a monarch: for this city is not governed by a single person, but is a free state; the people reigns here." These were his words, when at the same time he was both called and really was king there. The divine Plato likewise, in his eighth epistle: "Lycurgus," says he, "introduced the power of the senate and of the Ephori, a thing very preservative of kingly government, which by this means has honorably flourished for so many ages, because the law in effect was made king." Now the law cannot be king, unless there be some, who, if there should be occasion, may put the law in execution against the king. A kingly government so bounded and limited he himself commends to the Sicilians: "Let the people enjoy their liberty under a kingly government; let the king himself be accountable; let the law take place even against kings themselves, if they act contrary to law." Aristotle likewise, in the third book of his Politics: "Of all kingdoms," says he, "that are governed by laws, that of the Lacedemonians seems to be most truly and properly so." And he says, all forms of kingly governments are according to settled and established laws; but one, which he calls *παμβασιλεία,* or Absolute Monarchy, which he does not mention ever to have obtained in any nation. So that Aristotle thought such a kingdom as that of the Lacedemonians was to be and deserve the name of a kingdom more properly than any other; and consequently that a king, though subordinate to his own people, was nevertheless actually a king, and properly so called. Now since so many and so great authors assert, that a kingly government both in name and thing may very well subsist even where the people, though they do not ordinarily exercise the supreme power, yet have it actually residing in them, and exercise it upon occasion; be not you of so mean a soul as to fear the downfall of grammar, and the confusion of the signification of words to that degree, as to betray the liberty of mankind and the state, rather than your glossary should not hold water. . . . .

Let this stand then as a settled maxim of the law of nature, never to be shaken by any artifices of flatterers, that the senate, or the people, are superior to kings, be they good or bad: which is but what you yourself do in effect confess, when you tell us, that the authority of kings was derived from the people. For that power, which they transferred to princes, doth yet naturally, or, as I may say, virtually reside in themselves notwithstanding: for so natural causes, that produce any effect by a certain eminency of operation, do always retain more of their own virtue and energy than they impart; nor do they, by communicating to others, exhaust themselves. You see, the closer we keep to nature, the more evidently does the people's power appear to be above that of the prince. And this is likewise certain, that the people do not freely, and of choice, settle the government in the king absolutely, so as to give him a propriety in it, nor by nature can do so: but only for the public safety and liberty, which, when the king ceases to take care of, then the people in effect have given him nothing at all: for nature says, the people gave it him to a particular end and purpose; which end, if neither nature nor the people can attain, the people's gift becomes no more valid than any other void covenant or agreement. These reasons prove very fully, that the people are superior to the king; and so your "greatest and most convincing argument, that a king cannot be judged by his people, because he has no peer in his kingdom," nor any superior, falls to the ground. . . . .

Since, therefore, by our law, as appears by that old book called "The Mirror," the king has his peers, who in Parliament have cognizance of wrongs done by the king to any of his people; and since it is notoriously known that the meanest man in the kingdom may even in inferior courts have the benefit of the law against the king himself, in case of any injury or wrong sustained; how much more consonant to justice, how much more necessary is it that in case the king oppress all his people, there should be such as have authority not only to restrain him and keep him within bounds, but to judge and punish him! for that government must needs be very ill, and most ridiculously constituted, in which remedy is provided in case of little injuries done by the prince to private persons, and no remedy, no redress for greater, no care taken for the safety of the whole; no provision made to the contrary, but that the king may, without any law, ruin all his subjects, when at the same time he cannot by law so much as hurt any one of them. And since I have shown that it is neither good manners, nor expedient, that the lords should be the king's judges; it follows, that the power of judicature in that case does wholly, and by very good right, belong to the commons, who are both peers of the realm and barons, and have the power and authority of all the people committed to them. For since (as we find it expressly in our written law, which I have already cited) the commons together with the king made a good Parliament without either lords or bishops, because before either lords or bishops had a being, kings held Parliaments with their commons only; by the very same reason the commons apart must have the sovereign power without the king, and a power of judging the king himself; because before there ever was a king, they, in the name of the whole body of the nation, held councils and Parliaments, had the power of judicature, made laws, and made the kings themselves, not to lord it over the people, but to administer their public affairs. Whom if the king, instead of so doing, shall endeavor to injure and oppress, our law pronounces him from time forward not so much as to retain the name of a king, to be no such thing as a king: and if he be no king, what need we trouble ourselves to find out peers for him? For being then by all good men adjudged to be a tyrant, there are none but who are peers good enough for him, and proper enough to pronounce sentence of death upon him judicially. These things being so, I think I have sufficiently proved what I undertook by many authorities, and written laws; to wit, that since the commons have authority by very good right to try the king, and since they have actually tried him, and put him to death, for the mischief he hath done both in church and state, and without all hope of amendment, they have done nothing therein but what was just and regular, for the interest of the state, in discharging of their trust, becoming their dignity, and according to the laws of the land. And I cannot upon this occasion but congratulate myself with the honor of having had such ancestors, who founded this government with no less prudence, and in as much liberty as the most worthy of the ancient Romans or Grecians ever founded any of theirs: and they must needs, if they have any knowledge of our affairs, rejoice over their posterity, who, when they were almost reduced to slavery, yet with so much wisdom and courage vindicated and asserted the state, which they so wisely founded upon so much liberty, from the unruly government of a king. . . . .

But who secluded those ill-affected members? "The English army," you say: so that it was not an army of foreigners, but of most valiant, and faithful, honest natives, whose officers for the most part were members of Parliament; and whom those good secluded members would have secluded their country, and banished into Ireland; while, in the mean time, the Scots, whose alliance began to be doubtful, had very considerable forces in four of our northern counties, and kept garrisons in the best towns of those parts, and had the king himself in custody; whilst they likewise encouraged the tumultuating of those of their own faction, who did more than threaten the Parliament, both in city and country, and through whose means not only a civil, but a war with Scotland too, shortly after brake out. If it has been always counted praiseworthy in private men to assist the state and promote the public good, whether by advice or action, our army sure was in no fault, who, being ordered by the Parliament to come to town, obeyed and came, and when they were come, quelled with ease the faction and uproar of the king's party, who sometimes threatened the House itself. For things were brought to that pass, that of necessity either we must be run down by them, or they by us. They had on their side most of the shopkeepers and handicraftsmen of London, and generally those of the ministers, that were most factious. On our side was the army, whose fidelity, moderation, and courage were sufficiently known. It being in our power by their means to retain our liberty, our state, our common safety, do you think we had not been fools to have lost all by our negligence and folly? They who had had places of command in the king's army, after their party were subdued, had laid down their arms indeed against their wills, but continued enemies to us in their hearts: and they flocked to town, and were here watching all opportunities of renewing the war. With these men, though they were the greatest enemies they had in the world, and thirsted after their blood, did the Presbyterians, because they were not permitted to exercise a civil as well as an ecclesiastical jurisdiction over all others, hold secret correspondence, and took measures very unworthy of what they had formerly both said and done; and they came to that spleen at last, that they would rather enthral themselves to the king again, than admit their own brethren to share in their liberty, which they likewise had purchased at the price of their own blood; they chose rather to be lorded over once more by a tyrant, polluted with the blood of so many of his own subjects, and who was enraged, and breathed out nothing but revenge against those of them that were left, than endure their brethren and friends to be upon the square with them. The Independents, as they are called, were the only men that, from first to last, kept to their point, and knew what use to make of their victory. They refused (and wisely, in my opinion) to make him king again, being then an enemy, who, when he was their king, had made himself their enemy: nor were they ever the less averse to a peace, but they very prudently dreaded a new war, or a perpetual slavery under the name of a peace. To load our army with the more reproaches, you begin a silly confused narrative of our affairs; in which, though I find many things false, many things frivolous, many things laid to our charge for which we rather merit; yet I think, it will be to no purpose for me to write a true relation in answer to your false one. . . . .

If any man should question whether you are an honest man or a knave, let him read these following lines of yours: "It is time to explain whence and at what time this sect [Independents] of enemies to kingship first began. Why truly these rare Puritans began in Queen Elizabeth's time to crawl out of hell, and disturb not only the Church, but the state likewise; for they are no less plagues to the latter than to the former." Now your very speech bewrays you to be a right Balaam; for where you designed to spit out the most bitter poison you could, there unwittingly and against your will you have pronounced a blessing. For it is notoriously known all over England, that if any endeavored to follow the example of those Churches, whether in France or Germany, which they accounted best reformed, and to exercise the public worship of God in a more pure manner, which our bishops had almost universally corrupted with their ceremonies and superstitions; or, if any seemed either in point of religion or morality to be better than others, such persons were by the favor of episcopacy termed Puritans. These are they whose principles, you say, are so opposite to kingship. Nor are they the only persons. "Most of the reformed religion, that have not sucked in the rest of their principles, yet seem to have approved of those that strike at kingly government." So that while you inveigh bitterly against the Independents, and endeavor to separate them from Christ's flock, with the same breath you praise them; and those principles which almost everywhere you affirm to be peculiar to the Independents, here you confess have been approved of by most of the reformed religion. . . . .

"But," say you, "there were added to those

judges, that were made choice of out of the House of Commons, some officers of the army, and it never was known, that soldiers had any right to try a subject for his life." I will silence you in a very few words: you may remember, that we are not now discoursing of a subject, but of an enemy; whom if a general of an army, after he has taken him prisoner, resolves to despatch, would he be thought to proceed otherwise than according to custom and martial law, if he himself with some of his officers should sit upon him, and try and condemn him? An enemy to a state, made a prisoner of war, cannot be looked upon to be so much as a member, much less a king in that state. This is declared by that sacred law of St. Edward, which denies that a bad king is a king at all, or ought to be called so. Whereas you say, it was "not the whole, but a part of the House of Commons, that tried and condemned the king," I give you this answer: the number of them, who gave their votes for putting the king to death, was far greater than is necessary, according to the custom of our Parliaments, to transact the greatest affairs of the kingdom, in the absence of the rest; who, since they were absent through their own fault, (for to revolt to the common enemy in their hearts is the worst sort of absence,) their absence ought not to hinder the rest who continued faithful to the cause from preserving the state; which when it was in a tottering condition, and almost quite reduced to slavery and utter ruin, the whole body of the people had at first committed to their fidelity, prudence, and courage. And they acted their parts like men; they set themselves in opposition to the unruly wilfulness, the rage, the secret designs of an inveterate and exasperated king; they preferred the common liberty and safety before their own; they outdid all former Parliaments, they outdid all their ancestors, in conduct, magnanimity, and steadiness to their cause. Yet these very men did a great part of the people ungratefully desert in the midst of their undertaking, though they had promised them all fidelity, all the help and assistance they could afford them. These were for slavery and peace, with sloth and luxury, upon any terms: others demanded their liberty, nor would accept of a peace that was not sure and honorable. What should the Parliament do in this case? Ought they to have defended this part of the people, that was sound, and continued faithful to them and their country, or to have sided with those that deserted both? I know what you will say they ought to have done. You are not Eurylochus, but Elpenor, a miserable enchanted beast, a filthy swine, accustomed to a sordid slavery, even under a woman; so that you have not the least relish of true magnanimity, nor consequently of liberty, which is the effect of it: you would have all other men slaves, because you find in yourself no generous, ingenuous inclinations; you say nothing, you breathe nothing, but what is mean and servile. . . . .

Here you lament his being condemned as a tyrant, a traitor, and a murderer. That he had no wrong done him, shall now be made appear. But let us define a tyrant, not according to vulgar conceits, but the judgment of Aristotle, and of all learned men. He is a tyrant who regards his own welfare and profit only, and not that of the people. So Aristotle defines one in the tenth book of his Ethics, and elsewhere; and so do very many others. Whether Charles regarded his own or the people's good, these few things of many that I shall but touch upon will evince. When his rents and other public revenues of the crown would not defray the expenses of the court, he laid most heavy taxes upon the people; and when they were squandered away, he invented new ones; not for the benefit, honor, or defence of the state, but that he might hoard up, or lavish out in one house, the riches and wealth, not of one, but of three nations. When at this rate he broke loose, and acted without any color of law to warrant his proceedings, knowing that the Parliament was the only thing that could give him check, he endeavored either wholly to lay aside the very calling of Parliaments, or calling them just as often, and no oftener, than to serve his own turn, to make them entirely at his devotion. Which bridle when he had cast off himself, he put another bridle upon the people: he put garrisons of German horse and Irish foot in many towns and cities, and that in time of peace. Do you think he does not begin to look like a tyrant? In which very thing, as in many other particulars, which you have formerly given me occasion to instance, though you scorn to have Charles compared with so cruel a tyrant as Nero, he resembled him extremely much. For Nero likewise often threatened to take away the senate. Besides, he bore extreme hard upon the consciences of good men, and compelled them to the use of ceremonies and superstitious worship, borrowed from Popery, and by him reintroduced into the Church. They that would not conform, were imprisoned or banished. He made war upon the Scots twice for no other cause than that. By all these actions he has surely deserved the name of a tyrant once over at least. Now I will tell you why the word traitor was put into his indictment: when he assured his Parliament by promises, by proclamations, by imprecations, that he had no design against the state, at that very time did he list Papists in Ireland, he sent a private embassy to the king of Denmark to beg assistance from him of arms, horses, and men, expressly against the Parliament; and was endeavoring to raise an army first in England, and then in Scotland. To the English he promised the plunder of the city of London; to the Scots, that the four northern counties should be added to Scotland, if they would but help him to get rid of the Parliament, by what means soever. These projects not succeeding, he sent over one Dillon, a traitor, into Ireland, with private instructions to the natives, to fall suddenly upon all the English that inhabited there. These are the most remarkable instances of his treasons, not taken up upon hearsay and idle reports, but discovered by letters under his own hand and seal. And finally I suppose no man will deny that he was a murderer, by whose order the Irish took arms, and put to death with most exquisite torments above a hundred thousand English, who lived peaceably by them, and without any apprehension of danger; and who raised so great a civil war in the other two kingdoms. Add to all this, that at the treaty in the Isle of Wight the king openly took upon himself the guilt of the war, and cleared the Parliament in the confession he made there, which is publicly known. Thus you have in short why King Charles was adjudged a tyrant, a traitor, and a murderer. . . . .

It would never have entered into the thoughts of this rascally foreign grammarian, to write a discourse of the rights of the crown of England, unless both Charles Stuart, now in banishment, and tainted with his father's principles, and those profligate tutors that he has along with him, had industriously suggested to him what they would have writ. They dictated to him, "that the whole Parliament were liable to be proceeded against as traitors, because they declared, without the king's assent, all them to be traitors who had taken up arms against the Parliament of England; and that Parliaments were but the king's vassals; that the oath which our kings take at their coronation is but a ceremony": and why not that a vassal too? So that no reverence of laws, no sacredness of an oath, will be sufficient to protect your lives and fortunes, either from the exorbitance of a furious, or the revenge of an exasperated prince, who has been so instructed from his cradle, as to think laws, religion, nay, and oaths themselves, ought to be subject to his will and pleasure. How much better is it, and more becoming yourselves, if you desire riches, liberty, peace, and empire, to obtain them assuredly by your own virtue, industry, prudence, and valor, than to long after and hope for them in vain under the rule of a king? They who are of opinion that these things cannot be compassed but under a king, and a lord, it cannot well be expressed how mean, how base, I do not say, how unworthy, thoughts they have of themselves; for in effect, what do they other than confess, that they themselves are lazy, weak, senseless, silly persons, and framed for slavery both in body and mind? And indeed all manner of slavery is scandalous and disgraceful to a freeborn ingenuous person; but for you, after you have recovered your lost liberty, by God's assistance and your own arms; after the performance of so many valiant exploits, and the making so remarkable an example of a most potent king, to desire to return again into a condition of bondage and slavery, will not only be scandalous and disgraceful, but an impious and wicked thing; and equal to that of the Israelites, who for desiring to return to the Egyptian slavery were so severely punished for that sordid, slavish temper of mind, and so many of them destroyed by that God who had been their deliverer. . . . .

And now I think, through God's assistance, I have finished the work I undertook, to wit, the defence of the noble actions of my countrymen at home and abroad, against the raging and envious madness of this distracted sophister; and the asserting of the common rights of the people against the unjust domination of kings, not out of any hatred to kings, but tyrants: nor have I purposely left unanswered any one argument alleged by my adversary, nor any one example or authority quoted by him, that seemed to have any force in it, or the least color of an argument. Perhaps I have been guilty rather of the other extreme, of replying to some of his fooleries and trifles, as if they were solid arguments, and thereby may seem to have attributed more to them than they deserved. One thing yet remains to be done, which perhaps is of the greatest concern of all, and that is, that you, my countrymen, refute this adversary of yours yourselves, which I do not see any other means of your affecting, than by a constant endeavor to outdo all men's bad words by your own good deeds. When you labored under more sorts of oppression than one, you betook yourselves to God for refuge, and he was graciously pleased to hear your most earnest prayer and desires. He has gloriously delivered you, the first of nations, from the two greatest mischiefs of this life, and most pernicious to virtue, tyranny and superstition; he has endued you with greatness of mind to be the first of mankind, who after having conquered their own king, and having had him delivered into their hands, have not scrupled to condemn him judicially, and, pursuant to that sentence of condemnation, to put him to death. After the performing so glorious an action as this, you ought to do nothing that is mean and little, not so much as to think of, much less to do, anything but what is great and sublime. Which to attain to, this is your only way: as you have subdued your enemies in the field, so to make appear, that unarmed, and in the highest outward peace and tranquillity, you of all mankind are best able to subdue ambition, avarice, the love of riches, and can best avoid the corruptions that prosperity is apt to introduce, (which generally subdue and triumph over other nations,) to show as great justice, temperance, and moderation in the maintaining your liberty, as you have shown courage in freeing yourselves from slavery. These are the only arguments by which you will be able to evince that you are not such persons as this fellow represents you, — Traitors, Robbers, Murderers, Parricides, Madmen; that you did not put your king to death out of any ambitious design, or a desire of invading the rights of others; not out of any seditious principles or sinister ends; that it was not an act of fury or madness; but that it was wholly out of love to your liberty, your religion, to justice, virtue, and your country, that you punished a tyrant. But if it should fall out otherwise, (which God forbid,) if as you have been valiant in war, you should grow debauched in peace, you that have had such visible demonstrations of the goodness of God to yourselves, and his wrath against your enemies; and that you should not have learned by so eminent, so remarkable an example before your eyes, to fear God, and work righteousness; for my part, I shall easily grant and confess (for I cannot deny it) whatever ill men may speak or think of you, to be very true. And you will find in a little time, that God's displeasure against you will be greater than it has been against your adversaries, greater than his grace and favor has been to yourselves, which you have had larger experience of than any other nation under heaven.

FROM

THE SECOND DEFENCE OF THE PEOPLE OF ENGLAND.

GRATEFUL recollection of the divine goodness is the first of human obligations; and extraordinary favors demand more solemn and devout acknowledgments: with such acknowledgments I feel it my duty to begin this work. First, because I was born at a time when the virtue of my fellow-citizens, far exceeding that of their progenitors in greatness of soul and vigor of enterprise, having invoked Heaven to witness the justice of their cause, and been clearly governed by its directions, has succeeded in delivering the commonwealth from the most grievous tyranny, and religion from the most ignominious degradation. And next, because when there suddenly arose many who, as is usual with the vulgar, basely calumniated the most illustrious achievements, and when one, eminent above the rest, inflated with literary pride, and the zealous applauses of his partisans, had in a scandalous publication, which was particularly levelled against me, nefariously undertaken to plead the cause of despotism, I, who was neither deemed unequal to so renowned an adversary, nor to so great a subject, was particularly selected by the deliverers of our country, and by the general suffrage of the public, openly to vindicate the rights of the English nation, and consequently of liberty itself. Lastly, because in a matter of so much moment, and which excited such ardent expectations, I did not disappoint the hopes nor the opinions of my fellow-citizens; while men of learning and eminence abroad honored me with unmingled approbation; while I obtained such a victory over my opponent, that, notwithstanding his unparalleled assurance, he was obliged to quit the field with his courage broken and his reputation lost; and for the three years which he lived afterwards, much as he menaced and furiously as he raved, he gave me no further trouble, except that he procured the paltry aid of some despicable hirelings, and suborned some of his silly and extravagant admirers, to support him under the weight of the unexpected and recent disgrace which he had experienced. This will immediately appear. Such are the signal favors which I ascribe to the divine beneficence, and which I thought it right devoutly to commemorate, not only that I might discharge a debt of gratitude, but particularly because they seem auspicious to the success of my present undertaking. For who is there who does not identify the honor of his country with his own? And what can conduce more to the beauty or glory of one's country, than the recovery, not only of its civil but its religious liberty? And what nation or state ever obtained both, by more successful or more valorous exertion? For fortitude is seen resplendent, not only in the field of battle and amid the clash of arms, but displays its energy under every difficulty and against every assailant. Those Greeks and Romans, who are the objects of our admiration, employed hardly any other virtue in the extirpation of tyrants, than that love of liberty which made them prompt in seizing the sword, and gave them strength to use it. With facility they accomplished the undertaking, amid the general shout of praise and joy; nor did they engage in the attempt so much as an enterprise of perilous and doubtful issue, as in a contest the most glorious in which virtue could be signalized; which infallibly led to present recompense; which bound their brows with wreaths of laurel, and consigned their memories to immortal fame. For as yet, tyrants were not beheld with a superstitious reverence; as yet they were not regarded with tenderness and complacency, as the vicegerents or deputies of Christ, as they have suddenly professed to be; as yet the vulgar, stupefied by the subtle casuistry of the priest, had not degenerated into a state of barbarism, more gross than that which disgraces the most senseless natives of Hindostan. For these make mischievous demons, whose malice they cannot resist, the objects of their religious adoration: while those elevate impotent tyrants, in order to shield them from destruction, into the rank of gods; and, to their own cost, consecrate the pests of the human race. But against this dark array of long-received opinions, superstitions, obloquy, and fears, which some dread even more than the enemy himself, the English had to contend; and all this, under the light of better information, and favored by an impulse from above, they overcame with such singular enthusiasm and bravery, that, great as were the numbers engaged in the contest, the grandeur of conception, and loftiness of spirit which were universally displayed, merited for each individual more than a mediocrity of fame; and Britain, which was formerly styled the hot-bed of tyranny, will hereafter deserve to be celebrated, for endless ages, as a soil most genial to the growth of liberty. During the mighty struggle, no anarchy, no licentiousness was seen; no illusions of glory, no extravagant emulation of the ancients inflamed them with a thirst for ideal liberty; but the rectitude of their lives, and the sobriety of their habits, taught them the only true and safe road to real liberty; and they took up arms only to defend the sanctity of the laws and the rights of conscience. Relying on the divine assistance, they used every honorable exertion to break the yoke of slavery; of the praise of which, though I claim no share to myself, yet I can easily repel any charge which may be adduced against me, either of want of courage, or want of zeal. For though I did not participate in the toils or dangers of the war, yet I was at the same time engaged in a service not less hazardous to myself and more beneficial to my fellow-citizens; nor, in the adverse turns of our affairs, did I ever betray any symptoms of pusillanimity and dejection; or show myself more afraid than became me of malice or of death. For since from my youth I was devoted to the pursuits of literature, and my mind had always been stronger than my body, I did not court the labors of a camp, in which any common person would have been of more service than myself, but resorted to that employment in which my exertions were likely to be of most avail. Thus, with the better part of my frame I contributed as much as possible to the good of my country, and to the success of the glorious cause in which we were engaged; and I thought that if God willed the success of such glorious achievements, it was equally agreeable to his will that there should be others by whom those achievements should be recorded with dignity and elegance; and that the truth, which had been defended by arms, should also be defended by reason; which is the best and only legitimate means of defending it. Hence, while I applaud those who were victorious in the field, I will not complain of the province which was assigned me; but rather congratulate myself upon it, and thank the Author of all good for having placed me in a station, which may be an object of envy to others rather than of regret to myself. I am far from wishing to make any vain or arrogant comparisons, or to speak ostentatiously of myself; but, in a cause so great and glorious, and particularly on an occasion when I am called by the general suffrage to defend the very defenders of that cause, I can hardly refrain from assuming a more lofty and swelling tone than the simplicity of an exordium may seem to justify: and much as I may be surpassed in the powers of eloquence and copiousness of diction, by the illustrious orators of antiquity, yet the subject of which I treat was never surpassed in any age, in dignity, or in interest. It has excited such general and such ardent expectation, that I imagine myself not in the forum or on the rostra, surrounded only by the people of Athens or of Rome, but about to address in this, as I did in my former Defence, the whole collective body of people, cities, states, and councils of the wise and eminent, through the wide expanse of anxious and listening Europe. I seem to survey, as from a towering height, the far-extended tracts of sea and land, and innumerable crowds of spectators, betraying in their looks the liveliest interest, and sensations the most congenial with my own. Here I behold the stout and manly prowess of the Germans disdaining servitude; there the generous and lively impetuosity of the

French ; on this side, the calm and stately valor of the Spaniard ; on that the composed and wary magnanimity of the Italian. Of all the lovers of liberty and virtue, the magnanimous and the wise, in whatever quarter they may be found, some secretly favor, others openly approve ; some greet me with congratulations and applause ; others, who had long been proof against conviction, at last yield themselves captive to the force of truth. Surrounded by congregated multitudes, I now imagine that, from the columns of Hercules to the Indian Ocean, I behold the nations of the earth recovering that liberty which they so long had lost ; and that the people of this island are transporting to other countries a plant of more beneficial qualities, and more noble growth, than that which Triptolemus is reported to have carried from region to region ; that they are disseminating the blessings of civilization and freedom among cities, kingdoms, and nations. . . . .

The prerogative which I deny to kings, I would persist in denying in any legitimate monarchy ; for no sovereign could injure me without first condemning himself by a confession of his despotism. If I inveigh against tyrants, what is this to kings? whom I am far from associating with tyrants. As much as an honest man differs from a rogue, so much I contend that a king differs from a tyrant. Whence it is clear, that a tyrant is so far from being a king, that he is always in direct opposition to a king. And he who peruses the records of history, will find that more kings have been subverted by tyrants than by their subjects. He, therefore, who would authorize the destruction of tyrants, does not authorize the destruction of kings, but of the most inveterate enemies to kings. But that right, which you concede to kings, the right of doing what they please, is not justice, but injustice, ruin, and despair. By that envenomed present you yourselves destroy those whom you extol as if they were above the reach of danger and oppression; and you quite obliterate the difference between a king and a tyrant, if you invest both with the same arbitrary power. For, if a king does not exercise that power, (and no king will exercise it as long as he is not a tyrant,) the power must be ascribed, not to the king, but to the individual. For, what can be imagined more absurd than that regal prerogative, which, if any one uses, as often as he wishes to act the king, so often he ceases to be an honest man; and as often as he chooses to be an honest man, so often he must evince that he is not a king? Can any more bitter reproach be cast upon kings? He who maintains this prerogative must himself be a monster of injustice and iniquity; for how can there be a worse person than him, who must himself first verify the exaggerated picture of atrocity which he delineates? But if every good man, as an ancient sect of philosophers magnificently taught, is a king, it follows that every bad one is, according to his capacity, a tyrant; nor does the name of tyrant signify anything soaring or illustrious, but the meanest reptile on the earth; for in proportion as he is great, he is contemptible and abject. Others are vicious only for themselves; but tyrants are vicious, not only for themselves, but are even involuntarily obliged to participate in the crimes of their importunate menials and favorites, and to intrust certain portions of their despotism to the vilest of their dependants. Tyrants are thus the most abject of slaves, for they are the servants of those who are themselves in servitude. . . . .

Let us now come to the charges which were brought against myself. Is there anything reprehensible in my manners or my conduct? Surely nothing. What no one, not totally divested of all generous sensibility, would have done, he reproaches me with want of beauty and loss of sight,—

> "A monster huge and hideous, void of sight."

I certainly never supposed that I should have been obliged to enter into a competition for beauty with the Cyclops; but he immediately corrects himself, and says, "though not indeed huge, for there cannot be a more spare, shrivelled, and bloodless form." It is of no moment to say anything of personal appearance, yet lest (as the Spanish vulgar, implicitly confiding in the relations of their priests, believe of heretics) any one, from the representations of my enemies, should be led to imagine that I have either the head of a dog, or the horn of a rhinoceros, I will say something on the subject, that I may have an opportunity of paying my grateful acknowledgments to the Deity, and of refuting the most shameless lies. I do not believe that I was ever once noted for deformity, by any one who ever saw me; but the praise of beauty I am not anxious to obtain. My stature certainly is not tall; but it rather approaches the middle than the diminutive. Yet what if it were diminutive, when so many men, illustrious both in peace and war, have been the same? And how can that be called diminutive, which is great enough for every virtuous achievement? Nor, though very thin, was I ever deficient in courage or in strength; and I was wont constantly to exercise myself in the use of the broadsword, as long as it comported with my habit and my years. Armed with this weapon, as I usually was, I should have thought myself quite a match for any one, though much stronger than myself; and I felt perfectly secure against the assault of any open enemy. At this moment I have the same courage, the same strength, though not the same eyes; yet so little do they betray any external appearance of injury, that they are as unclouded and bright as the eyes of those who most distinctly see. In this instance alone I am a dissembler against my will.

My face, which is said to indicate a total privation of blood, is of a complexion entirely opposite to the pale and the cadaverous; so that, though I am more than forty years old, there is scarcely any one to whom I do not appear ten years younger than I am; and the smoothness of my skin is not, in the least, affected by the wrinkles of age. If there be one particle of falsehood in this relation, I should deservedly incur the ridicule of many thousands of my countrymen, and even many foreigners, to whom I am personally known. But if he, in a matter so foreign to his purpose, shall be found to have asserted so many shameless and gratuitous falsehoods, you may the more readily estimate the quantity of his veracity on other topics. Thus much necessity compelled me to assert concerning my personal appearance. Respecting yours, though I have been informed that it is most insignificant and contemptible, a perfect mirror of the worthlessness of your character and the malevolence of your heart, I say nothing, and no one will be anxious that anything should be said. I wish that I could with equal facility refute what this barbarous opponent has said of my blindness; but I cannot do it; and I must submit to the affliction. It is not so wretched to be blind, as it is not to be capable of enduring blindness. But why should I not endure a misfortune, which it behoves every one to be prepared to endure if it should happen; which may, in the common course of things, happen to any man; and which has been known to happen to the most distinguished and virtuous persons in history. Shall I mention those wise and ancient bards, whose misfortunes the gods are said to have compensated by superior endowments, and whom men so much revered, that they chose rather to impute their want of sight to the injustice of Heaven than to their own want of innocence or virtue? What is reported of the Augur Tiresias is well known; of whom Apollonius sung thus in his Argonauts: —

"To men he dared the will divine disclose,
Nor feared what Jove might in his wrath impose.
The gods assigned him age, without decay,
But snatched the blessing of his sight away."

But God himself is truth; in propagating which, as men display a greater integrity and zeal, they approach nearer to the similitude of God, and possess a greater portion of his love. We cannot suppose the Deity envious of truth, or unwilling that it should be freely communicated to mankind. The loss of sight, therefore, which this inspired sage, who was so eager in promoting knowledge among men, sustained, cannot be considered as a judicial punishment. Or shall I mention those worthies, who were as distinguished for wisdom in the cabinet as for valor in the field? And first, Timoleon of Corinth, who delivered his city and all Sicily from the yoke of slavery; than whom there never lived in any age, a more virtuous man, or a more incorrupt statesman: next Appius Claudius, whose discreet counsels in the Senate, though they could not restore sight to his own eyes, saved Italy from the formidable inroads of Pyrrhus: then Cæcilius Metellus the high-priest, who lost his sight, while he saved, not only the city, but the palladium, the protection of the city, and the most sacred relics, from the destruction of the flames. On other occasions Providence has indeed given conspicuous proofs of its regard for such singular exertions of patriotism and virtue; what, therefore, happened to so great and so good a man, I can hardly place in the catalogue of misfortunes. Why should I mention others of later times, as Dandolo of Venice, the incomparable Doge; of Boemar Zisca, the bravest of generals, and the champion of the cross; or Jerome Zanchius, and some other theologians of the highest reputation? For it is evident that the patriarch Isaac, than whom no man ever enjoyed more of the divine regard, lived blind for many years; and perhaps also his son Jacob, who was equally an object of the divine benevolence. And in short, did not our Saviour himself clearly declare that that poor man whom he restored to sight had not been born blind either on account of his own sins or those of his progenitors? And with respect to myself, though I have accurately examined my conduct, and scrutinized my soul, I call thee, O God, the searcher of hearts, to witness, that I am not conscious, either in the more early or in the later periods of my life, of having committed any enormity, which might deservedly have marked me out as a fit object for such a calamitous visitation. But since my enemies boast that this affliction is only a retribution for the transgressions of my pen, I again invoke the Almighty to witness, that I never, at any time, wrote anything which I did not think agreeable to truth, to justice, and to piety. This was my persuasion then, and I feel the same persuasion now. Nor was I ever prompted to such exertions by the influence of ambition, by the lust of lucre or of praise; it was only by the conviction of duty and the feeling of patriotism, a disinterested passion for the extension of civil and religious liberty. Thus, therefore, when I was publicly solicited to write a reply to the Defence of the royal cause, when I had to contend with the pressure of sickness, and with the apprehension of soon losing the sight of my remaining eye, and when my medical attendants clearly announced, that if I did engage in the work, it would be irreparably lost, their premonitions caused no hesitation and inspired no dismay. I would not have listened to the voice even of Esculapius himself from the shrine of Epidauris, in preference to the suggestions of the heavenly monitor within my breast; my resolution was unshaken, though the alternative was either the loss of my sight, or the desertion of my duty: and I called to mind those two destinies, which the oracle of Delphi announced to the son of Thetis: —

> "Two fates may lead me to the realms of night;
> If staying here, around Troy's wall I fight,
> To my dear home no more must I return;
> But lasting glory will adorn my urn.
> But, if I withdraw from the martial strife,
> Short is my fame, but long will be my life." — *Il.* ix.

I considered that many had purchased a less good by a greater evil, the meed of glory by the loss of life; but that I might procure great good by little suffering; that though I am blind, I might still discharge the most honorable duties, the performance of which, as it is something more durable than glory, ought to be an object of superior admiration and esteem; I resolved, therefore, to make the short interval of sight, which was left me to enjoy, as beneficial as possible to the public interest. Thus it is clear by what motives I was governed in the measures which I took, and the losses which I sustained. Let then the calumniators of the divine goodness cease to revile, or to make me the object of their superstitious imaginations. Let them consider, that my situation, such as it is, is neither an object of my shame or my regret, that my resolutions are too firm to be shaken, that I am not depressed by any sense of the divine displeasure; that, on the other hand, in the most momentous periods, I have had full experience of the divine favor and protection; and that, in the solace and the strength which have been infused into me from above, I have been enabled to do the will of God; that I may oftener think on what he has bestowed, than on what he has withheld; that, in short, I am unwilling to exchange my consciousness of rectitude with that of any other person; and that I feel the recollection of a treasured store of tranquillity and delight. But, if the choice were necessary, I would, sir, prefer my blindness to yours; yours is a cloud spread over the mind, which darkens both the light of reason and of conscience; mine keeps from my view only the colored surfaces of things, while it leaves me at liberty to contemplate the beauty and stability of virtue and of truth. How many things are there besides which I would not willingly see; how many which I must see against my will; and how few which I feel any anxiety to see! There is, as the Apostle has remarked, a way to strength through weakness. Let me then be the most feeble creature alive, as long as that feebleness serves to invigorate the energies of my rational and immortal spirit; as long as in that obscurity in which I am enveloped the light of the divine presence more clearly shines, then, in proportion as I am weak, I shall be invincibly strong; and in proportion as I am blind, I shall more clearly see. O that I may thus be perfected by feebleness, and irradiated by obscurity! And, indeed, in my blindness, I enjoy in no inconsiderable degree the favor of the Deity, who regards me with more tenderness and compassion in proportion as I am able to behold nothing but himself. Alas! for him who insults me, who maligns and merits public execration! For the divine law not only shields me from injury, but almost renders me too sacred to attack; not indeed so much from the privation of my sight, as from the overshadowing of those heavenly wings which seem to have occasioned this obscurity; and which, when occasioned, he is wont to illuminate with an interior light, more precious and more pure. To this I ascribe the more tender assiduities of my friends, their soothing attentions, their kind visits, their reverential observances; among whom there are some with whom I may interchange the Pyladean and Thesean dialogue of inseparable friends:—

"*Orest.* Proceed, and be rudder of my feet, by showing me the most endearing love." — EURIP. *in Orest.*

And in another place,

"Lend your hand to your devoted friend,
Throw your arm round my neck, and I will conduct you on the way."

This extraordinary kindness, which I experience, cannot be any fortuitous combination; and friends, such as mine, do not suppose that all the virtues of a man are contained in his eyes. Nor do the persons of principal distinction in the commonwealth suffer me to be bereaved of comfort, when they see me bereaved of sight, amid the exertions which I made, the zeal which I showed, and the dangers which I run for the liberty which I love. But, soberly reflecting on the casualties of human life, they show me favor and indulgence, as to a soldier who has served his time, and kindly concede to me an exemption from care and toil. They do not strip me of the badges of honor which I have once worn; they do not deprive me of the places of public trust to which I have been appointed; they do not abridge my salary or emoluments; which, though I may not do so much to deserve as I did formerly, they are too considerate and too kind to take away; and, in short, they honor me as much as the Athenians did those whom they determined to support at the public expense in the Prytaneum. Thus, while both God and man unite in solacing me under the weight of my affliction, let no one lament my loss of sight in so honorable a cause. . . . .

He alone is worthy of the appellation [great] who does great things, or teaches how they may be done, or describes them with a suitable majesty when they have been done; but those only are great things, which tend to render life more happy, which increase the innocent enjoyments and comforts of existence, or which pave the way to a state of future bliss more permanent and more pure. . . . .

My work soon excited general approbation and delight; the author was lost sight of in the blaze of truth; and Salmasius, who had so lately been towering on the pinnacle of distinction, stripped of the mask which he had worn, soon dwindled into insignificance and contempt; from which, as long as he lived, he could never afterwards emerge, or recover his former consequence. But your penetrating mind, O serene queen of Sweden, soon detected his imposture; and, with a magnanimity almost above human, you taught sovereigns and the world to prefer truth to the interested clamors of faction. For though the splendor of his erudition, and the celebrity which he had acquired in the defence of the royal cause, had induced you to honor him with many marks of distinction, yet, when my answer appeared, which you perused with singular equanimity, you perceived that he had been convicted of the most palpable effrontery and misrepresentation; that he had betrayed the utmost indiscretion and intemperance, that he had uttered many falsehoods, many inconsistencies and contradictions. On this account, as it is said, you had him called into your presence; but when he was unable to vindicate himself, you were so visibly offended, that from that time you neither showed him the same attentions, nor held his talents nor his learning in the same esteem; and, what was entirely unexpected, you manifested a disposition to favor his adversary. You denied that what I had written against tyrants could have any reference to you; whence, in your own breast you enjoyed the sweets, and among others the fame, of a good conscience. For, since the whole tenor of your conduct sufficiently proves, that you are no tyrant, this unreserved expression of your sentiments makes it still more clear, that you are not even conscious to yourself of being one. How happy am I beyond my utmost expectations! (for to the praise of eloquence, except as far as eloquence consists in the force of truth, I lay no claim,) that, when the critical exigencies of my country demanded that I should undertake the arduous and invidious task of impugning the rights of kings, I should meet with so illustrious, so truly a royal evidence to my integrity, and to this truth, that I had not written a word against kings, but only against tyrants, the spots and the pests of royalty? But you, O Augusta, possessed not only so much magnanimity, but were so irradiated by the glorious beams of wisdom and of virtue, that you not only read with patience, with incredible impartiality, with a serene complacency of countenance, what might seem to be levelled against your rights and dignity; but expressed such an opinion of the defender of those rights, as may well be considered an adjudication of the palm of victory to his opponent. You, O queen! will forever be the object of my homage, my veneration, and my love; for it was your greatness of soul, so honorable to yourself and so auspicious to me, which served to efface the unfavorable impression against me at other courts, and to rescue me from the evil surmises of other sovereigns. What a high and favorable opinion must foreigners conceive, and your own subjects forever entertain, of your impartiality and justice, when, in a matter which so nearly interested the fate of sovereigns and the rights of your crown, they saw you sit down to the discussion with as much equanimity and composure, as you would to determine a dispute between two private individuals. It was not in vain that you made such large collections of books, and so many monuments of learning; not, indeed, that they could contribute much to your instruction, but because they so will teach your subjects to appreciate the merits of your reign, and the rare excellence of your virtue and your wisdom. For the Divinity himself seems to have inspired you with a love of wisdom, and a thirst for improvement, beyond what any books ever could have produced. It excites our astonishment to see a force of intellect so truly divine, a particle of celestial flame so resplendently pure, in a region so remote; of which an atmosphere, so darkened with clouds, and so chilled with frosts, could not extinguish the light, nor repress the operations. The rocky and barren soil, which is often as unfavorable to the growth of genius as of plants, has not impeded the maturation of your faculties; and that country so rich in metallic ore, which appears like a cruel step-mother to others, seems to have been a fostering parent to you; and after the most strenuous attempts to have at last produced a progeny of pure gold. I would invoke you, Christina! as the only child of the renowned and victorious Adolphus, if your merit did not as much eclipse his, as wisdom excels strength, and the arts of peace the havoc of war. Henceforth, the queen of the South will not be alone renowned in history; for there is a queen of the north, who would not only be worthy to appear in the court of the wise King of the Jews, or any king of equal wisdom; but to whose court others may from all parts repair, to behold so fair a heroine, so bright a pattern of all the royal virtues; and to the crown of whose praise this may well be added, that, neither in her conduct nor her appearance, is there any of the forbidding reserve, or the ostentatious parade, of royalty. She herself seems the least conscious of her own attributes of sovereignty; and her thoughts are always fixed on something greater and more sublime than the glitter of a crown. In this respect, her example may well make innumerable kings hide their diminished heads. She may, if such is the fatality of the Swedish nation, abdicate the sovereignty, but she can never lay aside the queen; for her reign has proved that she is fit to govern, not only Sweden, but the world. . . . .

I must therefore crave the indulgence of the reader if I have said already, or shall say hereafter, more of myself than I wish to say; that, if I cannot prevent the blindness of my eyes, the oblivion or the defamation of my name, I may at least rescue my life from that species of obscurity which is the associate of unprincipled depravity. This it will be necessary for me to do on more accounts than one; first, that so many good and learned men among the neighboring nations, who read my works, may not be induced by this fellow's calumnies to alter the favorable opinion which they have formed of me; but may be persuaded that I am not one who ever disgraced beauty of sentiment by deformity of conduct, or the maxims of a freeman by the actions of a slave; and that the whole tenor of my life has, by the grace of God, hitherto been unsullied by enormity or crime. Next, that those illustrious worthies, who are the objects of my praise, may know that nothing could afflict me with more shame than to have any vices of mine diminish the force or lessen the value of my panegyric upon them; and, lastly, that the people of England, whom fate, or duty, or their own virtues, have incited me to defend, may be convinced, from the purity and integrity of my life, that my defence, if it do not redound to their honor, can never be considered as their disgrace. I will now mention who and whence I am. I was born at London, of an honest family; my father was distinguished by the undeviating integrity of his life; my mother, by the esteem in which she was held, and the alms which she bestowed. My father destined me from a child to the pursuits of literature; and my appetite for knowledge was so voracious, that, from twelve years of age, I hardly ever left my studies, or went to bed before midnight. This primarily led to my loss of sight. My eyes were naturally weak, and I was subject to frequent headaches; which, however, could not chill the ardor of my curiosity, or retard the progress of my improvement. My father had me daily instructed in the grammar-school, and by other masters at home. He then, after I had acquired a proficiency in various languages, and had made a considerable progress in philosophy, sent me to the University of Cambridge. Here I passed seven years in the usual course of instruction and study, with the approbation of the good, and without any stain upon my character, till I took the degree of Master of Arts. After this I did not, as the miscreant feigns, run away into Italy, but of my own accord retired to my father's house, whither I was accompanied by the regrets of most of the fellows of the college, who showed me no common marks of friendship and esteem. On my father's estate, where he had determined to pass the remainder of his days, I enjoyed an interval of uninterrupted leisure, which I entirely devoted to the perusal of the Greek and Latin classics; though I occasionally visited the metropolis, either for the sake of purchasing books, or of learning something new in mathematics or in music, in which I, at that time, found a source of pleasure and amusement. In this manner I spent five years till my mother's death. I then became anxious to visit foreign parts, and particularly Italy. My father gave me his permission, and I left home with one servant. On my departure, the celebrated Henry Wootton, who had long been King James's ambassador at Venice, gave me a signal proof of his regard, in an elegant letter which he wrote, breathing not only the warmest friendship, but containing some maxims of conduct which I found very useful in my travels. The noble Thomas Scudamore, King Charles's ambassador, to whom I carried letters of recommendation, received me most courteously at Paris. His lordship gave me a card of introduction to the learned Hugo Grotius, at that time ambassador from the queen of Sweden to the French court; whose acquaintance I anxiously desired, and to whose house I was accompanied by some of his lordship's friends. A few days after, when I set out for Italy, he gave me letters to the English merchants on my route, that they might show me any civilities in their power. Taking ship at Nice, I arrived at Genoa, and afterwards visited Leghorn, Pisa, and Florence. In the latter city, which I have always more particularly esteemed for the elegance of its dialect, its genius, and its taste, I stopped about two months; when I contracted an intimacy with many persons of rank and learning; and was a constant attendant at their literary parties; a practice which prevails there, and tends so much to the diffusion of knowledge, and the preservation of friendship. No time will ever abolish the agreeable recollections which I cherish of Jacob Gaddi, Carolo Dati, Frescobaldo, Cultellero, Bonomatthai, Clementillo, Francisco, and many others. From Florence I went to Siena, thence to Rome, where, after I had spent about two months in viewing the antiquities of that renowned city, where I experienced the most friendly attentions from Lucas Holstein, and other learned and ingenious men, I continued my route to Naples. There I was introduced by a certain recluse, with whom I had travelled from Rome, to John Baptista Manso, Marquis of Villa, a nobleman of distinguished rank and authority, to whom Torquato Tasso, the illustrious poet, inscribed his book on friendship. During my stay, he gave me singular proofs of his regard; he himself conducted me round the city, and to the palace of the viceroy; and more than once paid me a visit at my lodgings. On my departure he gravely apologized for not having shown me more civility, which he said he had been restrained from doing, because I had spoken with so little reserve on matters of religion. When I was preparing to pass over into Sicily and Greece, the melancholy intelligence which I received of the civil commotions in England made me alter my purpose; for I thought it base to be travelling for amusement abroad, while my fellow-citizens were fighting for liberty at home. While I was on my way back to Rome, some merchants informed me that the English Jesuits had formed a plot against me if I returned to Rome, because I had spoken too freely on religion; for it was a rule which I laid down to myself in these places, never to be the first to begin any conversation on religion; but if any questions were put to me concerning my faith, to declare it without any reserve or fear. I, nevertheless, returned to Rome. I took no steps to conceal either my person or my character; and for about the space of two months I again openly defended, as I had done before, the reformed religion in the very metropolis of Popery. By the favor of God, I got safe back to Florence, where I was received with as much affection as if I had returned to my native country. There I stopped as many months as I had done before, except that I made an excursion for a few days to Lucca; and, crossing the Apennines, passed through Bologna and Ferrara to Venice. After I had spent a month in surveying the curiosities of this city, and put on board a ship the books which I had collected in Italy, I proceeded through Verona and Milan, and along the Leman lake to Geneva. The mention of this city brings to my recollection the slandering More, and makes me again call the Deity to witness, that in all those places in which vice meets with so little discouragement, and is practised with so little shame, I never once deviated from the paths of integrity and virtue, and perpetually reflected that, though my conduct might escape the notice of men, it could not elude the inspection of God. At Geneva I held daily converses with John Deodati, the learned Professor of Theology. Then pursuing my former route through France, I returned to my native country, after an absence of one year and about three months; at the time when Charles, having broken the peace, was renewing what is called the Episcopal war with the Scots, in which the royalists being routed in the first encounter, and the English being universally and justly disaffected, the necessity of his affairs at last obliged him to convene a Parliament. As soon as I was able, I hired a spacious house in the city for myself and my books; where I again with rapture renewed my literary pursuits, and where I calmly awaited the issue of the contest, which I trusted to the wise conduct of Providence, and to the courage of the people. The vigor of the Parliament had begun to humble the pride of the bishops. As long as the liberty of speech was no longer subject to control, all mouths began to be opened against the bishops; some complained of the vices of the individuals, others of those of the order. They said that it was unjust that they alone should differ from the model of other reformed churches; that the government of the Church should be according to the pattern of other churches, and particularly the word of God. This awakened all my attention and my zeal. I saw that a way was opening for the establishment of real liberty; that the foundation was laying for the deliverance of man from the yoke of slavery and superstition; that the principles of religion, which were the first objects of our care, would exert a salutary influence on the manners and constitution of the republic; and as I had from my youth studied the distinctions between religious and civil rights, I perceived that if I ever wished to be of use, I ought at least not to be wanting to my country, to the Church, and to so many of my fellow-Christians, in a crisis of so much danger; I therefore determined to relinquish the other pursuits in which I was engaged, and to transfer the whole force of my talents and my industry to this one important object. I accordingly wrote two books to a friend concerning the reformation of the Church of England. Afterwards, when two bishops of superior distinction vindicated their privileges against some principal ministers, I thought that on those topics, to the consideration of which I was led solely by my love of truth, and my reverence for Christianity, I should not probably write worse than those who were contending only for their own emoluments and usurpations. I therefore answered the one in two books, of which the first is inscribed, Concerning Prelatical Episcopacy, and the other, Concerning the Mode of Ecclesiastical

Government; and I replied to the other in some Animadversions, and soon after in an Apology. On this occasion it was supposed that I brought a timely succor to the ministers, who were hardly a match for the eloquence of their opponents; and from that time I was actively employed in refuting any answers that appeared. When the bishops could no longer resist the multitude of their assailants, I had leisure to turn my thoughts to other subjects; to the promotion of real and substantial liberty; which is rather to be sought from within than from without; and whose existence depends, not so much on the terror of the sword, as on sobriety of conduct, and integrity of life. When, therefore, I perceived that there were three species of liberty which are essential to the happiness of social life, — religious, domestic, and civil; and as I had already written concerning the first, and the magistrates were strenuously active in obtaining the third, I determined to turn my attention to the second, or the domestic species. As this seemed to involve three material questions, the conditions of the conjugal tie, the education of the children, and the free publication of the thoughts, I made them objects of distinct consideration. I explained my sentiments, not only concerning the solemnization of the marriage, but the dissolution, if circumstances rendered it necessary; and I drew my arguments from the divine law, which Christ did not abolish, or publish another more grievous than that of Moses. I stated my own opinions, and those of others, concerning the exclusive exception of fornication, which our illustrious Selden has since, in his Hebrew Wife, more copiously discussed; for he in vain makes a vaunt of liberty in the senate or in the forum, who languishes under the vilest servitude, to an inferior at home. On this subject, therefore, I published some books which were more particularly necessary at that time, when man and wife were often the most inveterate foes, when the man often stayed to take care of his children at home, while the mother of the family was seen in the camp of the enemy, threatening death and destruction to her husband. I then discussed the principles of education in a summary manner, but sufficiently copious for those who attend seriously to the subject; than which nothing can be more necessary to principle the minds of men in virtue, the only genuine source of political and individual liberty, the only true safeguard of states, the bulwark of their prosperity and renown. Lastly, I wrote my Areopagitica, in order to deliver the press from the restraints with which it was encumbered, that the power of determining what was true and what was false, what ought to be published and what to be suppressed, might no longer be intrusted to a few illiterate and illiberal individuals, who refused their sanction to any work which contained views or sentiments at all above the level of the vulgar superstition. On the last species of civil liberty, I said nothing, because I saw that sufficient attention was paid to it by the magistrates; nor did I write anything on the prerogative of the crown, till the king, voted an enemy by the Parliament, and vanquished in the field, was summoned before the tribunal which condemned him to lose his head. But when, at length, some Presbyterian ministers, who had formerly been the most bitter enemies to Charles, became jealous of the growth of the Independents, and of their ascendency in the Parliament, most tumultuously clamored against the sentence, and did all in their power to prevent the execution, though they were not angry, so much on account of the act itself, as because it was not the act of their party; and when they dared to affirm, that the doctrine of the Protestants, and of all the reformed churches, was abhorrent to such an atrocious proceeding against kings; I thought that it became me to oppose such a glaring falsehood; and accordingly, without any immediate or personal application to Charles, I showed, in an abstract consideration of the question, what might lawfully be done against tyrants; and in support of what I advanced, produced the opinions of the most celebrated divines; while I vehemently inveighed against the egregious ignorance or effrontery of men, who professed better things, and from whom better things might have been expected. That book did not make its appearance till after the death of Charles; and was written rather to reconcile the minds of the people to the event, than to discuss the legitimacy of that particular sentence which concerned the magistrates, and which was already executed. Such were the fruits of my private studies, which I gratuitously presented to the church and to the state: and for which I was recompensed by nothing but impunity; though the actions themselves procured me peace of conscience, and the approbation of the good; while I exercised that freedom of discussion which I loved. Others, without labor or desert, got possession of honors and emoluments; but no one ever knew me either soliciting anything myself or through the medium of my friends, ever beheld me in a supplicating posture at the doors of the senate, or the levees of the great. I usually kept myself secluded at home, where my own property, part of which had been withheld during the civil commotions, and part of which had been absorbed in the oppressive contributions which I had to sustain, afforded me a scanty subsistence. When I was released from these engagements, and thought that I was about to enjoy an interval of uninterrupted ease, I turned my thoughts to a continued history of my country, from the earliest times to the present period. I had already finished four books, when, after the subversion of the monarchy, and the establishment of a republic, I was surprised by an invitation from the Council of State, who desired my services in the office for foreign affairs. A book appeared soon after, which was ascribed to the king, and contained the most invidious charges against the Parliament. I was ordered to answer it; and opposed the Iconoclast to his Icon. I did not insult over fallen majesty, as is pretended; I only preferred Queen Truth to King Charles. The charge of insult, which I saw that the malevolent would urge, I was at some pains to remove in the beginning of the work: and as often as possible in other places. Salmasius then appeared, to whom they were not, as More says, long in looking about for an opponent, but immediately appointed me, who happened at the time to be present in the council. I have thus, sir, given some account of myself, in order to stop your mouth, and to remove any prejudices which your falsehoods and misrepresentations might cause even good men to entertain against me. I tell thee then, thou mass of corruption, to hold thy peace; for the more you malign, the more you will compel me to confute; which will only serve to render your iniquity more glaring, and my integrity more manifest. . . . .

John Bradshaw (a name which will be repeated with applause wherever liberty is cherished or is known) was sprung from a noble family. All his early life he sedulously employed in making himself acquainted with the laws of his country; he then practised with singular success and reputation at the bar; he showed himself an intrepid and unwearied advocate for the liberties of the people: he took an active part in the most momentous affairs of the state, and occasionally discharged the functions of a judge with the most inviolable integrity. At last, when he was entreated by the Parliament to preside in the trial of the king, he did not refuse the dangerous office. To a profound knowledge of the law, he added the most comprehensive views, the most generous sentiments, manners the most obliging and the most pure. Hence he discharged that office with a propriety almost without a parallel; he inspired both respect and awe; and though menaced by the daggers of so many assassins, he conducted himself with so much consistency and gravity, with so much presence of mind and so much dignity of demeanor, that he seems to have been purposely destined by Providence for that part which he so nobly acted on the theatre of the world. And his glory is as much exalted above that of all other tyrannicides, as it is both more humane, more just, and more strikingly grand, judicially to condemn a tyrant, than to put him to death without a trial. In other respects there was no forbidding austerity, no moroseness in his manner; he was courteous and benign; but the great character which he then sustained, he with perfect consistency still sustains, so that you would suppose that not only then, but in every future period of his life, he was sitting in judgment upon the king. In the public business his activity is unwearied; and he alone is equal to a host. At home his hospitality is as splendid as his fortune will permit: in his friendships there is the most inflexible fidelity; and no one more readily discerns merit, or more liberally rewards it. Men of piety and learning, ingenious persons in all professions, those who have been distinguished by their courage or their misfortunes, are free to participate his bounty; and if they want not his bounty, they are sure to share his friendship and esteem. He never ceases to extol the merits of others, or to conceal his own; and no one was ever more ready to accept the excuses, or to pardon the hostility, of his political opponents. If he undertake to plead the cause of the oppressed, to solicit the favor or deprecate the resentment of the powerful, to reprove the public ingratitude towards any particular individual, his address and his perseverance are beyond all praise. On such occasions no one could desire a patron or a friend more able, more zealous, or more eloquent. No menace could divert him from his purpose; no intimidation on the one hand, and no promise of emolument or promotion on the other, could alter the serenity of his countenance, or shake the firmness of his soul. . . . .

"The army is a hydra-headed monster of accumulated heresies." Those who speak the truth, acknowledge that our army excels all others, not only in courage, but in virtue and in piety. Other camps are the scenes of gambling, swearing, riot, and debauchery; in ours, the troops employ what leisure they have in searching the Scriptures and hearing the word; nor is there one who thinks it more honorable to vanquish the enemy than to propagate the truth; and they not only carry on a military warfare against their enemies, but an evangelical one against themselves. And indeed if we consider the proper objects of war, what employment can be more becoming soldiers, who are raised to defend the laws, to be the support of our political and religious institutions? Ought they not then to be less conspicuous for ferocity than for the civil and the softer virtues, and to consider it as their true and proper destination, not merely to sow the seeds of strife, and reap the harvest of destruction, but to procure peace and security for the whole human race? If there be any who, either from the mistakes of others, or the infirmities of their own minds, deviate from these noble ends, we ought not to punish them with the sword, but rather labor to reform them by reason, by admonition, by pious supplications to God, to whom alone it belongs to dispel all the errors of the mind, and to impart to whom he will the celestial light of truth. We approve no heresies which are truly such; we do not even tolerate some; we wish them extirpated, but by those means which are best suited to the purpose, — by reason and instruction, the only safe remedies for disorders of the mind; and not by the knife or the scourge, as if they were seated in the body. . . . .

Oliver Cromwell was sprung from a line of illustrious ancestors, who were distinguished for the civil functions which they sustained under the monarchy, and still more for the part which they took in restoring and establishing true religion in this country. In the vigor and maturity of his life, which he passed in retirement, he was conspicuous for nothing more than for the strictness of his religious habits, and the innocence of his life; and he had tacitly cherished in his breast that flame of piety which was afterwards to stand him in so much stead on the greatest occasions, and in the most critical exigencies. In the last Parliament which was called by the king, he was elected to represent his native town, when he soon became distinguished by the justness of his opinions, and the vigor and decision of his councils. When the sword was drawn, he offered his services, and was appointed to a troop of horse, whose numbers were soon increased by the pious and the good, who flocked from all quarters to his standard; and in a short time he almost surpassed the greatest generals in the magnitude and the rapidity of his achievements. Nor is this surprising; for he was a soldier disciplined to perfection in the knowledge of himself. He had either extinguished, or by habit had learned to subdue, the whole host of vain hopes, fears, and passions, which infest the soul. He first acquired the government of himself, and over himself acquired the most signal victories; so that on the first day he took the field against the external enemy, he was a veteran in arms, consummately practised in the toils and exigencies of war. It is not possible for me, in the narrow limits in which I circumscribe myself on this occasion, to enumerate the many towns which he has taken, the many battles which he has won. The whole surface of the British empire has been the scene of his exploits, and the theatre of his triumphs; which alone would furnish ample materials for a history, and want a copiousness of narration not inferior to the magnitude and diversity of the transactions. This alone seems to be a sufficient proof of his extraordinary and almost supernatural virtue, that by the vigor of his genius, or the excellence of his discipline, adapted, not more to the necessities of war than to the precepts of Christianity, the good and the brave were from all quarters attracted to his camp, not only as to the best school of military talents, but of piety and virtue; and that during the whole war, and the occasional intervals of peace, amid so many vicissitudes of faction and of events, he retained and still retains the obedience of his troops, not by largesses or indulgence, but by his sole authority and the regularity of his pay. In this instance his fame may rival that of Cyrus, of Epaminondas, or any of the great generals of antiquity. Hence he collected an army as numerous and as well equipped as any one ever did in so short a time; which was uniformly obedient to his orders, and dear to the affections of the citizens; which was formidable to the enemy in the field, but never cruel to those who laid down their arms; which committed no lawless ravages on the persons or the property of the inhabitants; who, when they compared their conduct with the turbulence, the intemperance, the impiety, and the debauchery of the royalists, were wont to salute them as friends, and to consider them as guests. They were a stay to the good, a terror to the evil, and the warmest advocates for every exertion of piety and virtue. Nor would it be right to pass over the name of Fairfax, who united the utmost fortitude with the utmost courage; and the spotless innocence of whose life seemed to point him out as the peculiar favorite of Heaven. Justly, indeed, may you be excited to receive this wreath of praise; though you have retired as much as possible from the world, and seek those shades of privacy which were the delight of Scipio. Nor was it only the enemy whom you subdued, but you have triumphed over that flame of ambition and that lust of glory which are wont to make the best and the greatest of men their slaves. The purity of your virtues and the splendor of your actions consecrate those sweets of ease which you enjoy, and which constitute the wished-for haven of the toils of man. Such was the ease which, when the heroes of antiquity possessed, after a life of exertion and glory not greater than yours, the poets, in despair of finding ideas or expressions better suited to the subject, feigned that they were received into heaven, and invited to recline at the tables of the gods. But whether it were your health, which I principally believe, or any other motive which caused you to retire, of this I am convinced, that nothing could have induced you to relinquish the service of your country, if you had not known that in your successor liberty would meet with a protector, and England with a stay to its safety, and a pillar to its glory. For while you, O Cromwell, are left among us, he hardly shows a proper confidence in the Supreme, who distrusts the security of England; when he sees that you are in so special a manner the favored object of the divine regard. But there was another department of the war, which was destined for your exclusive exertions.

Without entering into any length of detail, I will, if possible, describe some of the most memorable actions, with as much brevity as you performed them with celerity. After the loss of all Ireland, with the exception of one city, you in one battle immediately discomfited the forces of the rebels; and were busily employed in settling the country, when you were suddenly recalled to the war in Scotland. Hence you proceeded with unwearied diligence against the Scots, who were on the point of making an irruption into England with the king in their train: and in about the space of one year you entirely subdued, and added to the English dominion, that kingdom which all our monarchs, during a period of eight hundred years, had in vain struggled to subject. In one battle you almost annihilated the remainder of their forces, who, in a fit of desperation, had made a sudden incursion into England, then almost destitute of garrisons, and got as far as Worcester; where you came up with them by forced marches, and captured almost the whole of their nobility. A profound peace ensued; when we found, though indeed not then for the first time, that you were as wise in the cabinet as valiant in the field. It was your constant endeavor in the Senate either to induce them to adhere to those treaties which they had entered into with the enemy, or speedily to adjust others which promised to be beneficial to the country. But when you saw that the business was artfully procrastinated, that every one was more intent on his own selfish interest than on the public good, that the people complained of the disappointments which they had experienced, and the fallacious promises by which they had been gulled, that they were the dupes of a few overbearing individuals, you put an end to their domination. A new Parliament is summoned; and the right of election given to those to whom it was expedient. They meet; but do nothing; and, after having wearied themselves by their mutual dissensions, and fully exposed their incapacity to the observation of the country, they consent to a voluntary dissolution. In this state of desolation, to which we were reduced, you, O Cromwell! alone remained to conduct the government, and to save the country. We all willingly yield the palm of sovereignty to your unrivalled ability and virtue, except the few among us, who, either ambitious of honors which they have not the capacity to sustain, or who envy those which are conferred on one more worthy than themselves, or else who do not know that nothing in the world is more pleasing to God, more agreeable to reason, more politically just, or more generally useful, than that the supreme power should be vested in the best and the wisest of men. Such, O Cromwell, all acknowledge you to be; such are the services which you have rendered, as the leader of our councils, the general of our armies, and the father of your country. For this is the tender appellation by which all the good among us salute you from the very soul. Other names you neither have nor could endure; and you deservedly reject that pomp of title which attracts the gaze and admiration of the multitude. For what is a title but a certain definite mode of dignity; but actions such as yours surpass, not only the bounds of our admiration, but our titles; and, like the points of pyramids, which are lost in the clouds, they soar above the possibilities of titular commendation. But since, though it be not fit, it may be expedient, that the highest pitch of virtue should be circumscribed within the bounds of some human appellation, you endured to receive, for the public good, a title most like to that of the father of your country; not to exalt, but rather to bring you nearer to the level of ordinary men; the title of king was unworthy the transcendent majesty of your character. For if you had been captivated by a name over which, as a private man, you had so completely triumphed and crumbled into dust, you would have been doing the same thing as if, after having subdued some idolatrous nation by the help of the true God, you should afterwards fall down and worship the gods which you had vanquished. Do you then, sir, continue your course with the same unrivalled magnanimity; it sits well upon you; — to you our country owes its liberties; nor can you sustain a character at once more momentous and more august than that of the author, the guardian, and the preserver of our liberties; and hence you have not only eclipsed the achievements of all our kings, but even those which have been fabled of our heroes. Often reflect what a dear pledge the beloved land of your nativity has intrusted to your care; and that liberty which she once expected only from the chosen flower of her talents and her virtues, she now expects from you only, and by you only hopes to obtain. Revere the fond expectations which we cherish, the solicitudes of your anxious country; revere the looks and the wounds of your brave companions in arms, who, under your banners, have so strenuously fought for liberty; revere the shades of those who perished in the contest; revere also the opinions and the hopes which foreign states entertain concerning us, who promise to themselves so many advantages from that liberty which we have so bravely acquired, from the establishment of that new government which has begun to shed its splendor on the world, which, if it be suffered to vanish like a dream, would involve us in the deepest abyss of shame; and lastly, revere yourself; and, after having endured so many sufferings and encountered so many perils for the sake of liberty, do not suffer it, now it is obtained, either to be violated by yourself, or in any one instance impaired by others. You cannot be truly free unless we are free too; for such is the nature of things, that he who entrenches on the liberty of others, is the first to lose his own and become a slave. But if you, who have hitherto been the patron and tutelary genius of liberty, if you, who are exceeded by no one in justice, in piety, and goodness, should hereafter invade that liberty which you have defended, your conduct must be fatally operative, not only against the cause of liberty, but the general interests of piety and virtue. Your integrity and virtue will appear to have evaporated; your faith in religion to have been small; your character with posterity will dwindle into insignificance, by which a most destructive blow will be levelled against the happiness of mankind. The work which you have undertaken is of incalculable moment, which will thoroughly sift and expose every principle and sensation of your heart, which will fully display the vigor and genius of your character, which will evince whether you really possess those great qualities of piety, fidelity, justice, and self-denial, which made us believe that you were elevated by the special direction of the Deity to the highest pinnacle of power. At once wisely and discreetly to hold the sceptre over three powerful nations, to persuade people to relinquish inveterate and corrupt for new and more beneficial maxims and institutions, to penetrate into the remotest parts of the country, to have the mind present and operative in every quarter, to watch against surprise, to provide against danger, to reject the blandishments of pleasure and pomp of power; — these are exertions compared with which the labor of war is mere pastime; which will require every energy and employ every faculty that you possess; which demand a man supported from above, and almost instructed by immediate inspiration. These and more than these are, no doubt, the objects which occupy your attention and engross your soul; as well as the means by which you may accomplish these important ends, and render our liberty at once more ample and more secure. And this you can, in my opinion, in no other way so readily effect, as by associating in your councils the companions of your dangers and your toils; men of exemplary modesty, integrity, and courage; whose hearts have not been hardened in cruelty, and rendered insensible to pity by the sight of so much ravage and so much death, but whom it has rather inspired with the love of justice, with a respect for religion, and with the feeling of compassion, and who are more zealously interested in the preservation of liberty, in proportion as they have encountered more perils in its defence. They are not strangers or foreigners, a hireling rout scraped together from the dregs of the people, but, for the most part, men of the better conditions in life, of families not disgraced if not ennobled, of fortunes either ample or moderate; and what if some among them are recommended by their poverty? for it was not the lust of ravage which brought them into the field; it was the calamitous aspect of the times, which, in the most critical circumstances, and often amid the most disastrous turn of fortune, roused them to attempt the deliverance of their country from the fangs of despotism. They were men prepared, not only to debate, but to fight; not only to argue in the Senate, but to engage the enemy in the field. But unless we will continually cherish indefinite and illusory expectations, I see not in whom we can place any confidence, if not in these men and such as these. We have the surest and most indubitable pledge of their fidelity in this, that they have already exposed themselves to death in the service of their country; of their piety in this, that they have been always wont to ascribe the whole glory of their successes to the favor of the Deity, whose help they have so suppliantly implored, and so conspicuously obtained; of their justice in this, that they even brought the king to trial, and when his guilt was proved, refused to save his life; of their moderation in our own uniform experience of its effects, and because, if by any outrage, they should disturb the peace which they have procured, they themselves will be the first to feel the miseries which it will occasion, the first to meet the havoc of the sword, and the first again to risk their lives for all those comforts and distinctions which they have so happily acquired; and lastly, of their fortitude in this, that there is no instance of any people who ever recovered their liberty with so much courage and success; and therefore let us not suppose, that there can be any persons who will be more zealous in preserving it. I now feel myself irresistibly compelled to commemorate the names of some of those who have most conspicuously signalized themselves in these times: and first thine, O Fleetwood! whom I have known from a boy, to the present blooming maturity of your military fame, to have been inferior to none in humanity, in gentleness, in benignity of disposition, whose intrepidity in the combat, and whose clemency in victory, have been acknowledged even by the enemy: next thine, O Lambert! who, with a mere handful of men, checked the progress, and sustained the attack, of the Duke of Hamilton, who was attended by the whole flower and vigor of the Scottish youth: next thine, O Desborough! and thine, O Hawley! who wast always conspicuous in the heat of the combat, and the thickest of the fight: thine, O Overton! who hast been most endeared to me now for so many years by the similitude of our studies, the suavity of your manners, and the more than fraternal sympathy of our hearts; you who, in the memorable battle of Marston Moor, when our left wing was put to the rout, were beheld with admiration, making head against the enemy with your infantry and repelling his attack, amid the thickest of the carnage: and lastly you, who, in the Scotch war, when under the auspices of Cromwell, occupied the coast of Fife, opened a passage beyond Stirling, and made the Scotch of the west, and of the north, and even the remotest Orkneys, confess your humanity, and submit to your power. Besides these, I will mention some as celebrated for their political wisdom and their civil virtues, whom you, sir, have admitted into your councils, and who are known to me by friendship or by fame. Whitlocke, Pickering, Strickland, Sydenham, Sydney (a name indissolubly attached to the interests of liberty), Montacute, Laurence, both of highly cultivated minds and polished taste; besides many other citizens of singular merit, some of whom were distinguished by their exertions in the senate, and others in the field. To these men, whose talents are so splendid, and whose worth has been so thoroughly tried, you would without doubt do right to trust the protection of our liberties; nor would it be easy to say to whom they might more safely be intrusted. Then, if you leave the Church to its own government, and relieve yourself and the other public functionaries from a charge so onerous, and so incompatible with your functions; and will no longer suffer two powers, so different as the civil and the ecclesiastical, to commit fornication together, and by their mutual and delusive aids in appearance to strengthen, but in reality to weaken and finally to subvert, each other; if you shall remove all power of persecution out of the Church, (but persecution will never cease, so long as men are bribed to preach the Gospel by a mercenary salary, which is forcibly extorted, rather than gratuitously bestowed, which serves only to poison religion and to strangle truth,) you will then effectually have cast those money-changers out of the temple, who do not merely truckle with doves but with the Dove itself, with the Spirit of the Most High. Then, since there are often in a republic men who have the same itch for making a multiplicity of laws as some poetasters have for making many verses, and since laws are usually worse in proportion as they are more numerous, if you shall not enact so many new laws as you abolish old, which do not operate so much as warnings against evil, as impediments in the way of good; and if you shall retain only those which are necessary, which do not confound the distinctions of good and evil, which while they prevent the frauds of the wicked do not prohibit the innocent freedoms of the good, which punish crimes, without interdicting those things which are lawful only on account of the abuses to which they may occasionally be exposed. For the intention of laws is to check the commission of vice; but liberty is the best school of virtue, and affords the strongest encouragements to the practice. Then, if you make a better provision for the education of our youth than has hitherto been made, if you prevent the promiscuous instruction of the docile and the indocile, of the idle and the diligent, at the public cost, but reserve the rewards of learning for the learned, and of merit for the meritorious; if you permit the free discussion of truth without any hazard to the author, or any subjection to the caprice of an individual, which is the best way to make truth flourish and knowledge abound, the censure of the half-learned, the envy, the pusillanimity, or the prejudice which measures the discoveries of others, and in short every degree of wisdom, by the measure of its own capacity, will be prevented from doling out information to us according to their own arbitrary choice. Lastly, if you shall not dread to hear any truth or any falsehood, whatever it may be, but if you shall least of all listen to those who think that they can never be free till the liberties of others depend on their caprice, and who attempt nothing with so much zeal and vehemence as to fetter, not only the bodies but the minds of men, who labor to introduce into the state the worst of all tyrannies, the tyranny of their own depraved habits and pernicious opinions; you will always be dear to those who think not merely that their own sect or faction, but that all citizens of all descriptions, should enjoy equal rights and equal laws. If there be any one who thinks that this is not liberty enough, he appears to me to be rather inflamed with the lust of ambition or of anarchy, than with the love of a genuine and well-regulated liberty; and particularly since the circumstances of the country, which have been so convulsed by the storms of faction, which are yet hardly still, do not permit us to adopt a more perfect or desirable form of government.

For it is of no little consequence O citizens, by what principles you are governed, either in acquiring liberty, or in attaining it when acquired. And unless that liberty, which is of such a kind as arms can neither procure nor take away, which alone is the fruit of piety, of justice, of temperance, and unadulterated virtue, shall have taken deep root in your minds and hearts, there will not long be wanting one who will snatch from you by treachery what you have acquired by arms. War has made many great whom peace makes small. If, after being released from the toils of war, you neglect the arts of peace, if your peace and your liberty be a state of warfare, if war be your only virtue, the summit of your praise, you will, believe me, soon find peace the most adverse to your interests. Your peace will be only a more distressing war; and that which you imagined liberty will prove the worst of slavery. Unless by the means of piety, not frothy and loquacious, but operative, unadulterated, and sincere, you clear the horizon of the mind from those mists of superstition which arise from the ignorance of true religion, you will always have those who will bend your necks to the yoke as if you were brutes, who, notwithstanding all your triumphs, will put you up to the highest bidder, as if you were mere booty made in war; and will find an exuberant source of wealth in your ignorance and superstition. Unless you will subjugate the propensity to avarice, to ambition, and sensuality, and expel all luxury from yourselves and from your families, you will find that you have cherished a more stubborn and intractable despot at home than you ever encountered in the field; and even your very bowels will be continually teeming with an intolerable progeny of tyrants. Let those be the first enemies whom you subdue;

this constitutes the campaign of peace; these are triumphs, difficult indeed, but bloodless; and far more honorable than those trophies which are purchased only by slaughter and by rapine. Unless you are victors in this service, it is in vain that you have been victorious over the despotic enemy in the field. For if you think that it is a more grand, a more beneficial, or a more wise policy, to invent subtle expedients for increasing the revenue, to multiply our naval and military force, to rival in craft the ambassadors of foreign states, to form skilful treaties and alliances, than to administer unpolluted justice to the people, to redress the injured, and to succor the distressed, and speedily to restore to every one his own, you are involved in a cloud of error; and too late will you perceive, when the illusion of those mighty benefits has vanished, that in neglecting these, which you now think inferior considerations, you have only been precipitating your own ruin and despair. The fidelity of enemies and allies is frail and perishing, unless it be cemented by the principles of justice; that wealth and those honors, which most covet, readily change masters; they forsake the idle, and repair where virtue, where industry, where patience flourish most. Thus nation precipitates the downfall of nation; thus the more sound part of one people subverts the more corrupt; thus you obtained the ascendant over the royalists. If you plunge into the same depravity, if you imitate their excesses, and hanker after the same vanities, you will become royalists as well as they, and liable to be subdued by the same enemies, or by others in your turn; who, placing their reliance on the same religious principles, the same patience, the same integrity and discretion which made you strong, will deservedly triumph over you who are immersed in debauchery, in the luxury and the sloth of kings. Then, as if God was weary of protecting you, you will be seen to have passed through the fire, that you might perish in the smoke; the contempt which you will then experience will be great as the admiration which you now enjoy; and, what may in future profit others, but cannot benefit yourselves, you will leave a salutary proof what great things the solid reality of virtue and of piety might have effected, when the mere counterfeit and varnished resemblance could attempt such mighty achievements, and make such considerable advances toward the execution. For, if either through your want of knowledge, your want of constancy, or your want of virtue, attempts so noble, and actions so glorious, have had an issue so unfortunate, it does not therefore follow, that better men should be either less daring in their projects or less sanguine in their hopes. But from such an abyss of corruption into which you so readily fall, no one, not even Cromwell himself, nor a whole nation of Brutuses, if they were alive, could deliver you if they would, or would deliver you if they could. For who would vindicate your right of unrestrained suffrage, or of choosing what representatives you liked best, merely that you might elect the creatures of your own faction, whoever they might be, or him, however small might be his worth, who would give you the most lavish feasts, and enable you to drink to the greatest excess? Thus not wisdom and authority, but turbulence and gluttony, would soon exalt the vilest miscreants from our taverns and our brothels, from our towns and villages, to the rank and dignity of senators. For, should the management of the republic be intrusted to persons to whom no one would willingly intrust the management of his private concerns; and the treasury of the state be left to the care of those who had lavished their own fortunes in an infamous prodigality? Should they have the charge of the public purse, which they would soon convert into a private, by their unprincipled peculations? Are they fit to be the legislators of a whole people who themselves know not what law, what reason, what right and wrong, what crooked and straight, what licit and illicit means? who think that all power consists in outrage, all dignity in the parade of insolence? who neglect every other consideration for the corrupt gratification of their friendships, or the prosecution of their resentments? who disperse their own relations and creatures through the provinces, for the sake of levying taxes and confiscating goods;

men, for the greater part, the most profligate and vile, who buy up for themselves what they pretend to expose to sale, who thence collect an exorbitant mass of wealth, which they fraudulently divert from the public service; who thus spread their pillage through the country, and in a moment emerge from penury and rags to a state of splendor and of wealth? Who could endure such thievish servants, such vicegerents of their lords? Who could believe that the masters and the patrons of a banditti could be the proper guardians of liberty? or who would suppose that he should ever be made one hair more free by such a set of public functionaries, (though they might amount to five hundred elected in this manner from the counties and boroughs,) when among them who are the very guardians of liberty, and to whose custody it is committed, there must be so many, who know not either how to use or to enjoy liberty, who neither understand the principles, nor merit the possession? But, what is worthy of remark, those who are the most unworthy of liberty are wont to behave most ungratefully towards their deliverers. Among such persons, who would be willing either to fight for liberty, or to encounter the least peril in its defence? It is not agreeable to the nature of things that such persons ever should be free. However much they may brawl about liberty, they are slaves, both at home and abroad, but without perceiving it; and when they do perceive it, like unruly horses that are impatient of the bit, they will endeavor to throw off the yoke, not from the love of genuine liberty, (which a good man only loves and knows how to obtain,) but from the impulses of pride and little passions. But though they often attempt it by arms, they will make no advances to the execution; they may change their masters, but will never be able to get rid of their servitude. This often happened to the ancient Romans, wasted by excess, and enervated by luxury: and it has still more so been the fate of the moderns; when, after a long interval of years, they aspired, under the auspices of Crescentius, Nomentanus, and afterwards of Nicholas Rentius, who had assumed the title of Tribune of the People, to restore the splendor and re-establish the government of ancient Rome. For, instead of fretting with vexation, or thinking that you can lay the blame on any one but yourselves, know that to be free is the same thing as to be pious, to be wise, to be temperate and just, to be frugal and abstinent, and lastly, to be magnanimous and brave; so to be the opposite of all these is the same as to be a slave; and it usually happens, by the appointment, and as it were retributive justice of the Deity, that that people which cannot govern themselves, and moderate their passions, but crouch under the slavery of their lusts, should be delivered up to the sway of those whom they abhor, and made to submit to an involuntary servitude. It is also sanctioned by the dictates of justice and by the constitution of nature, that he who, from the imbecility or derangement of his intellect, is incapable of governing himself, should, like a minor, be committed to the government of another; and least of all should he be appointed to superintend the affairs of others or the interests of the state. You, therefore, who wish to remain free, either instantly be wise, or, as soon as possible, cease to be fools; if you think slavery an intolerable evil, learn obedience to reason and the government of yourselves; and finally bid adieu to your dissensions, your jealousies, your superstitions, your outrages, your rapine, and your lusts. Unless you will spare no pains to effect this, you must be judged unfit, both by God and mankind, to be intrusted with the possession of liberty and the administration of the government; but will rather, like a nation in a state of pupilage, want some active and courageous guardian to undertake the management of your affairs.

FROM

A TREATISE OF CIVIL POWER IN ECCLESIASTICAL CAUSES.

TWO things there be, which have been ever found working much mischief to the Church of God and the advancement of truth: force on one side restraining, and hire on the other side corrupting, the teachers thereof. Few ages have been since the ascension of our Saviour, wherein the one of these two, or both together, have not prevailed. It can be at no time, therefore, unseasonable to speak of these things; since by them the Church is either in continual detriment and oppression, or in continual danger. . . . .

It will require no great labor of exposition to unfold what is here meant by matters of religion; being as soon apprehended as defined, such things as belong chiefly to the knowledge and service of God; and are either above the reach and light of nature without revelation from above, and therefore liable to be variously understood by human reason, or such things as are enjoined or forbidden by divine precept, which else by the light of reason would seem indifferent to be done or not done; and so likewise must needs appear to every man as the precept is understood. Whence I here mean *by conscience or religion that full* persuasion, whereby we are assured, that our belief and practice, as far as we are able to apprehend and probably make appear, is according to the will of God and his Holy Spirit within us, which we ought to follow much rather than any law of man, as not only his word everywhere bids us, but the very dictate of reason tells us. . . . .

It cannot be denied, being the main foundation of our Protestant religion, that we of these ages, having no other divine rule or authority from without us, warrantable to one another as a common ground, but the holy Scripture, and no other within us but the illumination of the Holy Spirit, so interpreting that Scripture as warrantable only to ourselves, and to such whose consciences we can so persuade, can have no other ground in matters of religion but only from the Scriptures. And these being not possible to be understood without this divine illumination, which no man can know at all times to be in himself, much less to be at any time for certain in any other, it follows clearly, that no man or body of men in these times can be the infallible judges or determiners in matters of religion to any other men's consciences but their own. . . . .

Seeing, therefore, that no man, no synod, no session of men, though called the Church, can judge definitely the sense of Scripture to another man's conscience, which is well known to be a general maxim of the Protestant religion; it follows plainly, that he who holds in religion that belief, or those opinions, which to his conscience and utmost understanding appear with most evidence or probability in the Scripture, though to others he seem erroneous, can no more be justly censured for a heretic than his censurers; who do but the same thing themselves, while they censure him for so doing. For ask them, or any Protestant, which hath most authority, the Church or the Scripture? They will answer, doubtless, that the Scripture: and what hath most authority, that no doubt but they will confess is to be followed. He then, who to his best apprehension follows the Scripture, though against any point of doctrine by the whole Church received, is not the heretic; but he who follows the Church against his conscience and persuasion grounded on the Scripture. To make this yet more undeniable, I shall only borrow a plain simile, the same which our own writers, when they would demonstrate plainest, that we rightly prefer the Scripture before the Church, use frequently against the Papist in this manner. As the Samaritans believed Christ, first for the woman's word, but next and much rather for his own, so we the Scripture: first on the Church's word, but afterwards and much more for its own, as the Word of God; yea, the Church itself we believe then for the Scripture. The inference of itself follows: If by the Protestant doctrine we believe the Scripture, not for the Church's saying, but for its own, as the Word of God, then ought we to believe what in our conscience we apprehend the Scripture to say, though the visible Church, with all her doctors, gainsay: and being taught to believe them only for the Scripture, they who so do are not heretics, but the best Protestants: and by their opinions, whatever they be, can hurt no Protestant, whose rule is not to receive them but from the Scripture: which to interpret convincingly to his own conscience, none is able but himself, guided by the Holy Spirit; and not so guided, none than he to himself can be a worse deceiver. To Protestants, therefore, whose common rule and touchstone is the Scripture, nothing can with more conscience, more equity, nothing more Protestantly can be permitted, than a free and lawful debate at all times by writing, conference, or disputation of what opinion soever, disputable by Scripture: concluding that no man in religion is properly a heretic at this day, but he who maintains traditions or opinions not probable by Scripture, who, for aught I know, is the Papist only; he the only heretic, who counts all heretics but himself. . . . .

How many persecutions, then, imprisonments, banishments, penalties, and stripes; how much bloodshed have the forcers of conscience to answer for, and Protestants rather than Papists! For the Papist, judging by his principles, punishes them who believe not as the Church believes, though against the Scripture; but the Protestant, teaching every one to believe the Scripture, though against the Church, counts heretical, and persecutes against his own principles, them who in any particular so believe as he in general teaches them; them who most honor and believe divine Scripture, but not against it any human interpretation, though universal; them who interpret Scripture only to themselves, which, by his own position, none but they to themselves can interpret: them who use the Scripture no otherwise by his own doctrine to their edification, than he himself uses it to their punishing; and so whom his doctrine acknowledges a true believer, his discipline persecutes as a heretic. The Papist exacts our belief as to the Church due above Scripture; and by the Church, which is the whole people of God, understands the pope, the general councils, prelatical only, and the surnamed fathers: but the forcing Protestant, though he deny such belief to any Church whatsoever, yet takes it to himself and his teachers, of far less authority than to be called the Church, and above Scripture believed: which renders his practice both contrary to his belief, and far worse than that belief which he condemns in the Papist. By all which, well considered, the more he professes to be a true

Protestant, the more he hath to answer for his persecuting than a Papist. No Protestant, therefore, of what sect soever, following Scripture only, which is the common sect wherein they all agree, and the granted rule of every man's conscience to himself, ought by the common doctrine of Protestants to be forced or molested for religion. . . . .

Seducement is to be hindered by fit and proper means ordained in Church discipline, by instant and powerful demonstration to the contrary; by opposing truth to error, no unequal match; truth the strong, to error the weak, though sly and shifting. Force is no honest confutation, but uneffectual, and for the most part unsuccessful, ofttimes fatal to them who use it: sound doctrine, diligently and duly taught, is of herself both sufficient, and of herself (if some secret judgment of God hinder not) always prevalent against seducers. . . . .

Ill was our condition changed from legal to evangelical, and small advantage gotten by the Gospel, if, for the spirit of adoption to freedom promised us, we receive again the spirit of bondage to fear; if our fear, which was then servile towards God only, must be now servile in religion towards men: strange also and preposterous fear, if, when and wherein it hath attained by the redemption of our Saviour to be filial only towards God, it must be now servile towards the magistrate: who, by subjecting us to his punishment in these things, brings back into religion that law of terror and satisfaction belonging now only to civil crimes; and thereby in effect abolishes the Gospel, by establishing again the law to a far worse yoke of servitude upon us than before. It will therefore not misbecome the meanest Christian to put in mind Christian magistrates, and so much the more freely by how much the more they desire to be thought Christian, (for they will be thereby, as they ought to be in these things, the more our brethren and the less our lords,) that they meddle not rashly with Christian liberty, the birthright and outward testimony of our adoption; lest while they little think it, nay, think they do God service, they themselves, like the sons of that bondwoman, be found persecuting them who are freeborn of the Spirit, and, by a sacrilege of not the least aggravation, bereaving them of that sacred liberty, which our Saviour with his own blood purchased for them.

FROM

CONSIDERATIONS

TOUCHING THE LIKELIEST MEANS TO REMOVE HIRELINGS OUT OF THE CHURCH.

THE former treatise, which leads in this, began with two things ever found working much mischief to religion, force on the one side restraining, and hire on the other side corrupting, the teachers thereof. The latter of these is by much the more dangerous; for under force, though no thanks to the forcers, true religion ofttimes best thrives and flourishes; but the corruption of teachers, most commonly the effect of hire, is the very bane of truth in them who are so corrupted. Of force not to be used in matters of religion, I have already spoken; and so stated matters of conscience and religion in faith and divine worship, and so severed them from blasphemy and heresy, the one being such properly as is despiteful, the other such as stands not to the rule of Scripture, and so both of them not matters of religion, but rather against it, that to them who will yet use force, this only choice can be left, whether they will force them to believe, to whom it is not given from above, being not forced thereto by any principle of the Gospel, which is now the only dispensation of God to all men: or whether, being Protestants, they will punish in those things wherein the Protestant religion denies them to be judges, either in themselves infallible, or to the consciences of other men; or whether, lastly, they think fit to punish error, supposing they can be infallible that it is so, being not wilful but conscientious, and, according to the best light of him who errs, grounded on Scripture: which kind of error all men religious, or but only reasonable, have thought worthier of pardon, and the growth thereof to be prevented by spiritual means and Church discipline, not by civil laws and outward force, since it is God only who gives as well to believe aright, as to believe at all; and by those means, which he ordained sufficiently in his Church to the full execution of his divine purpose in the Gospel. It remains now to speak of hire, the other evil so mischievous in religion; whereof I promised then to speak further, when I should find God disposing me, and opportunity inviting. Opportunity I find now inviting; and apprehend therein the concurrence of God disposing; since the maintenance of Church ministers, a thing not properly belonging to the magistrate, and yet with such importunity called for, and expected from him, is at present under public debate. Wherein, lest anything may happen to be determined and established prejudicial to the right and freedom of the Church, or advantageous to such as may be found hirelings therein, it will be now most seasonable, and in these matters, wherein every Christian hath his free suffrage, no way misbecoming Christian meekness to offer freely, without disparagement to the wisest, such advice as God shall incline him and enable him to propound: since heretofore in commonwealths of most fame for government, civil laws were not established till they had been first for certain days published to the view of all men, that whoso pleased might speak freely his opinion thereof, and give in his exceptions, ere the law could pass to a full establishment. And where ought this equity to have more place, than in the liberty which is inseparable from Christian religion? This, I am not ignorant, will be a work unpleasing to some: but what truth is not hateful to some or other, as this, in likelihood, will be to none but hirelings. And if there be among them who hold it their duty to speak impartial truth, as the work of their ministry, though not performed without money, let them not envy others who think the same no less their duty by the general office of Christianity, to speak truth, as in all reason may be thought, more impartially and unsuspectedly without money.

Hire of itself is neither a thing unlawful, nor a word of any evil note, signifying no more than a due recompense or reward; as when our Saviour saith, "The laborer is worthy of his hire." That which makes it so dangerous in the Church, and properly makes the hireling, a word always of evil signification, is either the excess thereof, or the undue manner of giving and taking it. What harm the excess thereof brought to the Church, perhaps was not found by experience till the days of Constantine; who out of his zeal thinking he could be never too liberally a nursing father of the Church, might be not unfitly said to have either overlaid it or choked it in the nursing. Which was foretold, as is recorded in ecclesiastical traditions, by a voice heard from heaven, on the very day that those great donations and Church revenues were given, crying aloud, "This day is poison poured into the Church." Which the event soon after verified, as appears by another no less ancient observation, "That religion brought forth wealth, and the daughter devoured the mother." But long ere wealth came into the Church, so soon as any gain appeared in religion, hirelings were apparent; drawn in long before by the very scent thereof. Judas therefore, the first hireling, for want of present hire answerable to his coveting, from the small number or the meanness of such as then were the religious, sold the religion itself with the founder thereof, his master. Simon Magus the next, in hope only that preaching and the gifts of the Holy Ghost would prove gainful, offered beforehand a sum of money to obtain them. Not long after, as the apostle foretold, hirelings like wolves came in by herds. . . . . Neither came they in of themselves only, but invited ofttimes by a corrupt audience: 2 Tim. iv. 3. . . . .

Thus we see, that not only the excess of hire in wealthiest times, but also the undue and vicious taking or giving it, though but small or mean, as in the primitive times, gave to hirelings occasion, though not intended, yet sufficient to creep at first into the Church. Which argues also the difficulty, or rather the impossibility, to remove them quite, unless every minister were, as St. Paul, contented to preach gratis; but few such are to be found. As therefore we cannot justly take away all hire in the Church, because we cannot otherwise quite remove all hirelings, so are we not, for the impossibility of removing them all, to use therefore no endeavor that fewest may come in; but rather, in regard the evil, do what we can, will always be incumbent and unavoidable, to use our utmost diligence how it may be least dangerous. . . . .

What recompense ought to be given to Church ministers, God hath answerably ordained according to that difference which he hath manifestly put between those his two great dispensations, the Law and the Gospel. Under the Law he gave them tithes; under the Gospel, having left all things in his Church to charity and Christian freedom, he hath given them only what is justly given them.

That, as well under the Gospel as under the Law, say our English divines, and they only of all Protestants, is tithes: and they say true, if any man be so minded to give them of his own the tenth or twentieth; but that the law therefore of tithes is in force under the Gospel, all other Protestant divines, though equally concerned, yet constantly deny. For although hire to the laborer be of moral and perpetual right, yet that special kind of hire, the tenth, can be of no right or necessity, but to that special labor for which God ordained it. . . . .

What if they who are to be instructed be not able to maintain a minister, as in many villages? I answer that the Scripture shows in many places what ought to be done herein. First, I offer it to the reason of any man, whether he think the knowledge of Christian religion harder than any other art or science to attain. I suppose he will grant that it is far easier, both of itself, and in regard of God's assisting Spirit, not particularly promised us to the attainment of any other knowledge, but of this only: since it was preached as well to the shepherds of Bethlehem by angels, as to the Eastern wise men by that star: and our Saviour declares himself anointed to preach the Gospel to the poor, Luke iv. 18; then surely to their capacity. They who after him first taught it, were otherwise unlearned men: they who before Hus and Luther first reformed it, were for the meanness of their condition called, "the poor men of Lyons": and in Flanders at this day, "le Gueus," which is to say, beggars. Therefore are the Scriptures translated into every vulgar tongue, as being held in main matters of belief and salvation plain and easy to the poorest: and such no less than their teachers have the spirit to guide them in all truth, John xiv. 26, and xvi. 13. Hence we may conclude, if men be not all their lifetime under a teacher to learn logic, natural philosophy, ethics, or mathematics, which are more difficult, that certainly it is not necessary to the attainment of Christian knowledge, that men should sit all their life long at the feet of a pulpited divine; while he, indeed a lollard over his elbow-cushion, in almost the seventh part of forty or fifty years teaches them scarce half the principles of religion; and his sheep ofttimes sit the while to as little purpose of benefiting, as the sheep in their pews at Smithfield; and for the most part by some simony or other bought and sold like them: or, if this comparison be too low, like those women, 1 Tim. iii. 7, "Ever learning and never attaining"; yet not so much through their own fault, as through the unskilful and immethodical teaching of their pastor, teaching here and there at random out of this or that text, as his ease or fancy, and ofttimes as his stealth guides him. Seeing then that Christian religion may be so easily attained, and by meanest capacities, it cannot be much difficult to find ways, both how the poor, yea, all men, may be soon taught what is to be known of Christianity, and they who teach them, recompensed. First, if ministers of their own accord, who pretend that they are called and sent to preach the Gospel, those especially who have no particular flock, would imitate our Saviour and his disciples, who went preaching through the villages, not only through the cities, and there preached to the poor as well as to the rich, looking for no recompense but in heaven.

. . . . .

But they will soon reply, We ourselves have not wherewithal; who shall bear the charges of our journey? To whom it may as soon be answered, that in likelihood they are not poorer than they who did thus; and if they have not the same faith which those disciples had to trust in God and the promise of Christ for their maintenance as they did, and yet intrude into the ministry without any livelihood of their own, they cast themselves into miserable hazard or temptation, and ofttimes into a more miserable necessity, either to starve, or to please their paymasters rather than God; and give men just cause to suspect, that they came, neither called nor sent from above to preach the word, but from below, by the instinct of their own hunger, to feed upon the Church. Yet grant it needful to allow them both the charges of their journey and the hire of their labor, it will belong next to the charity of richer congregations, where most commonly they abound with teachers, to send some of their number to the villages round, as the Apostles from Jerusalem sent Peter and John to the city and villages of Samaria, Acts viii. 14, 25; or as the church at Jerusalem sent Barnabas to Antioch, chap. xi. 22, and other churches joining sent Luke to travel with Paul, 2 Cor. viii. 19: though whether they had their charges borne by the church or no, it be not recorded. If it be objected, that this itinerary preaching will not serve to plant the Gospel in those places, unless they who are sent abide there some competent time; I answer, that if they stay there a year or two, which was the longest time usually stayed by the apostles in one place, it may suffice to teach them who will attend and learn all the points of religion necessary to salvation; then sorting them into several congregations of a moderate number, out of the ablest and zealousest among them to create elders, who, exercising and requiring from themselves what they have learned, (for no learning is retained without constant exercise and methodical repetition,) may teach and govern the rest: and so exhorted to continue faithful and steadfast, they may securely be committed to the providence of God and the guidance of his Holy Spirit, till God may offer some opportunity to visit them again, and to confirm them: which when they have done, they have done as much as the Apostles were wont to do in propagating the Gospel. . . . .

To these I might add other helps, which we enjoy now, to make more easy the attainment of Christian religion by the meanest: the entire Scripture translated into English with plenty of notes; and somewhere or other, I trust, may be found some wholesome body of divinity, as they call it, without school-terms and metaphysical notions, which have obscured rather than explained our religion, and made it seem difficult without cause. Thus taught once for all, and thus now and then visited and confirmed, in the most destitute and poorest places of the land, under the government of their own elders performing all ministerial offices among them, they may be trusted to meet and edify one another, whether in church or chapel, or to save them the trudging of many miles thither, nearer home, though in a house or barn. For notwithstanding the gaudy superstition of some devoted still ignorantly to temples, we may be well assured, that he who disdained not to be laid in a manger, disdains not to be preached in a barn; and that by such meetings as these, being indeed most apostolical and primitive, they will in a short time advance more in Christian knowledge and reformation of life, than by the many years' preaching of such an incumbent, I may say, such an incubus ofttimes, as will be meanly hired to abide long in those places. They have this left perhaps to object further; that to send thus, and to maintain, though but for a year or two, ministers and teachers in several places, would prove chargeable to the churches, though in towns and cities roundabout. To whom again I answer, that it was not thought so by them who first thus propagated the Gospel, though but few in number to us, and much less able to sustain the expense. Yet this expense would be much less than to hire incumbents, or rather incumbrances, for lifetime; and a great means (which is the subject of this discourse) to diminish hirelings. . . . .

But that the magistrate either out of that Church revenue which remains yet in his hand, or establishing any other maintenance instead of tithe, should take into his own power the stipendiary maintenance of church-ministers, or compel it by law, can stand neither with the people's right, nor with Christian liberty, but would suspend the Church wholly upon the state, and turn her ministers into state pensioners. And for the magistrate in person of a nursing father to make the Church his mere ward, as always in minority, the Church to whom he ought as a magistrate, Isa. xlix. 23, "to bow down with his face toward the earth, and lick up the dust of her feet"; her to subject to his political drifts or conceived opinions, by mastering her revenue; and so by his examinant committees to circumscribe her free election of ministers, is neither just nor pious; no honor done to the Church, but a plain dishonor: and upon her whose only head is in heaven, yea, upon him, who is only head, sets another in effect, and, which is most monstrous, a human on a heavenly, a carnal on a spiritual, a political head on an ecclesiastical body; which, at length, by such heterogeneal, such incestuous conjunction, transforms her ofttimes into a beast of many heads and many horns. For if the Church be of all societies the holiest on earth, and so to be reverenced by the magistrate; not to trust her with her own belief and integrity, and therefore not with the keeping, at least with the disposing, of what revenue should be found justly and lawfully her own, is to count the Church not a holy congregation, but a pack of giddy or dishonest persons, to be ruled by civil power in sacred affairs. . . . .

Heretofore in the first evangelic times, (and it were happy for Christendom if it were so again,) ministers of the Gospel were by nothing else distinguished from other Christians, but by their spiritual knowledge and sanctity of life, for which the Church elected them to be her teachers and overseers, though not thereby to separate them from whatever calling she then found them following besides; as the example of St. Paul declares, and the first times of Christianity. When once they affected to be called a clergy, and became, as it were, a peculiar tribe of Levites, a party, a distinct order in the commonwealth, bred up for divines in babbling schools, and fed at the public cost, good for nothing else but what was good for nothing, they soon grew idle: that idleness, with fulness of bread, begat pride and perpetual contention with their feeders, the despised laity, through all ages ever since; to the perverting of religion, and the disturbance of all Christendom. And we may confidently conclude, it never will be otherwise while they are thus upheld undepending on the Church, on which alone they anciently depended, and are by the magistrate publicly maintained, a numerous faction of indigent persons, crept for the most part out of extreme want and bad nurture, claiming by divine right and freehold the tenth of our estates, to monopolize the ministry as their peculiar, which is free and open to all able Christians, elected by any church. Under this pretence, exempt from all other employment, and enriching themselves on the public, they last of all prove common incendiaries, and exalt their horns against the magistrate himself that maintains them, as the priest of Rome did soon after against his benefactor the emperor, and the presbyters of late in Scotland. Of which hireling crew, together with all the mischiefs, dissensions, troubles, wars merely of their kindling, Christendom might soon rid herself and be happy, if Christians would but know their own dignity, their liberty, their adoption, and, let it not be wondered if I say, their spiritual priesthood, whereby they have all equally access to any ministerial function, whenever called by their own abilities, and the Church, though they never came near commencement or university. But while Protestants, to avoid the due labor of understanding their own religion, are content to lodge it in the breast, or rather in the books, of a clergyman, and to take it thence by scraps and mammocks, as he dispenses it in his Sunday's dole, they will be always learning and never knowing; always infants; always either his vassals, as lay Papists are to their priests; or at odds with him, as reformed principles give them some light to be not wholly conformable; whence infinite disturbances in the state, as they do, must needs follow. Thus much I had to say; and, I suppose, what may be enough to them who are not avariciously bent otherwise, touching the likeliest means to remove hirelings out of the Church; than which nothing can more conduce to truth, to peace and all happiness, both in church and state. If I be not heard nor believed, the event will have borne me witness to have spoken truth; and I in the mean while have borne my witness, not out of season, to the Church and to my country.

FROM

THE READY AND EASY WAY TO ESTABLISH A FREE COMMONWEALTH.

AFTER our liberty and religion thus prosperously fought for, gained, and many years possessed, except in those unhappy interruptions which God hath removed; now that nothing remains, but in all reason the certain hopes of a speedy and immediate settlement forever in a firm and free commonwealth, for this extolled and magnified nation, regardless both of honor won, or deliverances vouchsafed from Heaven, to fall back, or rather to creep back so poorly, as it seems the multitude would, to their once abjured and detested thraldom of kingship, to be ourselves the slanderers of our own just and religious deeds, though done by some to covetous and ambitious ends, yet not therefore to be stained with their infamy, or they to asperse the integrity of others; and yet these, now by revolting from the conscience of deeds well done, both in church and state, to throw away and forsake, or rather to betray a just and noble cause for the mixture of bad men who have ill-managed and abused it, (which had our fathers done heretofore, and on the same pretence deserted true religion, what had long ere this become of our Gospel, and all Protestant reformation, so much intermixed with the avarice and ambition of some reformers?) and by thus relapsing, to verify all the bitter predictions of our triumphing enemies, who will now think they wisely discerned and justly censured both us and all our actions as rash, rebellious, hypocritical, and impious; not only argues a strange, degenerate contagion suddenly spread among us, fitted and prepared for new slavery, but will render us a scorn and derision to all our neighbors.

And what will they at best say of us, and of the whole English name, but scoffingly, as of that foolish builder mentioned by our Saviour, who began to build a tower, and was not able to finish it? Where is this goodly tower of a commonwealth, which the English boasted they would build to overshadow kings, and be another Rome in the West? The foundation indeed they lay gallantly, but fell into a worse confusion, not of tongues, but of factions, than those at the tower of Babel; and have left no memorial of their work behind them remaining but in the common laughter of Europe! Which must needs redound the more to our shame, if we but look on our neighbors the United Provinces, to us inferior in all outward advantages; who, notwithstanding, in the midst of greater difficulties, courageously, wisely, constantly went through with the same work, and are settled in all the happy enjoyments of a potent and flourishing republic to this day.

Besides this, if we return to kingship, and soon repent, (as undoubtedly we shall, when we begin to find the old encroachment coming on by little and little upon our consciences, which must necessarily proceed from king and bishop united inseparably in one interest,) we may be forced perhaps to fight over again all that we have fought, and spend over again all that we have spent, but are never like to attain thus far as we are now advanced to the recovery of our freedom, never to have it in possession as we now have it, never to be vouchsafed hereafter the like mercies and signal assistances from Heaven in our cause, if by our ingrateful backsliding we make these fruitless; flying now to regal concessions from his divine condescensions and gracious answers to our once importuning prayers against the tyranny which we then groaned under; making vain and viler than dirt the blood of so many thousand faithful and valiant Englishmen, who left us in this liberty, bought with their lives; losing by a strange after-game of folly all the battles we have won, together with all Scotland as to our conquest, hereby lost, which never any of our kings could conquer, all the treasure we have spent, not that corruptible treasure only, but that far more precious of all our late miraculous deliverances; treading back again with lost labor all our happy steps in the progress of reformation, and most pitifully depriving ourselves the instant fruition of that free government, which we have so dearly purchased, a free commonwealth, not only held by wisest men in all ages the noblest, the manliest, the equallest, the justest government, the most agreeable to all due liberty and proportioned equality, both human, civil, and Christian, most cherishing to virtue and true religion, but also (I may say it with greatest probability) plainly commended, or rather enjoined by our Saviour himself, to all Christians, not without remarkable disallowance, and the brand of Gentilism upon kingship. . . . .

It may be well wondered that any nation, styling themselves free, can suffer any man to pretend hereditary right over them as their lord; whenas, by acknowledging that right, they conclude themselves his servants and his vassals, and so renounce their own freedom. Which how a people and their leaders especially can do, who have fought so gloriously for liberty; how they can change their noble words and actions, heretofore so becoming the majesty of a free people, into the base necessity of court flatteries and prostrations, is not only strange and admirable, but lamentable to think on. That a nation should be so valorous and courageous to win their liberty in the field, and when they have won it, should be so heartless and unwise in their counsels, as not to know how to use it, value it, what to do with it, or with themselves; but after ten or twelve years' prosperous war and contestation with tyranny, basely and besottedly to run their necks again into the yoke which they have broken, and prostrate all the fruits of their victory for naught at the feet of the vanquished, besides our loss of glory, and such an example as kings or tyrants never yet had the like to boast of, will be an ignominy if it befall us, that never yet befell any nation possessed of their liberty; worthy indeed themselves, whatsoever they be, to be forever slaves, but that part of the nation which consents not with them, as I persuade me of a great number, far worthier than by their means to be brought into the same bondage.

Considering these things so plain, so rational, I cannot but yet further admire on the other side, how any man, who hath the true principles of justice and religion in him, can presume or take upon him to be a king and lord over his brethren, whom he cannot but know, whether as men or Christians, to be for the most part every way equal or superior to himself: how he can display with such vanity and ostentation his regal splendor, so supereminently above other mortal men; or, being a Christian, can assume such extraordinary honor and worship to himself, while the kingdom of Christ, our common king and lord, is hid to this world, and such Gentilish imitation forbid in express words by himself to all his disciples. All Protestants hold that Christ in his Church hath left no vicegerent of his power; but himself, without deputy, is the only head thereof, governing it from heaven: how then can any Christian man derive his kingship from Christ, but with worse usurpation than the pope his headship over the Church, since Christ not only hath not left the least shadow of a command for any such vicegerence from him in the state, as the pope pretends for his in the Church, but hath expressly declared that such regal dominion is from the Gentiles, not from him, and hath strictly charged us not to imitate them therein? . . . .

To make the people fittest to choose, and the chosen fittest to govern, will be to mend our corrupt and faulty education, to teach the people faith, not without virtue, temperance, modesty, sobriety, parsimony, justice; not to admire wealth or honor; to hate turbulence and ambition; to place every one his private welfare and happiness in the public peace, liberty, and safety. . . . .

The whole freedom of man consists either in spiritual or civil liberty. As for spiritual, who can be at rest, who can enjoy anything in this world with contentment, who hath not liberty to serve God, and to save his own soul, according to the best light which God hath planted in him to that purpose, by the reading of his revealed will, and the guidance of his Holy Spirit? That this is best pleasing to God, and that the whole Protestant Church allows no supreme judge or ruler in matters of religion, but the Scriptures; and these to be interpreted by the Scriptures themselves, which necessarily infers liberty of conscience, I have heretofore proved at large in another treatise; and might yet further, by the public declarations, confessions, and admonitions of whole churches and states, obvious in all histories since the Reformation.

This liberty of conscience, which above all other things ought to be to all men dearest and most precious, no government more inclinable not to favor only, but to protect, than a free commonwealth; as being most magnanimous, most fearless, and confident of its own fair proceedings. Whereas kingship, though looking big, yet indeed most pusillanimous, full of fears, full of jealousies, startled at every umbrage, as it hath been observed of old to have ever suspected most and mistrusted them who were in most esteem for virtue and generosity of mind, so it is now known to have most in doubt and suspicion them who are most reputed to be religious. Queen Elizabeth, though herself accounted so good a Protestant, so moderate, so confident of her subjects' love, would never give way so much as to Presbyterian reformation in this land, though once and again besought, as Camden relates; but imprisoned and persecuted the very proposers thereof, alleging it as her mind and maxim unalterable, that such reformation would diminish regal authority.

What liberty of conscience can we then expect of others, far worse principled from the cradle, trained up and governed by Popish and Spanish counsels, and on such depending hitherto for subsistence? Especially what can this last Parliament expect, who, having revived lately and published the covenant, have re-engaged themselves, never to readmit Episcopacy? Which no son of Charles returning but will most certainly bring back with him, if he regard the last and strictest charge of his father, "to persevere in, not the doctrine only, but government of the Church of England, not to neglect the speedy and effectual suppressing of errors and schisms"; among which he accounted Presbytery one of the chief.

Or if, notwithstanding that charge of his father, he submit to the covenant, how will he keep faith to us, with disobedience to him; or regard that faith given, which must be founded on the breach of that last and solemnest paternal charge, and the reluctance, I may say the antipathy, which is in all kings, against Presbyterian and Independent discipline? For they hear the Gospel speaking much of liberty; a word which monarchy and her bishops both fear and hate, but a free commonwealth both favors and promotes; and not the word only, but the thing itself. But let our governors beware in time, lest their hard measure to liberty of conscience be found the rock whereon they shipwreck themselves, as others have now done before them in the course wherein God was directing their steerage to a free commonwealth; and the abandoning of all those whom they call sectaries, for the detected falsehood and ambition of some, be a wilful rejection of their own chief strength and interest in the freedom of all Protestant religion, under what abusive name soever calumniated.

The other part of our freedom consists in the civil rights and advancements of every person according to his merit: the enjoyment of those never more certain, and the access to these never more open, than in a free commonwealth. Both which, in my opinion, may be best and soonest obtained, if every county in the land were made a kind of subordinate commonalty or commonwealth, and one chief town or more, according as the shire is in circuit, made cities, if they be not so called already; where the nobility and chief gentry, from a proportionable compass of territory annexed to each city, may build houses or palaces befitting their quality; may bear part in the government, make their own judicial laws, or use those that are, and execute them by their own elected judicatures and judges without appeal, in all things of civil government between man and man. So they shall have justice in their own hands, law executed fully and finally in their own counties and precincts, long wished and spoken of, but never yet obtained. They shall have none then to blame but themselves, if it be not well administered; and fewer laws to expect or fear from the supreme authority; or to those that shall be made, of any great concernment to public liberty, they may, without much trouble in these commonalties, or in more general assemblies called to their cities from the whole territory on such occasion, declare and publish their assent or dissent by deputies, within a time limited, sent to the grand council; yet so as this their judgment declared shall submit to the greater number of other counties or commonalties, and not avail them to any exemption of themselves, or refusal of agreement with the rest, as it may in any of the United Provinces, being sovereign within itself, ofttimes to the great disadvantage of that union.

In these employments they may, much better than they do now, exercise and fit themselves till their lot fall to be chosen into the grand council, according as their worth and merit shall be taken notice of by the people. As for controversies that shall happen between men of several counties, they may repair, as they do now, to the capital city, or any other more commodious, indifferent place, and equal judges. And this I find to have been practised in the old Athenian commonwealth, reputed the first and ancientest place of civility in all Greece; that they had in their several cities a peculiar, in Athens a common government; and their right, as it befell them, to the administration of both.

They should have here also schools and academies at their own choice, wherein their children may be bred up in their own sight to all learning and noble education; not in grammar only, but in all liberal arts and exercises. This would soon spread much more knowledge and civility, yea, religion, through all parts of the land, by communicating the natural heat of government and culture more distributively to all extreme parts, which now lie numb and neglected; would soon make the whole nature more industrious, more ingenious at home, more potent, more honorable abroad. To this a free commonwealth will easily assent; (nay, the Parliament hath had already some such thing in design;) for of all governments a commonwealth aims most to make the people flourishing, virtuous, noble, and high-spirited. Monarchs will never permit; whose aim is to make the people wealthy indeed perhaps, and well fleeced, for their own shearing, and the supply of regal prodigality; but otherwise softest, basest, viciousest, servilest, easiest to be kept under. And not only in fleece, but in mind also sheepishest; and will have all the benches of judicature annexed to the throne, as a gift of royal grace, that we have justice done us; whenas nothing can be more essential to the freedom of a people, than to have the administration of justice, and all public ornaments, in their own election, and within their own bounds, without long travelling or depending upon remote places to obtain their right, or any civil accomplishment; so it be not supreme, but subordinate to the general power and union of the whole republic. . . . .

I have no more to say at present: few words will save us, well considered; few and easy things, now seasonably done. But if the people be so affected as to prostitute religion and liberty to the vain and groundless apprehension, that nothing but kingship can restore trade, not remembering the frequent plagues and pestilences that then wasted this city, such as through God's mercy we never have felt since; and that trade flourishes nowhere more than in the free commonwealths of Italy, Germany, and the Low Countries, before their eyes at this day; yet if trade be grown so craving and importunate through the profuse living of tradesmen, that nothing can support it but the luxurious expenses of a nation upon trifles or superfluities; so as if the people generally should betake themselves to frugality, it might prove a dangerous matter, lest tradesmen should mutiny for want of trading; and that therefore we must forego and set to sale religion, liberty, honor, safety, all concernments divine or human, to keep up trading: if, lastly, after all this light among us, the same reason shall pass for current, to put our necks again under kingship, as was made use of by the

Jews to return back to Egypt, and to the worship of their idol queen, because they falsely imagined that they then lived in more plenty and prosperity; our condition is not sound, but rotten, both in religion and all civil prudence; and will bring us soon, the way we are marching, to those calamities, which attend always and unavoidably on luxury, all national judgments under foreign and domestic slavery: so far we shall be from mending our condition by monarchizing our government, whatever new conceit now possesses us.

FROM

THE HISTORY OF BRITAIN.

BY this time, like one who had set out on his way by night, and travelled through a region of smooth or idle dreams, our history now arrives on the confines, where daylight and truth meet us with a clear dawn, representing to our view, though at a far distance, true colors and shapes. . . . .

Worthy deeds are not often destitute of worthy relaters; as, by a certain fate, great acts and great eloquence have most commonly gone hand in hand, equalling and honoring each other in the same ages. It is true, that in obscurest times, by shallow and unskilful writers, the indistinct noise of many battles and devastations of many kingdoms, overrun and lost, hath come to our ears. For what wonder, if in all ages, ambition and the love of rapine hath stirred up greedy and violent men to bold attempts in wasting and ruining wars, which to posterity have left the work of wild beasts and destroyers, rather than the deeds and monuments of men and conquerors? But he whose just and true valor uses the necessity of war and dominion not to destroy, but to prevent destruction, to bring in liberty against tyrants, law and civility among barbarous nations, knowing that when he conquers all things else, he cannot conquer Time or Detraction, wisely conscious of this his want, as well as of his worth not to be forgotten or concealed, honors and hath recourse to the aid of eloquence, his friendliest and best supply; by whose immortal record his noble deeds, which else were transitory, become fixed and durable against the force of years and generations, he fails not to continue through all posterity, over Envy, Death, and Time also victorious. Therefore, when the esteem of science and liberal study waxes low in the commonwealth, we may presume that also there all civil virtue and worthy action is grown as low to a decline: and then eloquence as it were consorted in the same destiny, with the decrease and fall of virtue, corrupts also and fades; at least resigns her office of relating to illiterate and frivolous historians, such as the persons themselves both deserve, and are best pleased with; whilst they want either the understanding to choose better, or the innocence to dare invite the examining and searching style of an intelligent and faithful writer to the survey of their unsound exploits, better befriended by obscurity than fame. . . . .

Thus expired this great empire of the Romans;

first in Britain, soon after in Italy itself; having borne chief sway in this island, though never thoroughly subdued, or all at once in subjection, if we reckon from the coming in of Julius, to the taking of Rome by Alaric, in which year Honorius wrote those letters of discharge into Britain, the space of four hundred and sixty-two years. And with the empire fell also what before in this Western world was chiefly Roman; learning, valor, eloquence, history, civility, and even language itself, all these together, as it were, with equal peace, diminishing and decaying. Henceforth we are to steer by another sort of authors; near enough to the things they write, as in their own country, if that would serve; in time not much belated, some of equal age; in expression barbarous, and to say how judicious, I suspend a while: this we must expect; in civil matters to find them dubious relaters, and still to the best advantage of what they term the Holy Church, meaning indeed themselves: in most other matters of religion, blind, astonished, and struck with superstition as with a planet; in one word, monks. Yet these guides, where can be had no better, must be followed; in gross, it may be true enough; in circumstances each man, as his judgment gives him, may reserve his faith, or bestow it. . . . .

Of these who swayed most in the late troubles, a few words as to this point may suffice. They had arms, leaders, and successes to their wish, but to make use of so great an advantage was not their skill.

To other causes therefore, and not to the want of force, or warlike manhood in the Britons, both those, and these lately, we must impute the ill husbanding of those fair opportunities, which might seem to have put liberty, so long desired, like a bridle into their hands. Of which other causes, equally belonging to ruler, priest, and people, above hath been related: which, as they brought those ancient natives to misery and ruin, by liberty, which rightly used, might have made them happy; so brought they these of late, after many labors, much bloodshed, and vast expense, to ridiculous frustration, in whom the like defects, the like miscarriages notoriously appeared, with vices not less hateful or inexcusable.

For a Parliament being called, to address many things, as it was thought, the people with great courage, and expectation to be eased of what discontented them, chose their behoof in Parliament, such as they thought best affected to the public good, and some indeed men of wisdom and integrity; the rest, (to be sure the greater part,) whom wealth or ample possessions, or bold and active ambition (rather than merit) had commended to the same place.

But when once the superficial zeal and popular fumes that acted their New magistracy were cooled, and spent in them, straight every one betook himself (setting the commonwealth behind, his private ends before) to do as his own profit or ambition led him. Then was justice delayed, and soon after denied: spite and favor determined all; hence faction, thence treachery, both at home and in the field: everywhere wrong and oppression: foul and horrid deeds committed daily, or maintained in secret, or in open. Some who had been called from shops and warehouses, without other merit, to sit in supreme councils and committees, (as their breeding was,) fell to huckster the commonwealth. Others did thereafter as men could soothe and humor them best; so he who would give most, or, under cover of hypocritical zeal, insinuate basest, enjoyed unworthily the rewards of learning and fidelity; or escaped the punishment of his crimes and misdeeds. Their votes and ordinances, which men looked should have contained the repealing of bad laws, and the immediate constitution of better, resounded with nothing else but new impositions, taxes, excises; yearly, monthly, weekly. Not to reckon the offices, gifts, and preferments bestowed and shared among themselves: they in the mean while, who were ever faithfullest to this cause, and freely aided them in person, or with their substance, when they durst not compel either, slighted and bereaved after of their just debts by greedy sequestrations, were tossed up and down after miserable attendance from one committee to another with petitions in their hands, yet either missed the obtaining of their suit, or though it were at length granted, (mere shame and reason ofttimes extorting from them at least a show of justice,) yet by their sequestrators and sub-committees abroad, men for the most part of insatiable hands, and noted disloyalty, those orders were commonly disobeyed: which for certain durst not have been, without secret compliance, if not compact, with some superiors able to bear them out. Thus were their friends confiscate with their enemies, while they forfeited their debtors to the state, as they called it, but indeed to the ravening seizure of innumerable thieves in office: yet withal no less burdened in all extraordinary assessments and oppressions, than those whom they took to be disaffected: nor were we happier creditors to what we called the state, than to them who were sequestered as the state's enemies.

For that faith which ought to have been kept as sacred and inviolable as anything holy, "the Public Faith," after infinite sums received, and all the wealth of the Church not better employed, but swallowed up into a private gulf, was not erelong ashamed to confess bankrupt. And now beside the sweetness of bribery, and other gain, with the love of rule, their own guiltiness and the dreaded name of Just Account, which the people had long called for, discovered plainly that there were of their own number, who secretly contrived and fomented those troubles and combustions in the land, which openly they sat to remedy; and would continually find such work, as should keep them from being ever brought to that Terrible Stand of laying down their authority for lack of new business, or not drawing it out to any length of time, though upon the ruin of a whole nation.

And if the state were in this plight, religion was not in much better; to reform which, a certain number of divines were called, neither chosen by any rule or custom ecclesiastical, nor eminent for either piety or knowledge above others left out; only as each member of Parliament in his private fancy thought fit, so elected one by one. The most part of them were such as had preached and cried down, with great show of zeal, the avarice and pluralities of bishops and prelates; that one cure of souls was a full employment for one spiritual pastor, how able soever, if not a charge rather above human strength. Yet these conscientious men (ere any part of the work done for which they came together, and that on the public salary) wanted not boldness, to the ignominy and scandal of their pastorlike profession, and especially of their boasted reformation, to seize into their hands, or not unwillingly to accept (besides one, sometimes two or more of the best livings) collegiate masterships in the universities, rich lectures in the city, setting sail to all winds that might blow gain into their covetous bosoms; by which means these great rebukers of non-residence, among so many distant cures, were not ashamed to be seen so quickly pluralists and non-residents themselves, to a fearful condemnation, doubtless by their own mouths. And yet the main doctrine for which they took such pay, and insisted upon with more vehemence than Gospel, was but to tell us in effect, that their doctrine was worth nothing, and the spiritual power of their ministry less available than bodily compulsion; persuading the magistrate to use it, as a stronger means to subdue and bring in conscience, than evangelical persuasion: distrusting the virtue of their own spiritual weapons, which were given them, if they be rightly called, with full warrant of sufficiency to pull down all thoughts and imaginations that exalt themselves against God. But while they taught compulsion without convincement, which not long before they complained of as executed unchristianly, against themselves; these intents are clear to have been no better than antichristian; setting up a spiritual tyranny by a secular power, to the advancing of their own authority above the magistrate, whom they would have made their executioner, to punish Church-delinquencies, whereof civil laws have no cognizance.

And well did their disciples manifest themselves to be no better principled than their teachers, trusted with committeeships and other gainful offices, upon their commendations for zealous, (and as they sticked not to term them,) godly men; but executing their places like children of the Devil, unfaithfully, unjustly, unmercifully, and, where not corruptly, stupidly. So that between them the teachers, and these the disciples, there hath not been a more ignominious and mortal wound to faith, to piety, to the work of reformation, nor more cause of blaspheming given to the enemies of God and truth, since the first preaching of reformation.

The people therefore looking one while on the statists, whom they beheld without constancy or firmness laboring doubtfully beneath the weight of their own too high undertakings, busiest in petty things, trifling in the main, deluded and quite alienated, expressed divers ways their disaffection; some despising whom before they honored, some deserting, some inveighing, some conspiring against them. Then looking on the churchmen, whom they saw under subtle hypocrisy to have preached their own follies, most of them not the Gospel, timeservers, covetous, illiterate persecutors, not lovers of the truth, like in most things whereof they accused their predecessors; looking on all this, the people which had been kept warm awhile with counterfeit zeal of their pulpits, after a false heat, became more cold and obdurate than before, some turning to lewdness, some to flat atheism, put beside their old religion, and foully scandalized in what they expected should be new.

Thus they who of late were extolled as our

greatest deliverers, and had the people wholly at their devotion, by so discharging their trust as we see, did not only weaken and unfit themselves to be dispensers of what liberty they pretended, but unfitted also the people, now grown worse and more disordinate, to receive or to digest any liberty at all. For stories teach us, that liberty sought out of season, in a corrupt and degenerate age, brought Rome itself to a farther slavery: for liberty hath a sharp and double edge, fit only to be handled by just and virtuous men; to bad and dissolute, it becomes a mischief unwieldy in their own hands: neither is it completely given, but by them who have the happy skill to know what is grievance and unjust to a people, and how to remove it wisely; what good laws are wanting, and how to frame them substantially, that good men may enjoy the freedom whch they merit, and the bad the curb which they need. But to do this, and to know these exquisite proportions, the heroic wisdom which is required, surmounted far the principles of these narrow politicians: what wonder then if they sunk as these unfortunate Britons before them, entangled and oppressed with things too hard and generous above their strain and temper? For Britain, to speak a truth not often spoken, as it is a land fruitful enough of men stout and courageous in war, so it is naturally not over-fertile of men able to govern justly and prudently in peace, trusting only in their mother-wit; who consider not justly, that civility, prudence, love of the public good, more than of money or vain honor, are to this soil in a manner outlandish ; grow not here, but in minds well implanted with solid and elaborate breeding, too impolitic else and rude, if not headstrong and intractable to the industry and virtue either of executing or understanding true civil government. Valiant indeed, and prosperous to win a field ; but to know the end and reason of winning unjudicious and unwise: in good or bad success alike unteachable. For the sun, which we want, ripens wits as well as fruits ; and as wine and oil are imported to us from abroad, so must ripe understanding, and many civil virtues, be imported into our minds from foreign writings, and examples of best ages: we shall else miscarry still, and come short in the attempts of any great enterprise. Hence did their victories prove as fruitless as their losses dangerous ; and left them still conquering under the same grievances that men suffer conquered ; which was indeed unlikely to go otherwise, unless men more than vulgar bred up, as few of them were, in the knowledge of ancient and illustrious deeds, invincible against many and vain titles, impartial to friendships and relations, had conducted their affairs: but then from the chapman to the retailer, many whose ignorance was more audacious than the rest, were admitted, with all their sordid rudiments, to bear no mean sway among them, both in church and state.

From the confluence of all their errors, mischiefs, and misdemeanors, what in the eyes of men could be expected, but what befell those ancient inhabitants, whom they so much resembled, confusion in the end?

FROM THE TREATISE

OF TRUE RELIGION, HERESY, SCHISM, TOLERATION.

TRUE religion is the true worship and service of God, learned and believed from the word of God only. No man or angel can know how God would be worshipped and served unless God reveal it: he hath revealed and taught it us in the Holy Scriptures by inspired ministers, and in the Gospel by his own Son and his Apostles, with strictest command, to reject all other traditions or additions whatsoever. . . . .

With good and religious reason, therefore, all Protestant churches with one consent, and particularly the Church of England in her thirty-nine articles, article 6th, 19th, 20th, 21st, and elsewhere, maintain these two points, as the main principles of true religion,—that the rule of true religion is the word of God only; and that their faith ought not to be an implicit faith, that is, to believe, though as the Church believes, against or without express authority of Scripture. And if all Protestants, as universally as they hold these two principles, so attentively and religiously would observe them, they would avoid and cut off many debates and contentions, schisms and persecutions, which too oft have been among them, and more firmly unite against the common adversary. For hence it directly follows, that no true Protestant can persecute, or not tolerate, his fellow-Protestant, though dissenting from him in some opinions, but he must flatly deny and renounce these two his own main principles, whereon true religion is founded; while he compels his brother from that which he believes as the manifest word of God, to an implicit faith (which he himself condemns) to the endangering of his brother's soul, whether by rash belief, or outward conformity: for "whatsoever is not of faith is sin." . . . .

Let us now inquire whether Popery be tolerable or no. Popery is a double thing to deal with, and claims a twofold power, ecclesiastical and political, both usurped, and the one supporting the other.

But, ecclesiastical is ever pretended to political. The pope by this mixed faculty pretends right, to kingdoms and states, and especially to this of England, thrones and unthrones kings, and absolves the people from their obedience to them; sometimes interdicts to whole nations the public worship of God, shutting up their churches: and was wont to drain away greatest part of the wealth of this then miserable land, as part of his patrimony, to maintain the pride and luxury of his court and prelates; and now, since, through the infinite mercy and favor of God, we have shaken off his Babylonish yoke, hath not ceased by his spies and agents, bulls and emissaries, once to destroy both king and Parliament; perpetually to seduce, corrupt, and pervert as many as they can of the people. Whether therefore it be fit or reasonable to tolerate men thus principled in religion towards the state, I submit it to the consideration of all magistrates, who are best able to provide for their own and the public safety. As for tolerating the exercise of their religion, supposing their state-activities not to be dangerous, I answer, that toleration is either public or private; and the exercise of their religion, as far as it is idolatrous, can be tolerated neither way: not publicly, without grievous and unsufferable scandal given to all conscientious beholders; not privately, without great offence to God, declared against all kind of idolatry, though secret. Ezek. viii. 7, 8.

. . . . .

Having shown thus, that Popery, as being idolatrous, is not to be tolerated either in public or private; it must be now thought how to remove it, and hinder the growth thereof, I mean in our natives, and not foreigners, privileged by the law of nations. Are we to punish them by corporal punishment, or fines in their estates, upon account of their religion? I suppose it stands not with the clemency of the Gospel, more than what appertains to the security of the state: but first we must remove their idolatry, and all the furniture thereof, whether idols or the mass wherein they adore their God under bread and wine: for the commandment forbids to adore, not only "any graven image, but the likeness of anything in heaven above, or in the earth beneath, or in the water under the earth; thou shalt not bow down to them nor worship them, for I the Lord thy God am a jealous God." If they say, that by removing their idols we violate their consciences, we have no warrant to regard conscience which is not grounded on Scripture: and they themselves confess, in their late defences, that they hold not their images necessary to salvation, but only as they are enjoined them by tradition. . . . .

St. Paul judged, that not only to tolerate, but to examine and prove all things, was no danger to our holding fast that which is good. How shall we prove all things, which includes all opinions at least founded on Scripture, unless we not only tolerate them, but patiently hear them, and seriously read them? If he who thinks himself in the truth professes to have learnt it, not by implicit faith, but by attentive study of the Scriptures, and full persuasion of heart, with what equity can he refuse to hear or read him who demonstrates to have gained his knowledge by the same way? Is it a fair course to assert truth, by arrogating to himself the only freedom of speech, and stopping the mouths of others equally gifted? This is the direct way to bring in that Papistical implicit faith, which we all disclaim. They pretend it would unsettle the weaker sort; the same groundless fear is pretended by the Romish clergy. At least, then, let them have leave to write in Latin, which the common people understand not; that what they hold may be discussed among the learned only. We suffer the idolatrous books of Papists, without this fear, to be sold and read as common as our own: why not much rather of Anabaptists, Arians, Arminians, and Socinians? There is no learned man but will confess he hath much profited by reading controversies, his senses awakened, his judgment sharpened, and the truth which he holds more firmly established. If then it be profitable for him to read, why should it not at least be tolerable and free for his adversary to write? In logic they teach, that contraries laid together more evidently appear: it follows, then, that all controversy being permitted, falsehood will appear more false, and truth the more true; which must needs conduce much, not only to the confounding of Popery, but to the general confirmation of unimplicit truth.

FROM THE

FAMILIAR LETTERS.

To Benedetto Buonmattai, *a Florentine*.

I AM glad to hear, my dear Buonmattai, that you are preparing new institutes of your native language, and have just brought the work to a conclusion. The way to fame which you have chosen is the same as that which some persons of the first genius have embraced; and your fellow-citizens seem ardently to expect that you will either illustrate or amplify, or at least polish and methodize, the labors of your predecessors. By such a work, you will lay your countrymen under no common obligation, which they will be ungrateful if they do not acknowledge. For I hold him to deserve the highest praise who fixes the principles and forms the manners of a state, and makes the wisdom of his administration conspicuous both at home and abroad. But I assign the second place to him, who endeavors by precepts and by rules to perpetuate that style and idiom of speech and composition which have flourished in the purest periods of the language, and who, as it were, throws up such a trench around it, that people may be prevented from going beyond the boundary almost by the terrors of a Romulean prohibition. If we compare the benefits which each of these confer, we shall find that the former alone can render the intercourse of the citizens just and conscientious, but that the latter gives that gentility, that elegance, that refinement which are next to be desired. The one inspires lofty courage and intrepid ardor against the invasion of an enemy; the other exerts himself to annihilate that barbarism which commits more extensive ravages on the minds of men, which is the intestine enemy of genius and literature, by the taste which he inspires, and the good authors which he causes to be read. Nor do I think it a matter of little moment whether the language of a people be vitiated or refined, whether the popular idiom be erroneous or correct. This consideration was more than once found salutary at Athens. It is the opinion of Plato, that changes in the dress and habits of the citizens portend great commotions and changes in the state; and I am inclined to believe, that when the language in common use in any country becomes irregular and depraved, it is followed by their ruin or their degradation. For what do terms used without skill or meaning, which are at once corrupt and misapplied, denote, but a people listless, supine, and ripe for servitude? On the contrary, we have never heard of any people or state which has not flourished in some degree of prosperity as long as their language has retained its elegance and its purity. Hence, my Benedetto, you may be induced to proceed in executing a work so useful to your country, and may clearly see what an honorable and permanent claim you will have to the approbation and the gratitude of your fellow-citizens. Thus much I have said, not to make you acquainted with that of which you were ignorant, but because I was persuaded that you are more intent on serving your country than in considering the just title which you have to its remuneration. I will now mention the favorable opportunity which you have, if you wish to embrace it, of obliging foreigners, among whom there is no one at all conspicuous for genius or for elegance who does not make the Tuscan language his delight, and indeed consider it as an essential part of education, particularly if he be only slightly tinctured with the literature of Greece or of Rome. I, who certainly have not merely wetted the tip of my lips in the stream of those languages, but, in proportion to my years, have swallowed the most copious drafts, can yet sometimes retire with avidity and delight to feast on Dante, Petrarch, and many others; nor has Athens itself been able to confine me to the transparent wave of its Ilissus, nor ancient Rome to the banks of its Tiber, so as to prevent my visiting with delight the stream of the Arno, and the hills of

Fæsolæ. A stranger from the shores of the farthest ocean, I have now spent some days among you, and am become quite enamored of your nation. Consider whether there were sufficient reason for my preference, that you may more readily remember what I so earnestly importune; that you would, for the sake of foreigners, add something to the grammar which you have begun, and indeed almost finished, concerning the right pronunciation of the language, and made as easy as the nature of the subject will admit. The other critics in your language seem to this day to have had no other design than to satisfy their own countrymen, without taking any concern about anybody else. Though I think that they would have provided better for their own reputation and for the glory of the Italian language, if they had delivered their precepts in such a manner as if it was for the interest of all men to learn their language. But, for all them, we might think that you Italians wished to confine your wisdom within the pomærium of the Alps. This praise, therefore, which no one has anticipated, will be entirely yours, immaculate and pure; nor will it be less so if you will be at the pains to point out who may justly claim the second rank of fame after the renowned chiefs of the Florentine literature; who excels in the dignity of tragedy, or the festivity and elegance of comedy; who has shown acuteness of remark or depth of reflection in his epistles or dialogues; to whom belongs the grandeur of the historic style. Thus it will be easy for the student to choose the best writers in every department; and if he wishes to extend his researches further, he will know which way to take. Among the ancients, you will in this respect find Cicero and Fabius deserving of your imitation; but I know not one of your own countrymen who does. But though I think, as often as I have mentioned this subject, that your courtesy and benignity have induced you to comply with my request, I am unwilling that those qualities should deprive you of the homage of a more polished and elaborate entreaty. For since your singular modesty is so apt to depreciate your own performances; the dignity of the subject, and my respect for you, will not suffer me to rate them below their worth. And it is certainly just that he who shows the greatest facility in complying with a request, should not receive the less honor on account of his compliance. On this occasion I have employed the Latin rather than your own language, that I might in Latin confess my imperfect acquaintance with that language which I wish you by your precepts to embellish and adorn. And I hoped that if I invoked the venerable Latin mother, hoary with years, and crowned with the respect of ages, to plead the cause of her daughter, I should give to my request a force and authority which nothing could resist. Adieu.

FLORENCE, Sept. 10, 1638.

To Leonard Philaras, *the Athenian.*

I HAVE always been devotedly attached to the literature of Greece, and particularly to that of your Athens; and have never ceased to cherish the persuasion that that city would one day make me ample recompense for the warmth of my regard. The ancient genius of your renowned country has favored the completion of my prophecy in presenting me with your friendship and esteem. Though I was known to you only by my writings, and we were removed to such a distance from each other, you most courteously addressed me by letter; and when you unexpectedly came to London, and saw me who could no longer see, my affliction, which causes none to regard me with greater admiration, and perhaps many even with feelings of contempt, excited your tenderest sympathy and concern. You would not suffer me to abandon the hope of recovering my sight; and informed me that you had an intimate friend at Paris, Doctor Thevenot, who was particularly celebrated in disorders of the eyes, whom you would consult about mine, if I would enable you to lay before him the causes and symptoms of the complaint. I will do what you desire, lest I should seem to reject that aid which perhaps may be offered me by Heaven. It is now, I think, about ten years since I perceived my vision to grow weak and dull; and at the same time I was troubled with pain in my kidneys and bowels, accompanied with flatulency. In the morning, if I began to read, as was my custom, my eyes instantly ached intensely, but were refreshed after a little corporeal exercise. The candle which I looked at, seemed as it were encircled with a rainbow. Not long after the sight in the left part of the left eye (which I lost some years before the other) became quite obscured; and prevented me from discerning any object on that side. The sight in my other eye has now been gradually and sensibly vanishing away for about three years; some months before it had entirely perished, though I stood motionless, everything which I looked at, seemed in motion to and fro. A stiff cloudy vapor seemed to have settled on my forehead and temples, which usually occasions a sort of somnolent pressure upon my eyes, and particularly from dinner till the evening. So that I often recollect what is said of the poet Phineas in the Argonautics: —

> "A stupor deep his cloudy temples bound,
> And when he walked he seemed as whirling round,
> Or in a feeble trance he speechless lay."

I ought not to omit that while I had any sight left, as soon as I lay down on my bed and turned on either side, a flood of light used to gush from my closed eyelids. Then, as my sight became daily more impaired, the colors became more faint, and were emitted with a certain inward crackling sound; but at present, every species of illumination being, as it were, extinguished, there is diffused around me nothing but darkness, or darkness mingled and streaked with an ashy brown. Yet the darkness in which I am perpetually immersed, seems always, both by night and day, to approach nearer to white than black; and when the eye is rolling in its socket, it admits a little particle of light, as through a chink. And though your physician may kindle a small ray of hope, yet I make up my mind to the malady as quite incurable; and I often reflect, that as the wise man admonishes, days of darkness are destined to each of us, the darkness which I experience, less oppressive than that of the tomb, is, owing to the singular goodness of the Deity, passed amid the pursuits of literature and the cheering salutations of friendship. But if, as is written, "man shall not live by bread alone, but by every word that proceedeth from the mouth of God," why may not any one acquiesce in the privation of his sight, when God has so amply furnished his mind and his conscience with eyes? While he so tenderly provides for me, while he so graciously leads me by the hand, and conducts me on the way, I will, since it is his pleasure, rather rejoice than repine at being blind. And, my dear Philaras, whatever may be the event, I wish you adieu with no less courage and composure than if I had the eyes of a lynx.

WESTMINSTER, September 28, 1654.

To the Illustrious Lord Henry de Bras.

I SEE, my Lord, that you, unlike most of our modern youth who pass through foreign countries, wisely travel, like the ancient philosophers, for the sake of completing your juvenile studies, and of picking up knowledge wherever it may be found. Though as often as I consider the excellence of what you write, you appear to me to have gone among foreigners, not so much for the sake of procuring erudition yourself, as of imparting it to others, and rather to exchange than to purchase a stock of literature. I wish it were as easy for me in every way to promote the increase of your knowledge and the improvement of your intellect, as it is pleasing and flattering to me to have that assistance requested by talents and genius like yours. I have never attempted, and I should never dare to attempt, to solve those difficulties as you request, which seem to have cast a cloud over the writers of history for so many ages. Of Sallust I will speak, as you desire, without any hesitation or reserve. I prefer him to any of the Latin historians; which was also the general opinion of the ancients. Your favorite Tacitus deserves his meed of praise; but his highest praise, in my opinion, consists in his having imitated Sallust with all his might. By my conversation with you on this subject I seem, as far as I can guess from your letter, to have inspired you with sentiments very similar to my own, concerning that most energetic and animated writer. As he in the beginning of his Catilinarian war asserted that there was the greatest difficulty in historical composition, because the style should correspond with the nature of the narrative, you ask me how a writer of history may best attain that excellence. My opinion is that he who would describe actions and events in a way suited to their dignity and importance, ought to write with a mind endued with a spirit, and enlarged by an experience, as extensive as the actors in the scene, that he may have a capacity properly to comprehend and to estimate the most momentous affairs, and to relate them, when comprehended, with energy and distinctness, with purity and perspicuity of diction. The decorations of style I do not greatly heed: for I require an historian, and not a rhetorician. I do not want frequent interspersions of sentiment, or prolix dissertations on transactions, which interrupt the series of events, and cause the historian to intrench on the office of the politician, who, if, in explaining counsels and explaining facts, he follows truth rather than his own partialities and conjectures, excites the disgust or the aversion of his party. I will add a remark of Sallust, and which was one of the excellences he himself commends in Cato, that he should be able to say much in a few words; a perfection which I think no one can attain without the most discriminating judgment and a peculiar degree of moderation. There are many in whom you have not to regret either elegance of diction or copiousness of narrative, who have yet united copiousness with brevity. And among these Sallust is, in my opinion, the chief of the Latin writers. Such are the virtues which I think every historian ought to possess who would proportion his style to the facts which he records. But why do I mention this to you, when such is your genius that you need not my advice, and when such is your proficiency, that if it goes on increasing you will soon not be able to consult any one more learned than yourself? To the increase of that proficiency, though no exhortations can be necessary to stimulate your exertions, yet, that I may not seem entirely to frustrate your expectations, I will beseech you, with all my affection, all my authority, and all my zeal, to let nothing relax your diligence, or chill the ardor of your pursuit. Adieu! and may you ever successfully labor in the path of wisdom and of virtue!

WESTMINSTER, July 15, 1657.

FROM THE

LETTERS OF STATE.

To the most Illustrious and Noble Senators, SCULTETS, LANDAM, *and Senators of the Evangelic Cantons of* SWITZERLAND, ZURICK, BERN, GLARIS, BALE, SCHAFFHUSEN, APPENZEL, *also the Confederates of the same Religion in the country of the* GRISONS, *of* GENEVA, ST. GALL, MALHAUSEN, *and* BIENNE, *our dearest friends.*

OUR letters, most illustrious lords and dearest confederates, dated December twenty-four, full of civility, good will, and singular affection towards us and our republic, and what ought always to be greater and more sacred to us, breathing fraternal and truly Christian charity, we have received. And in the first place, we return thanks to Almighty God, who has raised and established both you and so many noble cities, not so much intrenched and fortified with those enclosures of mountains, as with your innate fortitude, piety, most prudent and just administration of government, and the faith of mutual confederacies, to be a firm and inaccessible shelter for all the truly

orthodox. Now then that you, who over all Europe were the first of mortals, who, after deluges of barbarous tyrants from the north, heaven prospering your valor, recovered your liberty, and, being obtained, for so many years have preserved it untainted, with no less prudence and moderation; that you should have such noble sentiments of our liberty recovered; that you, such sincere worshippers of the Gospel, should be so constantly persuaded of our love and affection for the orthodox faith, is that which is most acceptable and welcome to us. But as to your exhorting us to peace, with a pious and affectionate intent, as we are fully assured, certainly such an admonition ought to be of great weight with us, as well in respect of the thing itself which you persuade, and which of all things is chiefly to be desired, as also for the great authority, which is to be allowed your lordships above others in this particular, who in the midst of loud tumultuous wars on every side enjoy the sweets of peace both at home and abroad, and have approved yourselves the best example to all others of embracing and improving peace; and lastly, for that you persuade us to the very thing which we ourselves of our own accords, and that more than once, consulting as well our own as the interest of the whole evangelical communion, have begged by ambassadors, and other public ministers, namely, friendship and a most strict league with the United Provinces. But how they treated our ambassadors sent to them to negotiate, not a bare peace, but a brotherly amity and most strict league; what provocations to war they afterwards gave us; how they fell upon us in our own roads, in the midst of their ambassadors' negotiations for peace and allegiance, little dreaming any such violence; you will abundantly understand by our declaration set forth upon this subject, and sent you together with these our letters. But as for our parts, we are wholly intent upon this, by God's assistance, though prosperous hitherto, so to carry ourselves, that we may neither attribute anything to our own strength or forces, but all things to God alone, nor be insolently puffed up with our success; and we still retain the same ready inclinations to embrace all occasions of making a just and honest peace. In the mean time yourselves, illustrious and most excellent lords, in whom this noble and pious sedulity, out of mere evangelical affection, exerts itself to reconcile and pacify contending brethren, as ye are worthy of all applause among men, so doubtless will ye obtain the celestial reward of peacemakers with God; to whose supreme benignity and favor we heartily recommend in our prayers both you and yours, no less ready to make returns of all good offices, both of friends and brethren, if in anything we may be serviceable to your lordships.

Sealed with the Parliament seal, and subscribed, Speaker, &c.

WESTMINSTER, October, 1653.

OLIVER, *the Protector &c., to the most Serene Prince,* IMMANUEL, *Duke of Savoy, Prince of Piemont, Greeting:* —

MOST SERENE PRINCE: Letters have been sent us from Geneva, as also from the Dauphinate, and many other places bordering upon your territories, wherein we are given to understand, that such of your royal highness's subjects as profess the reformed religion, are commanded by your edict, and by your authority, within three days after the promulgation of your edict, to depart their native seats and habitations, upon pain of capital punishment, and forfeiture of all their fortunes and estates, unless they will give security to relinquish their religion within twenty days, and embrace the Roman Catholic faith. And that when they applied themselves to your royal highness in a most suppliant manner, imploring a revocation of the said edict, and that, being received into pristine favor, they might be restored to the liberty granted them by your predecessors, a part of your army fell upon them, most cruelly slew several, put others in chains, and compelled the rest to fly into desert places, and to the mountains covered with snow, where some hundreds of families are reduced to such distress, that it is greatly to be feared they will in a short time all miserably perish through cold and hunger. These things, when they were related to us, we could not choose but be touched with extreme grief, and compassion for the sufferings and calamities of this afflicted people. Now in regard we must acknowledge ourselves linked together, not only by the same tie of humanity, but by joint communion of the same religion, we thought it impossible for us to satisfy our duty to God, to brotherly charity, or our profession of the same religion, if we should only be affected with a bare sorrow for the misery and calamity of our brethren, and not contribute all our endeavors to relieve and succor them in their unexpected adversity, as much as in us lies. Therefore in a greater measure we most earnestly beseech and conjure your royal highness, that you would call back to your thoughts the moderation of your most serene predecessors, and the liberty by them granted and confirmed from time to time to their subjects the Vaudois. In granting and confirming which, as they did that which without all question was most grateful to God, who has been pleased to reserve the jurisdiction and power over the conscience to himself alone, so there is no doubt but that they had a due consideration of their subjects also, whom they found stout and most faithful in war, and always obedient in peace. And as your royal serenity in other things most laudably follows the footsteps of your immortal ancestors, so we again and again beseech your royal highness not to swerve from the path wherein they trod in this particular; but that you would vouchsafe to abrogate both this edict, and whatsoever else may be decreed to the disturbance of your subjects upon the account of the reformed religion; that you would ratify to them their conceded privileges and pristine liberty, and command their losses to be repaired, and that an end be put to their oppressions. Which if your royal highness shall be pleased to see performed, you will do a thing most acceptable to God, revive and comfort the miserable in dire calamity, and most highly oblige all your neighbors that profess the reformed religion, but more especially ourselves, who shall be bound to look upon your clemency and benignity toward your subjects as the fruit of our earnest solicitation. Which will both engage us to a reciprocal return to all good offices, and lay the solid foundations not only of establishing, but increasing, alliance and friendship between this republic and your dominions. Nor do we less promise this to ourselves from your justice and moderation; to which we beseech Almighty God to incline your mind and thoughts. And so we cordially implore just Heaven to bestow upon your highness and your people the blessings of peace and truth, and prosperous success in all your affairs.

WHITEHALL, May —, 1655.

OLIVER, PROTECTOR, *&c., to the High and Mighty Lords, the States of the* UNITED PROVINCES.

WE make no question but that you have already been informed by the Duke of Savoy's edict, set forth against his subjects inhabiting the valleys at the feet of the Alps, ancient professors of the orthodox faith; by which edict they are commanded to abandon their native habitations, stripped of all their fortunes, unless within twenty days they embrace the Roman faith; and with what cruelty the authority of this edict has raged against a needy and harmless people, many being slain by the soldiers, the rest plundered and driven from their houses, together with their wives and children, to combat cold and hunger among desert mountains, and perpetual snow. These things with what commotion of mind you heard related, what a fellow-feeling of the calamities of brethren pierced your breasts, we readily conjectured from the depth of our own sorrow, which certainly is most heavy and afflictive. For being engaged together by the same tie of religion, no wonder we should be so deeply moved with the same affections upon the dreadful and undeserved sufferings of our brethren. Besides, that your conspicuous piety and charity toward the orthodox, wherever overborne and oppressed, has been frequently experienced in the most urging straits and calamities of the churches. For my own part, unless my thoughts deceive me, there is nothing wherein I should desire more willingly to be overcome, than in good-will and charity toward brethren of the same religion, afflicted and wronged in their quiet enjoyments; as being one that would be accounted always ready to prefer the peace and safety of the churches before my particular interests. So far, therefore, as hitherto lay in our power, we have written to the Duke of Savoy, even almost to supplication, beseeching him that he would admit into his breast more placid thoughts and kinder effects of his favor towards his most innocent subjects and suppliants; that he would restore the miserable to their habitations and estates, and grant them their pristine freedom in the exercise of their religion. Moreover, we wrote to the chiefest princes and magistrates of the Protestants, whom we thought most nearly concerned in these matters, that they would lend us their assistance to entreat and pacify the Duke of Savoy in their behalf. And we make no doubt now but you have done the same, and perhaps much more. For this so dangerous a precedent, and lately removed severity of utmost cruelty toward the reformed, if the authors of it meet with prosperous success, to what apparent dangers it reduces our religion, we need not admonish your prudence. On the other side, if the Duke shall once but permit himself to be atoned and won by our united applications, not only our afflicted brethren, but we ourselves shall reap the noble and abounding harvest and reward of this laborious undertaking. But if he still persist in the same obstinate resolutions of reducing to utmost extremity those people, (among whom our religion was either disseminated by the first doctors of the

Gospel, and preserved from the defilement of superstition, or else restored to its pristine sincerity long before other nations obtained that felicity,) and determines their utter extirpation and destruction; we are ready to take such other course and councils with yourselves, in common with the rest of our reformed friends and confederates, as may be most necessary for the preservation of just and good men, upon the brink of inevitable ruin; and to make the Duke himself sensible that we can no longer neglect the heavy oppressions and calamities of our orthodox brethren. Farewell.

OLIVER, *Protector of the Commonwealth of* ENGLAND, *&c., to the most High and Mighty Lords, the States of the* UNITED PROVINCES.

MOST High and Mighty Lords, our dearest Friends and Confederates: — We make no doubt but that all men will bear us this testimony, that no considerations, in contracting foreign alliances, ever swayed us beyond those of defending the truth of religion, or that we accounted anything more sacred, than to unite the minds of all the friends and protectors of the Protestants, and of all others who at least were not their enemies. Whence it comes to pass, that we are touched with so much the more grief of mind, to hear that the Protestant princes and cities, whom it so much behoves to live in friendship and concord together, should begin to be so jealous of each other, and so ill disposed to mutual affection; more especially that your lordships and the King of Sweden, than whom the orthodox faith has not more magnanimous and courageous defenders, nor our republic confederates more strictly conjoined in interests, should seem to remit of your confidence in each other; or rather, that there should appear some too apparent signs of tottering friendship and growing discord between ye. What the causes are, and what progress this alienation of your affection has made, we protest ourselves to be altogether ignorant. However, we cannot but conceive an extraordinary trouble of mind for these beginnings of the least dissension arisen among brethren, which infallibly must greatly endanger the Protestant interests. Which if they should gather strength, how prejudicial it would prove to Protestant churches, what an occasion of triumph it would afford our enemies, and more especially the Spaniards, cannot be unknown to your prudence, and most industrious experience of affairs. As for the Spaniards, it has already so enlivened their confidence, and raised their courage, that they made no scruple, by their ambassador residing in your territories, boldly to obtrude their counsels upon your lordships, and that in reference to the highest concerns of your republic; presuming, partly with threats of renewing the war, to terrify, and partly with a false prospect of advantage, to solicit your lordships to forsake your ancient and most faithful friends, the English, French, and Danes, and enter into a strict confederacy with your old enemy, and once your domineering tyrant, now seemingly atoned; but, what is most to be feared, only at present treacherously fawning to advance his own designs. Certainly he who of an inveterate enemy lays hold of so slight an occasion of a sudden to become your counsellor, what is it that he would not take upon him? Where would his insolency stop, if once he could but see with his eyes what now he only ruminates and labors in his thoughts; that is to say, division and a civil war among the Protestants? We are not ignorant that your lordships, out of your deep wisdom, frequently revolve in your minds what the posture of all Europe is, and what more especially the condition of the Protestants: that the Cantons of Switzerland, adhering to the orthodox faith, are in daily expectation of new troubles to be raised by their countrymen embracing the Popish ceremonies; scarcely recovered from that war, which for the sake of religion was kindled and blown up by the Spaniards, who supplied their enemies both with commanders and money: that the counsels of the Spaniards are still contriving to continue the slaughter and destruction of the Piedmontois, which was cruelly put in execution the last year: that the Protestants under the jurisdiction of the emperor are most grievously harassed, having much ado to keep possession of their native homes:

that the King of Sweden, whom God, as we hope, has raised up to be a most stout defender of the orthodox faith, is at present waging, with all the force of his kingdom, a doubtful and bloody war with the most potent enemies of the reformed religion: that your own provinces are threatened with hostile confederacies of the princes your neighbors, headed by the Spaniards; and lastly, that we ourselves are busied in a war proclaimed against the King of Spain. In this posture of affairs, if any contest should happen between your lordships and the King of Sweden, how miserable would be the condition of all the reformed churches over all Europe, exposed to the cruelty and fury of unsanctified enemies! These cares not slightly seize us; and we hope your sentiments to be the same; and that out of your continued zeal for the common cause of the Protestants, and to the end the present peace between brethren professing the same faith, the same hope of eternity, may be preserved inviolable, your lordships will accommodate your counsels to those considerations, which are to be preferred before all others; and that you will leave nothing neglected that may conduce to the establishing tranquillity and union between your lordships and the King of Sweden. Wherein, if we can any way be useful, as far as our authority, and the favor you bear us will sway with your lordships, we freely offer our utmost assistance, prepared in like manner to be no less serviceable to the King of Sweden, to whom we design a speedy embassy, to the end we may declare our sentiments at large concerning these matters. We hope, moreover, that God will bend your minds on both sides to moderate counsels, and so restrain your animosities, that no provocation may be given, either by the one or the other, to fester your differences to extremity; but that, on the other side, both parties will remove whatever may give offence or occasion of jealousy to the other. Which, if you shall vouchsafe to do, you will disappoint your enemies, prove the consolation of your friends, and in the best manner provide for the welfare of your republic. And this we beseech you to be fully convinced of, that we shall use our utmost care to make appear, upon all occasions, our extraordinary affection and good will to the states of the United Provinces. And so we most earnestly implore the Almighty God to perpetuate his blessings of peace, wealth, and liberty, upon your republic: but above all things to preserve it always flourishing in the love of the Christian faith, and the true worship of his name.

Your high and mightinesses' most affectionate,

OLIVER, *Protector of the Commonwealth of England, &c.*

From our Palace at WESTMINSTER, Aug. —, 1656.

FROM THE

TREATISE ON CHRISTIAN DOCTRINE.

JOHN MILTON,

TO ALL THE CHURCHES OF CHRIST,

AND

TO ALL WHO PROFESS THE CHRISTIAN FAITH THROUGHOUT THE WORLD,

PEACE, AND THE RECOGNITION OF THE TRUTH, AND ETERNAL SALVATION IN GOD THE FATHER, AND IN OUR LORD JESUS CHRIST.

INCE the commencement of the last century, when religion began to be restored from the corruptions of more than thirteen hundred years to something of its original purity, many treatises of theology have been published, conducted according to sounder principles, wherein the chief heads of Christian doctrine are set forth, sometimes briefly, sometimes in a more enlarged and methodical order. I think myself obliged, therefore, to declare in the first instance why, if any works have already appeared as perfect as the nature of the subject will admit, I have not remained contented with them, — or, if all my predecessors have treated it unsuccessfully, why their failure has not deterred me from attempting an undertaking of a similar kind.

If I were to say that I had devoted myself to the study of the Christian religion because nothing else can so effectually rescue the lives and minds of men from those two detestable curses, slavery and superstition, I should seem to have acted rather from a regard to my highest earthly comforts, than from a religious motive.

But since it is only to the individual faith of each that the Deity has opened the way of eternal salvation, and as he requires that he who would be saved should have a personal belief of his own, I resolved not to repose on the faith or judgment of others in matters relating to God; but on the one hand, having taken the grounds of my faith from divine revelation alone, and on the other, having neglected nothing which depended on my own industry, I thought fit to scrutinize and ascertain for myself the several points of my religious belief, by the most careful perusal and meditation of the Holy Scriptures themselves.

If therefore I mention what has proved beneficial in my own practice, it is in the hope that others, who have a similar wish of improving themselves, may be thereby invited to pursue the same method. I entered upon an assiduous course of study in my youth, beginning with the books of the Old and New Testament in their original languages, and going diligently through a few of the shorter systems of divines, in imitation of whom I was in the habit of classing under certain heads whatever passages of Scripture occurred for extraction, to be made use of hereafter as occasion might require. At length I resorted with increased confidence to some of the more copious theological treatises, and to the examination of the arguments advanced by the conflicting parties respecting certain disputed points of faith. But, to speak the truth with freedom as well as candor, I was concerned to discover in many instances adverse reasonings either evaded by wretched shifts, or attempted to be refuted, rather speciously than with solidity, by an affected display of formal sophisms, or by a constant recourse to the quibbles of the grammarians; while what was most pertinaciously espoused as the true doctrine, seemed often defended, with more vehemence than strength of argument, by misconstructions of Scripture, or by the hasty deduction of erroneous inferences. Owing to these causes, the truth was sometimes as strenuously opposed as if it had been an error or a heresy, — while errors and heresies were substituted for the truth, and valued rather from deference to custom and the spirit of party than from the authority of Scripture.

According to my judgment, therefore, neither my creed nor my hope of salvation could be safely trusted to such guides; and yet it appeared highly requisite to possess some methodical tractate of Christian doctrine, or at least to attempt such a disquisition as might be useful in establishing my faith or assisting my memory. I deemed it therefore safest and most advisable to compile for myself, by my own labor and study, some original treatise which should be always at hand, derived solely from the word of God itself, and executed with all possible fidelity, seeing that I could have no wish to practise any imposition on myself in such a matter.

After a diligent perseverance in this plan for several years, I perceived that the strongholds of the reformed religion were sufficiently fortified, as far as it was in danger from the Papists, — but neglected many other quarters; neither competently strengthened with works of defence, nor adequately provided with champions. It was also evident to me, that in religion as in other things, the offers of God were all directed, not to an indolent credulity, but to constant diligence, and to an unwearied search after truth; and that more than I was aware of still remained, which required to be more rigidly examined by the rule of Scripture, and reformed after a more accurate model. I so far satisfied myself in the prosecution of this plan as at length to trust that I had discovered, with regard to religion, what was matter of belief, and what only matter of opinion. It was also a great solace to me to have compiled, by God's assistance, a precious aid for my faith, — or rather to have laid up for myself a treasure which would be a provision for my future life, and would remove from my mind all grounds for hesitation, as often as it behoved me to render an account of the principles of my belief.

If I communicate the result of my inquiries to the world at large; if, as God is my witness, it be with a friendly and benignant feeling towards mankind, that I readily give as wide a circulation as possible to what I esteem my best and richest possession, I hope to meet with a candid reception from all parties, and that none at least will take unjust offence, even though many things should be brought to light which will at once be seen to differ from certain received opinions. I earnestly beseech all lovers of truth, not to cry out that the Church is thrown into confusion by that freedom of discussion and inquiry which is granted to the schools, and ought certainly to be refused to no believer, since we are ordered "to prove all things," and since the daily progress of the light of truth is productive far less of disturbance to the Church, than of illumination and edification. Nor do I see how the Church can be more disturbed by the investigation of truth, than were the Gentiles by the first promulgation of the Gospel; since so far from recommending or imposing anything on my own authority, it is my particular advice that every one should suspend his opinion on whatever points he may not feel himself fully satisfied, till the evidence of Scripture prevail, and persuade his reason into assent and faith. Concealment is not my object; it is to the learned that I address myself, or if it be thought that the learned are not the best umpires and judges of such things, I should at least wish to submit my opinions to men of a mature and manly understanding, possessing a thorough knowledge of the doctrines of the Gospel; on whose judgments I should rely with far more confidence, than on those of novices in these matters. And whereas the greater part of those who have written most largely on these subjects have been wont to fill whole pages with explanations of their own opinions, thrusting into the margin the texts in support of their doctrine with a summary reference to the chapter and verse, I have chosen, on the contrary, to fill my pages, even to redundance, with quotations from Scripture, that so as little space as possible might be left for my own words, even when they arise from the context of revelation itself.

It has also been my object to make it appear from the opinions I shall be found to have advanced, whether new or old, of how much consequence to the Christian religion is the liberty not only of winnowing and sifting every doctrine, but also of thinking and even writing respecting it, according to our individual faith and persuasion; an inference which will be stronger in proportion to the weight and importance of those opinions, or rather in proportion to the authority of Scripture, on the abundant testimony of which they rest. Without this liberty there is neither religion nor Gospel, — force alone prevails, — by which it is disgraceful for the Christian religion to be supported. Without this liberty we are still enslaved, not indeed, as formerly, under the divine law, but, what is worst of all, under the law of man, or, to speak more truly, under a barbarous tyranny. But I do not expect from candid and judicious readers a conduct so unworthy of them, — that, like certain unjust and foolish men, they should stamp with the invidious name of heretic or heresy whatever appears to them to differ from the received opinions, without trying the doctrine by a comparison with Scripture testimonies. According to their notions, to have branded any one at random with this opprobrious mark, is to have refuted him without any trouble, by a single word. By the simple imputation of the name of heretic, they think that they have despatched their man at one blow. To men of this kind I answer, that in the time of the apostles, ere the New Testament was written, whenever the charge of heresy was applied as a term of reproach, that alone was considered as heresy which was at variance with their doctrine orally delivered, — and that those only were looked upon as heretics, who, according to Rom. xvi. 17, 18, "caused divisions and offences contrary to the doctrine" of the apostles. . . . "serving not our Lord Jesus Christ, but their own belly." By parity of reasoning therefore, since the compilation of the New Testament, I maintain that nothing but what is in contradiction to it can properly be called heresy.

For my own part, I adhere to the Holy Scriptures alone, — I follow no other heresy or sect. I had not even read any of the works of heretics, so called, when the mistakes of those who are reckoned for orthodox, and their incautious handling of Scripture, first taught me to agree with their opponents whenever those opponents agreed with Scripture. If this be heresy, I confess with St. Paul, Acts xxiv. 14, "that after the way which they call heresy, so worship I the God of my fathers, believing all things which are written in the law and the prophets," — to which I add, whatever is written in the New Testament. Any other judges or paramount interpreters of the Christian belief, together with all implicit faith, as it is called, I, in common with the whole Protestant Church, refuse to recognize.

For the rest, brethren, cultivate truth with brotherly love. Judge of my present undertaking according to the admonishing of the Spirit of God, — and neither adopt my sentiments nor reject them, unless every doubt has been removed from your belief by the clear testimony of revelation. Finally, live in the faith of our Lord and Saviour Jesus Christ. Farewell.

We must conclude, therefore, that God decreed nothing absolutely, which he left in the power of free agents, — a doctrine which is shown by the whole canon of Scripture. Gen. xix. 17, 21, "escape to the mountain, lest thou be consumed. . . . . see, I have accepted thee concerning this thing also, that I will not overthrow this city for the which thou hast spoken." Exod. iii. 8, 17, "I am come down to deliver them. . . . . and to bring them up unto a good land," — though these very individuals actually perished in the wilderness. God also had determined to deliver his people by the hand of Moses, whom he would nevertheless have put to death, Exod. iv. 24, if he had not immediately circumcised his son. 1 Sam. ii. 30, "I said indeed . . . but now Jehovah saith, be it far from me;" — and the reason for this change is added, — "for, them that honor me I will honor." xiii. 13, 14, "now would Jehovah have established thy kingdom . . . . but now thy kingdom shall not continue." Again, God had said, 2 Kings xx. 1, that Hezekiah should die immediately, which event, however, did not happen, and therefore could not have been decreed without reservation. The death of Josiah was not decreed peremptorily, but he would not hearken to the voice of Necho when he warned him according to the word of the Lord, not to come out against him; 2 Chron. xxxv. 22. Again, Jer. xviii. 9, 10, "at what instant I shall speak concerning a nation, and concerning a kingdom, to build and to plant it; if it do evil in my sight, that it obey not my voice, then I will repent of the good wherewith I said I would benefit them," — that is, I will rescind the decree, because that people hath not kept the condition on which the decree depended. Here then is a rule laid down by God himself, according to which he would always have his decrees understood, — namely, that regard should be paid to the conditionate terms attached to them. Jer. xxvi. 3, "if so be they will hearken, and turn every man from his evil way, that I may repent me of the evil, which I purpose to do unto them because of the evil of their doings." So also God had not even decreed absolutely the burning of Jerusalem. Jer. xxxviii. 17, &c., "thus saith Jehovah . . . . if thou wilt assuredly go forth unto the king of Babylon's princes, then thy soul shall live, and this city shall not be burned with fire." Jonah iii. iv., "yet forty days, and Nineveh shall be overthrown," — whereas it appears from the tenth verse, that when God saw that they turned from their evil way, he repented of his purpose, notwithstanding the anger of Jonah, who thought the change unworthy of God. Acts xxvii. 24, 31, "God hath given thee all them that sail with thee;" — and again, — "except these abide in the ship, ye cannot be saved," where Paul revokes the declaration he had previously made on the authority of God; or rather, God revokes the gift he had made to Paul, except on condition that they should consult for their own safety by their own personal exertions.

It appears, therefore, from these passages of Scripture, as well as from many others of the same kind, to which we must bow, as to a paramount authority, that the most high God has not decreed all things absolutely.

If, however, it be allowable to examine the divine decrees by the laws of human reason, since so many arguments have been maintained on this subject by controvertists on both sides, with more of subtlety than of solid argument, this theory of contingent decrees may be defended even on the principles of men, as most wise, and in no respect unworthy of the Deity. For if those decrees of God which have been referred to above, and such others of the same class as occur perpetually, were to be understood in an absolute sense, without any implied conditions, God would contradict himself, and appear inconsistent.

It is argued, however, that in such instances not only was the ultimate purpose predestinated, but even the means themselves were predestinated with a view to it. So, indeed, it is asserted, but not on the authority of Scripture; and the silence of Scripture would alone be a sufficient reason for rejecting the doctrine. But it is also attended by this additional inconvenience, that it would entirely take away from human affairs all liberty of action, all endeavor and desire to do right. For we might argue thus, — If God have at all events decreed my salvation, however I may act, I shall not perish. But God has also decreed as the means of salvation that you should act rightly. I cannot, therefore, but act rightly at some time or other, since God has so decreed, — in the mean time I will do as I please; if I never act rightly, it will be seen that I was never predestinated to salvation, and that whatever good I might have done would have been to no purpose. See more on this subject in the following Chapter.

Nor is it sufficient to affirm in reply, that it is not compulsory necessity which is here intended, but a necessity arising from the immutability of God, whereby all things are decreed, or a necessity arising from his infallibility or prescience, whereby all things are foreknown. I shall dispose hereafter of this twofold necessity of the schools; in the mean time no other law of necessity can be admitted than what logic, or, in other words, what sound reason teaches; that is to say, when the efficient either causes some determinate and uniform effect by its own inherent propensity, as, for example, when fire burns, which kind is denominated physical necessity; or when the efficient is compelled by some extraneous force to operate the effect, which is called compulsory necessity, and in the latter case, whatever effect the efficient produces, it produces *per accidens*. Now any necessity arising from external causes influences the agent either determinately or compulsorily; and it is apparent that on either alternative his liberty must be wholly annihilated. But though a certain immutable and internal necessity of acting rightly, independent of all extraneous influence whatever, may exist in God conjointly with the most perfect liberty, both which principles in the same divine nature tend to the same point, it does not therefore follow that the same thing can be conceded with regard to two different natures, as the nature of God and the nature of man, in which case the external immutability of one party may be in opposition to the internal liberty of the other, and may prevent unity of will. Nor is it admitted that the actions of God are in themselves necessary, but only that he has a necessary existence; for Scripture itself testifies that his decrees, and therefore his actions, of what kind soever they be, are perfectly free.

But it is objected that divine necessity, or a

first cause, imposes no constraint upon the liberty of free agents. I answer, — if it do not constrain, it either determines, or co-operates, or is wholly inefficient. If it determine or co-operate, it is either the sole or the joint and principal cause of every action, whether good or bad, of free agents. If it be wholly inefficient, it cannot be called a cause in any sense, much less can it be termed necessity.

Nor do we imagine anything unworthy of God, when we assert that those conditional events depend on the human will, which God himself has chosen to place at the free disposal of man; since the Deity purposely framed his own decrees with reference to particular circumstances, in order that he might permit free causes to act conformably to that liberty with which he had endued them. On the contrary, it would be much more unworthy of God, that man should nominally enjoy a liberty of which he was virtually deprived, which would be the case were that liberty to be oppressed or even obscured under the pretext of some sophistical necessity of immutability or infallibility, though not of compulsion, — a notion which has led, and still continues to lead, many individuals into error.

However, properly speaking, the divine counsels can be said to depend on nothing, but on the wisdom of God himself, whereby he perfectly foreknew in his own mind from the beginning what would be the nature and event of every future occurrence when its appointed season should arrive.

But it is asked how events, which are uncertain, inasmuch as they depend on the human will, can harmonize with the decrees of God, which are immutably fixed? for it is written, Psal. xxxiii. 11, "the counsel of Jehovah standeth for ever." See also Prov. xix. 21, and Isai. xlvi. 10, Heb. vi. 17, "the immutability of his counsel." To this objection it may be answered, first, that to God the issue of events is not uncertain, but foreknown with the utmost certainty, though they be not decreed necessarily, as will appear hereafter. — Secondly, in all the passages referred to, the divine counsel is said to stand against all human power and counsel, but not against liberty of will in things which God himself has placed at man's disposal, and had determined so to place from all eternity. For otherwise one of God's decrees would be in direct opposition to another, which would lead to the very consequence imputed by the objector to the doctrines of his opponents, inasmuch as by considering those things as necessary which the Deity has left to the uncontrolled decision of man, God would be rendered mutable. But God is not mutable, so long as he decrees nothing absolutely which could happen otherwise through the liberty assigned to man. He would indeed be mutable, neither would his *counsel stand*, if he were to obstruct by another decree that liberty which he had already decreed, or were to darken it with the least shadow of necessity.

It follows, therefore, that the liberty of man must be considered entirely independent of necessity, nor can any admission be made in favor of that modification of the principle which is founded on the doctrine of God's immutability and prescience. If there be any necessity at all, as has been stated before, it either determines free agents to a particular line of conduct, or it constrains them against their will, or it co-operates with them in conjunction with their will, or it is altogether inoperative. If it determine free agents to a particular line of conduct, man will be rendered the natural cause of all his actions, and consequently of his sins, and formed as it were with an inclination for sinning. If it constrain them against their will, man being subject to this compulsory decree, becomes the cause of sins only *per accidens*, God being the cause of sins *per se*. If it co-operate with them in conjunction with their will, then God becomes either the principal or the joint cause of sins with man. If finally it be altogether inoperative, there is no such thing as necessity, it virtually destroys itself by being without operation. For it is wholly impossible, that God should have fixed by a necessary decree what we know at the same time to be in the power of man; or that that should be immutable which it remains *for subsequent contingent circumstances* either to fulfil or frustrate.

Whatever, therefore, was left to the free will of our first parents, could not have been decreed immutably or absolutely from all eternity; and questionless, the Deity must either have never left anything in the power of man, or he cannot be said to have determined finally respecting whatever was so left without reference to possible contingencies.

If it be objected, that this doctrine leads to absurd consequences, we reply, either the consequences are not absurd, or they are not the consequences of the doctrine. For it is neither impious nor absurd to say, that the idea of certain things or events might be suggested to God from some extraneous source; since inasmuch as God had determined from all eternity, that man should so far be a free agent, that it remained with himself to decide whether he would stand or fall, the idea of that evil event, or of the fall of man, was suggested to God from an extraneous source, — a truth which all confess.

Nor does it follow from hence, that what is temporal becomes the cause of, or a restriction upon what is eternal, for it was not anything temporal, but the wisdom of the eternal mind that gave occasion for framing the divine counsel.

Seeing, therefore, that, in assigning the gift of free will, God suffered both men and angels to stand or fall at their own uncontrolled choice, there can be no doubt that the decree itself bore a strict analogy to the object which the divine counsel regarded, not necessitating the evil consequences which ensued, but leaving them contingent; hence the covenant was of this kind,—if thou stand, thou shalt abide in Paradise; if thou fall, thou shalt be cast out: if thou eat not the forbidden fruit, thou shalt live; if thou eat, thou shalt die.

Hence, those who contend that the liberty of actions is subject to an absolute decree, erroneously conclude that the decree of God is the cause of his foreknowledge, and antecedent in order of time. If we must apply to God a phraseology borrowed from our own habits and understanding, to consider his decrees as consequent upon his foreknowledge seems more agreeable to reason, as well as to Scripture, and to the nature of the Deity himself, who, as has just been proved, decreed everything according to his infinite wisdom by virtue of his foreknowledge.

That the will of God is the first cause of all things, is not intended to be denied, but his prescience and wisdom must not be separated from his will, much less considered as subsequent to the latter in point of time. The will of God, in fine, is not less the universal first cause, because he has himself decreed that some things should be left to our own free will, than if each particular event had been decreed necessarily.

To comprehend the whole matter in a few words, the sum of the argument may be thus stated in strict conformity with reason. God of his wisdom determined to create men and angels reasonable beings, and therefore free agents; foreseeing at the same time which way the bias of their will would incline, in the exercise of their own uncontrolled liberty. What then? shall we say that this foresight or foreknowledge on the part of God imposed on them the necessity of acting in any definite way? No more than if the future event had been foreseen by any human being. For what any human being has foreseen as certain to happen, will not less certainly happen than what God himself has predicted. Thus Elisha foresaw how much evil Hazael would bring upon the children of Israel in the course of a few years, 2 Kings viii. 12. Yet no one would affirm that the evil took place necessarily on account of the foreknowledge of Elisha; for had he never foreknown it, the event would have occurred with equal certainty, through the free will of the agent. In like manner nothing happens of necessity, because God has foreseen it; but he foresees the event of every action, because he is acquainted with their natural causes, which, in pursuance of his own decree, are left at liberty to exert their legitimate influence. Consequently the issue does not depend on God who foresees it, but on him alone who is the object of his foresight. Since, therefore, as has before been shown, there can be no absolute decree of God regarding free agents, undoubtedly the prescience of the Deity (which can no more bias free agents than the prescience of man, that is, not at all, since the action in both cases is intransitive, and has no external influence) can neither impose any necessity of itself, nor can it be considered at all as the cause of free actions. If it be so considered, the very name of liberty must be altogether abolished as an unmeaning sound; and that not only in matters of religion, but even in questions of morality and indifferent things. There can be nothing but what will happen necessarily, since there is nothing but what is foreknown by God.

That this long discussion may be at length concluded by a brief summary of the whole matter, we must hold that God foreknows all future events, but that he has not decreed them all absolutely: lest the consequence should be that sin in general would be imputed to the Deity, and evil spirits and wicked men exempted from blame. . . . .

From what has been said it is sufficiently evident, that free causes are not impeded by any law of necessity arising from the decrees or prescience of God. There are some who, in their zeal to oppose this doctrine, do not hesitate even to assert that God is himself the cause and origin of sin. Such men, if they are not to be looked upon as misguided rather that mischievous, should be ranked among the most abandoned of all blasphemers. An attempt to refute them, would be nothing more than an argument to prove that God was not the evil spirit. . . . .

Generation must be an external efficiency, since the Father and Son are different persons; and the divines themselves acknowledge this, who argue that there is a certain emanation of the Son from the Father (which will be explained when the doctrine concerning the Holy Spirit is under examination); for though they teach that the Spirit is co-essential with the Father, they do not deny its emanation, procession, spiration, and issuing from the Father, — which are all expressions denoting external efficiency. In conjunction with this doctrine they hold that the Son is also co-essential with the Father, and generated from all eternity. Hence this question, which is naturally very obscure, becomes involved in still greater difficulties if the received opinion respecting it be followed; for though the Father be said in Scripture to have begotten the Son in a double sense, the one literal, with reference to the production of the Son, the other metaphorical, with reference to his exaltation, many commentators have applied the passages which allude to the exaltation and mediatorial functions of Christ as proof of his generation from all eternity. They have indeed this excuse, if any excuse can be received in such a case, that it is impossible to find a single text in all Scripture to prove the eternal generation of the Son. Certain, however, it is, whatever some of the moderns may allege to the contrary, that the Son existed in the beginning, under the name of the logos, or word, and was the first of the whole creation, by whom afterwards all other things were made, both in heaven and earth. John i. 1–3, "in the beginning was the Word, and the Word was with God, and the Word was God," &c. xvii. 5, "and now, O Father, glorify me with thine own self with the glory which I had with thee before the world was." Col. i. 15, 18, "the first-born of every creature." Rev. iii. 14, "the beginning of the creation of God." 1 Cor. viii. 6, "Jesus Christ, by whom are all things." Eph. iii. 9, "who created all things by Jesus Christ." Col. i. 16, "all things were created by him and for him." Heb. i. 2, "by whom also he made the worlds," whence it is said, v. 10, "thou, Lord, in the beginning hast laid the foundation of the earth"; respecting which more will be said in the seventh chapter, on the Creation.

All these passages prove the existence of the Son before the world was made, but they conclude nothing respecting his generation from all eternity. The other texts which are produced relate only to his metaphorical generation, that is, to his resuscitation from the dead, or to his unction to the mediatorial office, according to St. Paul's own interpretation of the second Psalm: "I will declare the decree; Jehovah hath said unto me, Thou art my Son; this day have I begotten thee," — which the apostle thus explains, Acts xiii. 32, 33, "God hath fulfilled the promise unto us their children, in that he hath raised up Jesus again; as it is also written in the second Psalm, Thou art my Son; this day have I begotten thee." Rom. i. 4, "declared to be the Son of God with power, according to the spirit of holiness, by the resurrection from the dead." Hence, Col. i. 18, Rev. i. 4, "the first begotten of the dead." Heb. i. 5, speaking of the exaltation of the Son above the angels; "for unto which of the angels said he at any time, Thou art my Son, this day have I begotten thee? and again, I will be to him a Father, and he shall be to me a Son." Again, v. 5, 6, with reference to the priesthood of Christ; "so also Christ glorified not himself to be made an High Priest, but he that said unto him, Thou art my Son, this day have I begotten thee: as he said also in another place, Thou art a priest for ever," &c. Further, it will be apparent from the second Psalm, that God has begotten the Son, that is, has made him a king: v. 6, "yet have I set my King upon my holy hill of Sion"; and then in the next verse, after having anointed his King, whence the name of *Christ* is derived, he says, "this day have I begotten thee." Heb. i. 4, 5, "being made so much better than the angels, as he hath by inheritance obtained a more excellent name than they." No other name can be intended but that of Son, as the following verse proves: "for unto which of the angels said he at any time, Thou art my Son; this day have I begotten thee?" The Son also declares the same of himself. John x. 35, 36, "say ye of Him whom the Father hath sanctified, and sent into the world, Thou blasphemest, because I said, I am the Son of God?" By a similar figure of speech, though in a much lower sense, the saints are also said to be begotten of God.

It is evident, however, upon a careful comparison and examination of all these passages, and particularly from the whole of the second Psalm, that however the generation of the Son may have taken place, it arose from no natural necessity, as is generally contended, but was no less owing to the decree and will of the Father than his priesthood or kingly power, or his resuscitation from the dead. Nor is it any objection to this that he bears the title of *begotten*, in whatever sense that expression is to be understood, or of God's *own Son*, Rom. viii. 32. For he is called the own Son of God merely because he had no other Father besides God, whence he himself said, that *God was his Father*, John v. 18. For to Adam God stood less in the relation of Father, than of Creator, having only formed him from the dust of the earth; whereas he was properly the Father of the

Son made of his own substance. Yet it does not follow from hence that the Son is co-essential with the Father, for then the title of Son would be least of all applicable to him, since he who is properly the Son is not coeval with the Father, much less of the same numerical essence, otherwise the Father and the Son would be one person; nor did the Father beget him from any natural necessity, but of his own free will, — a mode more perfect and more agreeable to the paternal dignity; particularly since the Father is God, all whose works, and consequently the works of generation, are executed freely according to his own good pleasure, as has been already proved from Scripture.

For, questionless, it was in God's power consistently with the perfection of his own essence not to have begotten the Son, inasmuch as generation does not pertain to the nature of the Deity, who stands in no need of propagation; but whatever does not pertain to his own essence or nature, he does not effect like a natural agent from any physical necessity. If the generation of the Son proceeded from a physical necessity, the Father impaired himself by physically begetting a co-equal; which God could no more do than he could deny himself; therefore the generation of the Son cannot have proceeded otherwise than from a decree, and of the Father's own free will.

Thus the Son was begotten of the Father in consequence of his decree, and therefore within the limits of time, for the decree itself must have been anterior to the execution of the decree, as is sufficiently clear from the insertion of the word *to-day*. . . . .

According to the testimony of the Son, delivered in the clearest terms, the Father is that one true God, by whom are all things. Being asked by one of the scribes, Mark xii. 28, 29, 32, which was the first commandment of all, he answered from Deut. vi. 4, "the first of all the commandments is, 'Hear, O Israel, the Lord our God is one Lord'"; or as it is in the Hebrew, "Jehovah our God is one Jehovah." The scribe assented; "there is one God, and there is none other one but he"; and in the following verse Christ approves this answer. Nothing can be more clear than that it was the opinion of the scribe, as well as of the other Jews, that by the unity of God is intended his oneness of person. That this God was no other than God the Father, is proved from John viii. 41, 54, "we have one Father, even God . . . . it is my Father that honoreth me; of whom ye say that he is your God." iv. 21, "neither in this mountain, nor yet at Jerusalem, shall ye worship the Father." Christ therefore agrees with the whole people of God, that the Father is that one and only God. For who can believe it possible for the very first of the commandments to have been so obscure, and so ill understood by the Church through such a succession of ages, that two other persons, equally entitled to worship, should have remained wholly unknown to the people of God, and debarred of divine honors even to that very day? especially as God, where he is teaching his own people respecting the nature of their worship under the Gospel, forewarns them that they would have for their God the one Jehovah whom they had always served, and David, that is, Christ, for their King and Lord. Jer. xxx. 9, "they shall serve Jehovah their God, and David their King, whom I will raise up unto them." In this passage Christ, such as God willed that he should be known or worshipped by his people under the Gospel, is expressly distinguished from the one God Jehovah, both by nature and title. Christ himself therefore, the Son of God, teaches us nothing in the Gospel respecting the one God but what the law had before taught, and everywhere clearly asserts him to be his Father. John xvii. 3, "this is life eternal, that they might know thee, the only true God, and Jesus Christ whom thou hast sent." xx. 17, "I ascend unto my Father and your Father; and to my God and your God"; if therefore the Father be the God of Christ, and the same be our God, and if there be none other God but one, there can be no God beside the Father. . . .

Recurring, however, to the Gospel itself, on which, as on a foundation, our dependence should chiefly be placed, and adducing my proofs more especially from the evangelist John, the leading purpose of whose work was to declare explicitly the nature of the Son's divinity, I proceed to demonstrate the other proposition announced in my original division of the subject,—namely, that the Son himself professes to have received from the Father, not only the name of God and of Jehovah, but all that pertains to his own being,—that is to say, his individuality, his existence itself, his attributes, his works, his divine honors; to which doctrine the apostles also, subsequent to Christ, bear their testimony. John iii. 35, "the Father loveth the Son, and hath given all things unto him." xiii. 3, "Jesus knowing that the Father had given all things unto him, and that he was come from God." Mat. xi. 27, "all things are delivered unto me of my Father." . . . .

Christ therefore, having received all these things from the Father, and "being in the form of God, thought it not robbery to be equal with God," Philipp. ii. 5, namely, because he had obtained them by gift, not by robbery. For if this passage imply his co-equality with the Father, it rather refutes than proves his unity of essence; since equality cannot exist but between two or more essences. Further, the phrase *he did not think it*, —*he made himself of no reputation*, (literally, *he emptied himself*,) appear inapplicable to the supreme God. For *to think* is nothing else than to entertain an opinion, which cannot be properly said of God. Nor can the infinite God be said to empty himself, any more than to contradict himself; for infinity and emptiness are opposite terms. But since he emptied himself of that form of God in which he had previously existed, if the form of God is to be taken for the essence of the Deity itself, it would prove him to have emptied himself of that essence, which is impossible. . . . .

Such was the faith of the saints respecting the Son of God; such is the tenor of the celebrated confession of that faith; such is the doctrine which alone is taught in Scripture, which is acceptable to God, and has the promise of eternal salvation. . . .

Finally, this is the faith proposed to us in the Apostles' Creed, the most ancient and universally received compendium of belief in the possession of the Church. . . . .

The intent of SUPERNATURAL RENOVATION is not only to restore man more completely than before to the use of his natural faculties as regards his power to form right judgment, and to exercise free will; but to create afresh, as it were, the inward man, and infuse from above new and supernatural faculties into the minds of the renovated. This is called REGENERATION, and the regenerate are said to be PLANTED IN CHRIST.

REGENERATION IS THAT CHANGE OPERATED BY

THE WORD AND THE SPIRIT, WHEREBY THE OLD MAN BEING DESTROYED, THE INWARD MAN IS REGENERATED BY GOD AFTER HIS OWN IMAGE, IN ALL THE FACULTIES OF HIS MIND, INSOMUCH THAT HE BECOMES AS IT WERE A NEW CREATURE, AND THE WHOLE MAN IS SANCTIFIED BOTH IN BODY AND SOUL, FOR THE SERVICE OF GOD, AND THE PERFORMANCE OF GOOD WORKS. John iii. 3, 5, "except a man be born again, he cannot see the kingdom of God . . . . except a man be born of water and the Spirit." 1 Pet. i. 23, "being born again, not of corruptible seed, but of incorruptible."

IS REGENERATED BY GOD; namely, the Father; for no one regenerates, except the Father. Psal. li. 10, "create in me a clean heart, O God, and renew a right spirit within me." Ezek. xi. 19, "I will put a new spirit within you." John i. 12, 13, "to them gave he the power to become the sons of God . . . . which were born, not of blood . . . . but of God." iii. 5, 6, "except a man be born of water and the Spirit—"; where by *the Spirit* appears to be meant the divine power of the Father; for the Father is a Spirit; and, as was said before, no one generates except the Father. xvii. 17, "sanctify them through thy truth." Rom. viii. 11, 16, "but if the Spirit of him that raised up Jesus from the dead—: the Spirit itself beareth witness with our spirit, that we are the children of God." Gal. iv. 6, "because ye are sons, God hath sent forth the Spirit of his Son into your hearts, crying, Abba, Father." Eph. ii. 4, 5, "God who is rich in mercy . . . . hath quickened us together with Christ." 1 Thess. v. 23, "the very God of peace sanctify you wholly." Tit. iii. 5, "according to his mercy he saved us by the washing of regeneration and renewing of the Holy Ghost." Heb. xiii. 20, "the God of peace . . . . make you perfect in every good work." 1 Pet. i. 3, "blessed be the God and Father of our Lord Jesus Christ, which according to his abundant mercy hath begotten us again —." James i. 17, 18, "of his own will begat he us."

By the Word and the Spirit. John xvii. 17, "sanctify them through thy truth; thy word is truth." James i. 18, "of his own will begat he us with the word of truth." Eph. v. 26, "that he might cleanse it with the washing of water by the Word." 1 Cor. xii. 13, "by one Spirit we are all baptized into one body." Tit. iii. 5, "by the washing of regeneration and renewing of the Holy Ghost."

The inward man. John iii. 5, 6, "that which is born of the Spirit is spirit." Rom. vii. 22, "after the inward man."

The old man being destroyed. Rom. vi. 6, "knowing this, that our old man is crucified with him, that the body of sin might be destroyed." v. 11, "likewise reckon ye also yourselves to be dead indeed unto sin, but alive unto God through Jesus Christ our Lord." 2 Cor. v. 17, "old things are passed away; behold, all things are become new." Col. iii. 9-11, "that ye have put off the old man with his deeds, and have put on the new man."

IN ALL THE FACULTIES OF HIS MIND; that is to say, in understanding and will. Psal. li. 10, "create in me a clean heart, O God." Ezek. xi. 19, "I will put a new spirit within you . . . . and I will give them an heart of flesh." xxxvi. 26, "a new heart also will I give you, and a new spirit will I put within you." Rom. xii. 2, "be ye transformed by the renewing of your mind, that ye may prove what is that good . . . . will of God." Eph. iv. 23, "be renewed in the spirit of your mind." Philipp. ii. 13, "it is God which worketh in you both to will and do his good pleasure." This renewal of the will can mean nothing, but a restoration to its former liberty.

AFTER HIS OWN IMAGE. Eph. iv. 24, "put on the new man, which after God is created in righteousness and true holiness." Col. iii. 9-11, "which is renewed in knowledge after the image of him that created him." 2 Pet. i. 4, "that by these ye might be partakers of the divine nature, having escaped the corruption that is in the world through lust." If the choice were given us, we could ask nothing more of God, than that, being delivered from the slavery of sin, and restored to the divine image, we might have it in our power to obtain salvation if willing. Willing we shall undoubtedly be, if truly free; and he who is not willing, has no one to accuse but himself. But if the will of the regenerate be not made free, then we are not renewed, but compelled to embrace salvation in an unregenerate state.

A NEW CREATURE. 2 Cor. v. 17, "if any man be in Christ, he is a new creature." Gal. vi. 15, "a new creature." Eph. iv. 24, "the new man." See also Col. iii. 10, 11. Hence some, less properly, divide regeneration into two parts, *the mortification of the flesh*, and *the quickening of the spirit;* whereas mortification cannot be a constituent part of regeneration, inasmuch as it partly precedes it, (that is to say, as corruption precedes generation,) and partly follows it; in which latter capacity it belongs rather to repentance. On the other hand, *the quickening of the spirit* is as often used to signify resurrection as regeneration. John v. 21, "as the Father raiseth up the dead and quickeneth them, even so the Son quickeneth whom he will." v. 25, "the dead shall hear the voice of the Son of God, and they that hear shall live."

THE WHOLE MAN. 1 Cor. vi. 15, 19, "know ye not that your body is the temple of the Holy Ghost which is in you?" 1 Thess. v. 23, "the very God of peace sanctify you wholly, and I pray God your whole spirit and soul and body be preserved blameless unto the coming of our Lord Jesus Christ."

FOR THE PERFORMANCE OF GOOD WORKS. 1

John ii. 29, "if ye know that he is righteous, ye know that every one that doeth righteousness is born of him." Eph. ii. 10, "we are his workmanship, created in Christ Jesus unto good works."

Is SANCTIFIED. 1 John iii. 9, "whosoever is born of God, doth not commit sin, for his seed remaineth in him; and he cannot sin because he is born of God." v. 18, "whosoever is born of God, sinneth not, but he that is begotten of God keepeth himself, and that wicked one toucheth him not." Hence regeneration is sometimes termed sanctification, being the literal mode of expressing that, for which regeneration is merely a figurative phrase. 1 Cor. vi. 11, "such were some of you; but ye are washed, but ye are sanctified, but ye are justified." 1 Thess. iv. 7, "God hath not called us unto uncleanness, but unto holiness." 2 Thess. ii. 13. "because God hath from the beginning chosen you to salvation through sanctification of the Spirit." 1 Pet. i. 2, "according to the foreknowledge of God the Father, through the sanctification of the Spirit. " Deut. xxx. 6, "Jehovah thy God will circumcise thine heart, and the heart of thy seed, to love Jehovah thy God." Sanctification is also attributed to the Son. Eph. v. 25, 26, "Christ loved the church, and gave himself for it, that he might sanctify and cleanse it with the washing of water by the word." Tit. ii. 14, "that he might redeem us from all iniquity, and purify unto himself (unto himself as our Redeemer and King) a peculiar people."

Sanctification is sometimes used in a more extended sense, for any kind of election or separation, either of a whole nation to some particular form of worship, or of an individual to some office. Exod. xix. 10, "sanctify them to-day and to-morrow." xxxi. 13, "that ye may know that I am Jehovah that doth sanctify you." See also Ezek. xx. 12; Numb. xi. 18, "sanctify yourselves against to-morrow." Jer. i. 5, "before thou camest forth out of the womb, I sanctified thee, and I ordained thee a prophet unto the nations." Luke i. 15, "he shall be filled with the Holy Ghost, even from his mother's womb."

The external cause of regeneration or sanctification is the death and resurrection of Christ. Eph. ii. 4, 5, "when we were dead in sins, God hath quickened us together with Christ." v. 25, 26, "Christ gave himself for the church, that he might sanctify and cleanse it." Heb. ix. 14, "how much more shall the blood of Christ, who through the eternal Spirit offered himself without spot to God, purge your conscience from dead works to serve the living God." x. 10, "by the which will we are sanctified through the offering of the body of Jesus Christ." 1 Pet. i. 2, 3, "through sanctification of the Spirit, unto obedience and sprinkling of the blood of Jesus Christ . . . . which hath begotten us again by a lively hope, by the resurrection of Jesus Christ from the dead." 1 John i. 7, "the blood of Jesus Christ his Son cleanseth us from all sin."

Sanctification is attributed also to faith. Acts xv. 9, "purifying their hearts by faith"; not that faith is anterior to sanctification, but because faith is an instrumental and assisting cause in its gradual progress.

A LIST OF MILTON'S PROSE WORKS.

ARRANGED IN CHRONOLOGICAL ORDER.

1641. — 1. Of Reformation in England, and the Causes that hitherto have hindered it. In Two Books. Written to a Friend.

2. Of Prelatical Episcopacy, and whether it may be deduced from the Apostolical Times, by Virtue of those Testimonies which are alleged to that Purpose in some late Treatises; one whereof goes under the name of James, Archbishop of Armagh.

3. The Reason of Church Government urged against Prelaty. In Two Books.

4. Animadversions upon the Remonstrant's Defence against Smectymnuus.

1642. — 5. An Apology against a Pamphlet called "A Modest Confutation of the Animadversions upon the Remonstrant against Smectymnuus." (Better known by its briefer title, An Apology for Smectymnuus.)

1644. — 6. The Doctrine and Discipline of Divorce; restored to the Good of both Sexes, from the Bondage of Canon Law, and other Mistakes, to the true meaning of Scripture in the Law and Gospel compared. Wherein also are set down the bad Consequences of abolishing, or condemning as Sin, that which the Law of God allows, and Christ abolished not. Now the second time revised and much augmented. In Two Books. To the Parliament of England with the

Assembly. (Two editions were published in the same year. The title given above is of the second.)

1644. — 7. The Judgment of Martin Bucer, concerning Divorce: written to Edward the Sixth, in his Second Book of the Kingdom of Christ: and now Englished. Wherein a late Book, restoring "the Doctrine and Discipline of Divorce," is here confirmed and justified by the Authority of Martin Bucer. To the Parliament of England.

8. On Education. (In a Letter to Master Samuel Hartlib.)

9. Areopagitica: a Speech for the Liberty of Unlicensed Printing. To the Parliament of England.

1645. — 10. Tetrachordon: Expositions upon the Four Chief Places in Scripture which treat of Marriage, or Nullities in Marriage. Wherein "the Doctrine and Discipline of Divorce," as was lately published, is confirmed by Explanation of Scripture; by Testimony of Ancient Fathers; of Civil Laws in the Primitive Church; of famousest Reformed Divines; and lastly, by an intended Act of the Parliament and Church of England in the last Year of Edward the Sixth.

11. Colasterion: a Reply to a Nameless Answer against "the Doctrine and Discipline of Divorce." Wherein the trivial Author of that Answer is discovered, the Licenser conferred with, and the Opinion which they traduce defended.

1648–9 (Feb.). — 12. The Tenure of Kings and Magistrates: proving that it is lawful, and hath been held so through all Ages, for any who have the Power, to call to Account a Tyrant, or wicked King, and after due Conviction, to depose, and put him to Death, if the ordinary Magistrate have neglected or denied to do it. And that they who of late so much blame deposing, the Presbyterians, are the men that did it themselves.

1648–9. — 13. Observations on the Articles of Peace, between James Earl of Ormond for King Charles the First on the one hand, and the Irish Rebels and Papists on the other hand: and on a Letter sent by Ormond to Colonel Jones, Governor of Dublin. And a Representation of the Scots Presbytery at Belfast in Ireland. To which the said Articles, Letter, with Colonel Jones's Answer to it, and Representation, &c., are prefixed. (Published before his appointment as Latin Secretary, March 15th, 1648–9.)

1649. — 14. Eikonoklastes: in Answer to a Book entitled "Eikon Basilikè, The Portraiture of His Sacred Majesty in his Solitudes and Sufferings."

1650. — 15. Pro Populo Anglicano Defensio, contra Claudii anonymi alias Salmasii Defensionem Regiam. A Defence of the People of England; in Answer to Salmasius's Defence of the King. (The translation is ascribed by Toland to Mr. Washington of the Temple.)

1654. — 16. Defensio Secunda pro Populo Anglicano contra Infamem Libellum anonymum, cui titulus, Regii Sanguinis Clamor ad Cœlum adversus Parricidas Anglicanos. The Second Defence of the People of England: against an anonymous Libel, entitled "The Royal Blood crying to Heaven for Vengeance on the English Parricides." (The translation is by Robert Fellowes, A. M., Oxon.)

1655. — 17. Authoris pro se Defensio contra Alexandrum Morum Libelli, cui titulus, Regii Sanguinis, &c. Authorem recte dictum.

18. Authoris ad Alexandri Mori Supplementum Responsio. (These two polemic tracts have, I think, never been translated.)

19. A Manifesto of the Lord Protector to the Commonwealth of England, Scotland, Ireland, &c. Published by consent and advice of his Council.

Wherein is shown the Reasonableness of the Cause of this Republic against the Depredations of the Spaniards. (Written in Latin by John Milton, and first printed in 1655; translated into English in 1738.)

1659. — 20. A Treatise of Civil Power in Ecclesiastical Causes; showing that it is not lawful for any Power on Earth to compel in matters of Religion. To the Parliament of the Commonwealth of England, with the Dominions thereof.

21. Considerations touching the likeliest Means to remove Hirelings out of the Church. Wherein is also discoursed of Tithes, Church Fees, and Church Revenues; and whether any Maintenance of Ministers can be settled by Law. To the Parliament of England, with the Dominions thereof.

22. A Letter to a Friend concerning the Ruptures of the Commonwealth. (Dated Oct. 20, 1659, but first published by Toland in 1698.)

23. The Present Means and Brief Delineation of a Free Commonwealth, easy to be put in practice, and without delay. In a Letter to General Monk.

1660. — 24. The ready and easy Way to establish a free Commonwealth, and the Excellence thereof, compared with the Inconveniences and Dangers of re-admitting Kingship in this Nation.

25. Brief Notes upon a late Sermon titled, The Fear of God and the King; preached and since published by Matthew Griffith, D. D., and Chaplain to the late King. Wherein many notorious wrestings of Scripture, and other Falsities, are observed.

1661. — 26. Accedence Commenced Grammar, supplied with Sufficient Rules for the use of such as, younger or elder, are desirous, without more trouble than needs, to attain the Latin Tongue; the elder sort especially, with little teaching and their own industry. (It had probably been prepared some years before its publication.)

1670.—27. The History of Britain, that part especially now called England, from the first Traditional Beginning continued to the Norman Conquest; collected out of the ancientest and best Authors thereof. (This work, though published in 1670, was written mostly before the Restoration. The royal licenser expunged several passages, which appeared in a pamphlet by themselves in 1681, and were incorporated into an edition of Milton's Prose Works published in 1738. See a brief notice of this in D'Israeli's Curiosities of Literature, Vol. II., p. 408, and Vol. III., p. 206.)

1672.—28. Artis Logicæ Plenior Institutio ad Petri Rami Methodum concinnata. System of Logic after Peter Ramus. (Not translated. This too had been in manuscript many years before publication.)

1673.—29. Of True Religion, Heresy, Schism, Toleration; and what best Means may be used against the Growth of Popery.

1674.—30. Epistolarum Familiarum Liber Unus; quibus accesserunt Prolusiones quædam Oratoriæ in Collegio Christi habitæ. (The Familiar Letters, extending from 1625 to 1666, have been translated by Mr. Fellowes of Oxford. Of the "Prolusiones," or Academical Essays, seven in number, no complete translation has been published. Professor Masson, who has found them "full of biographical light," yet remarks: "I really have found no evidence that as many as ten persons have read them through before me." He has given a full account of these Essays, with copious extracts, in his Life of Milton, Vol. I. pp. 204–230.)

31. A Declaration, or Letters-Patent, for the Election of this present King of Poland, John the Third, elected on the 22nd of May last past, A. D. 1674.

Containing the Reasons of this Election, the great Virtues and Merits of the said serene Elect, his eminent Services in War, especially in his last great Victory against the Turks and Tartars, whereof many particulars are here related, not published before. Now faithfully translated from the Latin copy.

1676. — 32. Literæ Senatus Anglicani; necnon Cromwellii. The Letters of State. These were published in the original in 1676, then translated into English, and published in 1694.

1682. — 33. A brief History of Moscovia and of other best-known Countries lying eastward of Russia as far as Cathay; gathered from the Writings of several Eyewitnesses.

1823. — 34. Joannis Miltoni Angli de Doctrina Christiana ex sacris duntaxat Libris petitâ Disquisitionum Libri duo posthumia. The Christian Doctrine. (A Latin MS. bearing the above title was accidentally discovered in 1823 by Mr. Lemon in the State-Paper Office. It was edited and afterwards translated by Rev. Charles R. Sumner, Bishop of Winchester. The Christian Doctrine is generally supposed to have been written by Milton late in life; but a contrary view is ably maintained in an article of considerable length published in the Bibliotheca Sacra, Vol. XVI. p. 557, and Vol. XVII. p. 1.)

In addition to the works above mentioned, a few fragments have lately appeared. It is not likely that any important work of Milton remains now undiscovered.

INDEX.

THE END.

Cambridge: Stereotyped and Printed by Welch, Bigelow, & Co.

www.ingramcontent.com/pod-product-compliance
Lightning Source LLC
LaVergne TN
LVHW020917110826
845150LV00004B/698

9781425555641